Aldous Huxley and
the Search for Meaning

Aldous Huxley and the Search for Meaning

A Study of the Eleven Novels

RONALD T. SION

McFarland & Company, Inc., Publishers
Jefferson, North Carolina, and London

LIBRARY OF CONGRESS CATALOGUING-IN-PUBLICATION DATA

Sion, Ronald T.
   Aldous Huxley and the search for meaning : a study of the
eleven novels / Ronald T. Sion.
      p.   cm.
   Includes bibliographical references and index.

   ISBN 978-0-7864-4746-6
   softcover : 50# alkaline paper ∞

   1. Huxley, Aldous, 1894–1963.   I. Title.
PR6015.U9Z877   2010
823'.912 — dc22   2010018583

British Library cataloguing data are available

Front cover Aldous Huxley, ca. 1950s (Photofest)

Manufactured in the United States of America

McFarland & Company, Inc., Publishers

Table of Contents

Preface

"One can't have something for nothing." — Aldous Huxley[1]

How frequently these words of Huxley — whether directly to the reader in an essay or through the mouth of a character in a work of fiction — are repeated. Humanity is not always aware of the price it pays for progress, or at least what it renders as progress. Many times the price is far greater than the reward, especially when it means people must surrender their liberties, their freedoms, or the very essence of what it means to be human. A recent ad campaign for a popular cereal asks the question as to whether progress has improved our lives. It cites landfills, the reduction of natural resources, and climate change as just some of the challenges attributable to progress. Cleverly the ad goes on to state that the cereal has put the "no" in "innovation."[2] This may be a unique approach to sell a cereal, but the essence of the message speaks to Huxley's import that for every action there is a reaction — unfortunately, the reaction may be what our age has come to label the unintended consequences of progress. Global warming, pollution of the air and natural resources, AIDS, skin cancer, the sometimes deadly adverse reactions to medications, the ethical questions surrounding surrogate motherhood and cloning are only a small number of these unintended responses.

In an age when government has grown exponentially to soften the blow of an economic recession and the fear of terrorism has sometimes hindered our liberties, Huxley's prescient vision becomes all the more dramatic. First looking around at the somewhat frivolous nature of his counterparts, he wrote works of a satiric nature; later, in a journey to self-discovery, his leanings became more mystical in disposition as he became strikingly aware of Hamlet's words in Shakespeare's tragedy about "the undiscover'd country from whose bourn no traveler returns."[3] With an uncanny awareness of the complexities of the human condition and questions surrounding that con-

1

dition, his writings frequently border on the psychological as well as the spiritual. With a telescopic imagination, he peered into the lens of a future world and wondered if the human race would be happy with what it had achieved. In his words: "Who are we? What is our destiny? How can the frightful ways of God be justified? Before the rise of science the only answers to these questions came from the philosopher-poets and poet-philosophers."[4]

In fact, Aldous Huxley, as a writer of fiction in the 20th century, willingly assumes the role of a modern philosopher-king or literary prophet by examining the essence of what it means to be human in the modern age. As is evident in his fiction to be examined and supported by the artist's own words in selected essays and letters, Huxley was a prolific genius who was always searching throughout his life for an understanding of self and one's place within the universe. Engaging the reader in imaginative narratives, he was to ask numerous probing questions about humanity's relationship to its physical and metaphysical worlds.

The basis of Huxley's philosophical view of life is succinctly captured in the words of Boethius, an eminent Christian philosopher of the sixth century, whom he quotes in an epigraph to one of his chapters contained in an anthology on spirituality: "In other living creatures ignorance of self is nature; in man it is vice."[5] In the eleven novels of Huxley, one may discern a probing pattern in search of self-awareness and self-actualization. This self-awareness evolved across time through Huxley's own life experiences and his inquisitive mind that explored all the venues of human aspiration. Seeing with new eyes, this contemporary philosopher-king sought to warn humanity of its follies, especially the foolish belief that material progress would take care of all human woes. Huxley articulated early in his fiction that humanity's technological arrogance might have aided him in improving his physical standard of living but frequently at a significant cost. Living in sterile, crowded urban environments, modern man often finds himself isolated from his neighbor, alienated from meaningful achievements in a mechanized setting, and deprived of individual freedom. Controlled by an ever-growing power elite and conditioned to purchase an endless array of gadgets in a consumer-driven culture, the human race reflected in Huxley's fiction is generally discontent, restless, and spiritually bereft, having lost all sense of identity, meaning, and purpose. Huxley ardently believed that it was his responsibility as a literary artist to display the failings of humanity imaginatively. By doing so, he might facilitate the reader's entrance into the realm of self-examination.

Emphasizing that no one will ever get something for nothing, Huxley presses the issue that a pompous populace will pay the ultimate price in a loss of humane characteristics. Hoping that people would take the time to stand back and evaluate whether their human values were progressing along with their scientific innovations, Huxley optimistically concludes that it is never too late for humanity to change its ways. Change, however, will come about only with pain and a significant effort. Still, Huxley refused to give up the hope that people would come to seek out the ultimate meaning of life and move in the direction of spiritual awakening.

The journey to self-awareness came about gradually for Huxley; it is posited in this study that each work reflects the man — who he was, what he experienced, and what he thinks at a given point in time. Herein lies the uniqueness of this research since it focuses on a progression of Huxley's thinking and world view through the eleven works of fiction that encompass his life. While others have written works of a biographical nature, and certainly there are a number of volumes of critical analysis, the interfacing of Huxley's essays and letters woven within the fabric of his novels reflecting a progressive journey to self-awareness renders this study different, if not fully unique. In essence, this inquiry asks what Huxley was thinking and experiencing during the writing of each of his eleven novels. The answer comes in the form of his many essays and letters wherein the man expresses himself directly. The fiction, therefore, is the man in both his being and in his becoming. Huxley never rejected the notion that he was forever walking a slender tightrope between the development of story and narrative bent on social, political and moral instruction, but what he states indirectly through the mouths and actions of his characters, he speaks candidly in his multifarious essays and letters. It is noted in this analysis that Huxley stated that he wrote not for the reader, but for himself— as a means to explore and express what he was thinking at any given point in time. And his thoughts and feelings varied according to the times, the situations, and the personal experiences of a very probing mind. Never ashamed of the contradictory paths he sometimes chose, he consistently sought the wisdom of the ages to guide him on his own road to self-actualization. Accordingly, it is the very soul of the man that is woven skillfully and intricately within the framework of his fiction.

While numerous scholarly and critical studies have been researched in this undertaking, and Bedford's biography of Huxley has proved invaluable, it is Huxley's words as expressed in editor Smith's collection of letters and the prolific array of essays written by Huxley that prove to be the supportive heart of this study's thesis. No examination of a man of such profound intellect and creative talent can truly do him justice. This analysis in no way is the most critical endeavor, nor is it the most comprehensive in scope. It is, however, markedly definitive in its thematic intent. Deliberately written in a reader-friendly manner, it is intended to serve as a valuable tool to the novice or student of Huxley; it is also humbly offered as an innovative contribution to the current body of analytical studies examining the novels of Aldous Huxley.

Like Calamy and Beavis and Barnack and Farnaby, as well as the entourage of characters who seek a more meaningful path to life in Huxley's fiction, I was drawn to both the man and his narratives in my doctoral studies and dissertation, as well as my many years of teaching. In Huxley I found a compassionate comrade with whom to travel on the road to a more meaningful existence. Huxley — the man and the literary artist — searched persistently, and he came out on the other end of authentic understanding; his is a journey that all of us comprehend, and it is a nirvana for which all of us yearn.

So it is the young, avant-garde Huxley who brazenly satirizes the mores of his society and the diverse personalities that populate it (*Crome Yellow*, *Antic Hay* and *Those Barren Leaves*). Had he not seen so many of them at various social functions including those at Garsington Manor? Then there is the Huxley who writes to his father that he seeks to say more in his fiction than story — to display contrary views on life as in *Point Counter Point*. The Huxley who began writing a satire becomes more serious minded in displaying a humanity that has lost its way in a science-fictional narrative (*Brave New World*) set in the future. What would happen if a materialistic world bent on pleasure lost its soul? A thought-provoking Huxley moves to a more mystical perspective — to see with new eyes — in *Eyeless in Gaza*, a path that becomes far more pronounced in *After Many a Summer Dies the Swan* and *Time Must Have a Stop*. Across time, despite its serious shortcomings, Huxley still envisages hope for humanity following nuclear devastation in *Ape and Essence*, a hope that was lost to the likes of H.G. Wells following the desolation of World War II. This hope is blended with reminiscence in *The Genius and the Goddess* and culminates in profound wisdom in *Island*. The journey evolves but is unfortunately cut short because we are "all moving towards the same consummation — towards the progressive cutting of the lines of communications ... toward the final plunge, alone" in the cessation of life.[6]

In his quest for self-awareness in a loveless world, Huxley was to experiment with those means that would improve his vision and expand his mind. Ultimately, he came to believe that for all those who sought the kingdom of God first, all the rest would follow. Consequently, in his fiction, he prophetically characterizes what happens to those who invert the process. By taking his readers on journeys of discovery, he wanted to enable them to consciously observe and to question their own world, an exercise not always possible when one is trapped by the busyness of life. The image of the divided self— a being so involved in the present that he is unable to truly observe the world around him until sometime later, after the fact — is the figure, therefore, visited by Huxley in many of his novels.

Whether objectively observing a present or future generation dehumanized following the trauma of war; projected into the mindless existence of technological efficiency; absorbed into a morally depraved soul struggling to hold onto mortality; or converted to a new vision of the way the world could or ought to be, the spectrum of Huxley's insights blend with his satiric wit and search for a better way into literary works whose prophetic vision is astonishing.

Introduction

The 20th-century English novelist Aldous Huxley, both as a popular writer and an intellectual luminary, became a persuasive voice in protest against contemporary materialism and a future world dominated by science. His novels helped shape an awareness of what he saw as an inexorable trend toward technological power that would lead to dehumanization.

Huxley's creative years must be viewed against the temper of his times and his distinctive social background. His writing career began in Europe in the hectic years after World War I and continued in America through the Atomic Age following World War II. While his early novels satirized the frivolous lives of the English upper class in the twenties, his later fiction would focus on more probing moral issues and ethical dilemmas associated with the human quest for meaning and fulfillment.

Huxley had grown up in an age fascinated by a procession of new scientific marvels. The late 19th and early 20th centuries had become characterized by an increasing confidence in scientific progress and a fascination with inventions that promised a better life. Industrialization, a higher standard of living, medical breakthroughs — all such improvements encouraged the optimistic belief that applied technology would ultimately solve all human woes.

This buoyant outlook was reflected in the popular literature of the period. Jules Verne in the 19th century gained international fame for his fictional prophecies of fabulous scientific inventions that were to come. By the turn of the century in England, H.G. Wells, a student of Huxley's grandfather, was acclaimed in his writings as a passionate advocate of the coming dominance of science in everyday life. The popularity of the emerging genre of science fiction originated with these imaginative predictions of technical wonders that would transform the world.

This general optimism was shattered for many Europeans when World

War I introduced such technological marvels as poison gas and the machine gun that destroyed millions of lives. World War II brought even greater scientific horrors such as the Nazi gas ovens, and the added threat of nuclear annihilation raised even stronger doubts about the inevitability of continual favorable advances through science. Social critics and moralists with the benefit of hindsight began to recognize that technological progress could exact a very high price for the illusory promise of a perfect world awaiting humankind. Following World War I, popular thinkers such as Oswald Spengler, the German philosopher and historian, warned that, along with the power to control nature, a contrary social tendency toward disorder or disintegration — what had been termed entropy — could result in the collapse of Western civilization.

The comfortably optimistic world of the 19th century thus swiftly came to confront the brutality of world wars, worldwide economic depression, and the menace of communism and fascism in the 20th century. With individual freedoms on the decline and rapid industrial changes in the work place alienating the masses, common humanity simultaneously felt controlled, trapped, and helpless. Creative artists of the time like Picasso, Stravinsky, Eliot, and Joyce responded with a modernistic creative movement that broke with tradition and produced innovative and often disturbing forms of aesthetic expression.

In the 1920s, at the height of this artistic ferment, Aldous Huxley would emerge as a gifted young satirical novelist with a distinguished family background. He was heir to a lineage of intellectual brilliance, social concern, and creative talent. Huxley's Victorian forebears were particularly noteworthy. His grandfather, Thomas Henry Huxley, was a controversial 19th-century iconoclast who championed Darwin's theory of evolution. On his mother's side, he was a descendent of the noted Victorian educator Thomas Arnold; the poet Matthew Arnold; and Mrs. Humphry Ward, a widely read novelist whose themes dramatized the crisis of faith that afflicted Victorian society.

These family influences would affect Huxley's own attitudes as a writer. Radically opposed to his grandfather's faith in scientific progress, he would also seek through his imaginative fiction to warn society of the consequences of its folly and the need to reform. In this respect, Huxley seems to have inherited an idealistic family strain that repeatedly led him to warn society of the error of its ways. This idealism was to manifest itself later in an almost mystical search for spiritual reality — a search that was to take some rather unusual turns.

Huxley's impressive literary output explores many social, ethical, and religious themes. One of his most salient purposes was to expose a world so obsessed with material values that human progress, despite so many technological advancements, was actually in a state of regression. Scientific power was, according to Huxley, meaningless and destructive unless it enhanced the idealistic goals of human advancement.

Huxley's approach to these issues is that of a creative artist. While it is generally accepted that authentic literature should not be overtly didactic, serious fiction cannot be divorced from the dilemmas of real life. Through myth and allegory, literature has traditionally offered instructive insights on the human condition. Modern novels can also confront us with concrete moral contentions, and then describe personal human responses to life's challenges that involve the reader both intellectually and emotionally. They engage our feelings, and this engagement enriches our understanding of the meaning and purpose of life.

Huxley's incisive analysis of modern ills is in keeping with a strong literary tradition. Social criticism has always been a theme of imaginative writing. Classical authors such as Aristophanes and Horace first employed satire and irony to laugh humanity out of its follies. This critical mode was later adapted by such acerbic commentators as Jonathan Swift, of whom Aldous Huxley may be seen as a modern counterpart. Other well-known novelists as diverse as George Orwell and Alexander Solzhenitsyn have used their narrative art to decry social injustice — real or potential. Far from writing pure propaganda, these authors produced authentic literature that has profoundly affected public attitudes. It could further be claimed that these imaginative artists have been more influential than many contemporary philosophers and social thinkers because their books are more widely reviewed, publicized, and read. Huxley's granduncle, Matthew Arnold, had indicated that serious literature should expose the best and the worst of life for critical discernment. Aldous Huxley was to take this advice very seriously by brilliantly rendering imaginative tales probing diverse aspects of the human condition.

Any reader of Huxley will quickly recognize that he is a writer with a strong point of view. The failure in human fulfillment depicted in his fiction is evidence of the human cost of material progress. To Huxley, and the proponents of his perennial philosophy — wisdom of the ages that recognizes a divine reality sustaining the physical world — the question of whether physical progress is important or even possible is not of primary significance.

What is crucial for Huxley is the degree to which any scientific change aids or impedes society in the achievement of its ultimate human destiny.

This study seeks to analyze Aldous Huxley's novels, specifically demonstrating the maturation of his attitudes and concerns, from his first work published in 1921 through his last novel published in 1962, the year prior to his death. Reference to other books by the author will further illuminate his ideas, but these major examples from his imaginative works represent the most compelling evidence of his creative insight.

Throughout Huxley's literary career, he was always warning society about the human cost of scientific progress. He cautioned his readers that the harm caused by manipulating nature far exceeded the benefits achieved, a concept under close evaluation in our contemporary age. Huxley believed that humanity's overweening pride in its new powers and its blind trust in technological progress would invariably have to be paid for in human suffering. He wrote narratives that specifically questioned whether humanity was progressing toward or regressing from an ultimate goal. Ethical, moral, and social issues relating to the subject of industrial dominance in modern society are debated strongly in these novels. The relevance of key personal letters and essays written by Aldous Huxley in the period of each novel provide further evidence of the author's views.

Huxley's first four novels to be examined (*Crome Yellow*, *Antic Hay*, *Those Barren Leaves*, and *Point Counter Point*) may be categorized as novels of social criticism wherein Huxley employs satire or comic criticism to castigate the multiple social failings of his age. Three novels (*Eyeless in Gaza*, *After Many a Summer Dies the Swan*, and *Time Must Have a Stop*) maintain the satiric approach, but here the characters come to the realization that their pride, sensuality, and trust in material progress leave them devoid of spiritual worth — in each is a central character who seeks a better way through spiritual enlightenment. Three other narratives (*Brave New World*, *Ape and Essence*, and *Island*) may be generally labeled science fiction. The first two books project a future world that will result if technology continues at its present pace to exert greater control over humankind. Regarded by most critics as his seminal work, the study of *Brave New World*, therefore, is given more extensive scrutiny. Since the future depicted in both stories is far grimmer than 20th-century Western culture, they may be classified as dystopian novels — a variation on utopian fiction that describes a highly unfavorable future world. Huxley's final novel offers a synthesis of the two novels' conflicting themes by positing the possibility of a better world if limited technology and humane aspiration could achieve a harmonious union. Seven years after *Ape and Essence*, and likewise seven before his final synergistic work *Island*, is a small novella that stands alone: *The Genius and the Goddess*. Huxley's letters and other occasional writings, including transcripts of his lectures, also proved useful in elucidating the themes and motivations in the fiction he was working on at the time. Unfailingly instructive, he lost no occasion to inform his reader of the fascinating ideas that continually occupied his mind.

What is particularly striking is his skill as an imaginative artist to engage the reader in confronting moral predicaments that are more relevant today than ever before. The social and ethical alarm over the increasing influence of technology in today's world continues to sustain the reading public's interest in Huxley's fiction. While some of his predictions may seem quaint or outdated with the passage of time, on essential human issues his original satire remains right on target. Huxley was a remarkably clear-sighted visionary, and the thematic essence of his fiction is powerful, insightful, and resonates with the modern age.

Nuclear proliferation, the extreme power of the media, the lack of ecological responsibility, the economic and political dominance of technology, and the alienation and despair symptomatic of a materialistic society are but a few of his realized prophecies. While Aldous Huxley may not be listed among the supreme writers of the 20th century, he continues to maintain a significant influence. In 1960, Clifton Fadiman, the distinguished editor and critic, summed up Huxley's influence by stating: "I know no other single English or American writer who reflects with such clarity the last forty years of shifts and modulations in the Western intellect, including its latest shift toward the thought of the East."[1] Huxley's books are widely read and discussed by intellectuals, politicians, and the educated public. They remain on the reading lists of colleges and graduate schools throughout the world. They should endure of permanent interest as a vivid reflection of the social disquiet and spiritual uneasiness affecting Western culture immediately following the dawn of a new millennium.

ONE

The Man

Family Influences

Aldous Leonard Huxley's perception of the world as reflected in his novels was profoundly affected early on by the temper of the age in which he lived, by his family lineage, and by his life experiences. He was born toward the end of the Victorian era in 1894, a period when vast industrialization also brought to England the evils of mass unemployment and economic crisis. The conflict between religion and the new sciences continued to be argued, and traditional moral values were increasingly questioned. Huxley was to come to manhood during the catastrophic experience of World War I, and he was to write his first successful works during the turbulent postwar era of social unrest characterized as the Roaring Twenties. The Victorian social confidence that permeated the greater part of the 19th century had long been eroded. Young Huxley's association with his family's scientific and literary milieus was to contribute to a fascination with modern progress but also a somber recognition of the demands for social reform. The models for the conflicting views that he came to question surrounded him from an early age.

Queen Victoria's rule in England (1837–1901) had been characterized by a rapid growth in industry, an enormous increase in the urban population, greater agricultural production, and improved medical techniques. Great Britain seemed destined to continue as the leading industrial nation of the world. This swelling optimism and faith in the inevitability of progress was bolstered by the traditional beliefs of a national church, but these foundations were already under attack. One noteworthy controversy was over Charles Darwin's *The Origin of the Species* (1859) and the theory of evolution. Skeptics and free thinkers accepted the possibility that man was descended from a lower animal form of life. Religious leaders argued against it on the grounds that it attacked the literal meaning of the Bible, and in 1860 they selected a strong conservative, Bishop Samuel Wilberforce, as their spokesman. Much to Darwin's good fortune, one of his staunchest and most eloquent defenders was Thomas Henry Huxley, grandfather of Aldous Huxley.

Aldous Huxley's father, Leonard, was to summarize an 1860 debate held at Oxford between Bishop Wilberforce, nicknamed "Soapy Sam" for his smooth oratory style, and his father, Thomas Huxley, the champion of Charles Darwin who was dubbed "Darwin's Bulldog" in the press of his day. The elder patriarch was also affectionately called Grandfather in the Huxley home and came to be regarded as a lay saint by his descendants.[1] As a zealous advocate of evolution and new scientific theories, T.H. Huxley was at the center of the intellectual and social reform movement in the second half of the 19th century.[2] The common metaphor of the times — a war between science and religion — can be credited to Thomas Henry Huxley, who both captivated and outraged audiences with his talk of ape ancestors and who coined the fashionable term *agnostic*.[3] Although Thomas Huxley died when Aldous was less than a year old, his skeptical, inquiring mind and scientific interests were to influence his grandchild.

The early literary inclination of Aldous Huxley may be attributed to his parents, Leonard and Julia Arnold Huxley, who were distinct both in their ancestry and life pursuits. An assistant master at Charterhouse, a private school, when Aldous was born, Leonard Huxley wrote a two-volume biography of his famous father that was published in 1900 as *Life and Letters of Thomas Henry Huxley*. From 1901 onward, he served as the editor of *Cornhill Magazine*, and was also involved in editing the letters of Elizabeth Barrett Browning.[4]

Huxley's mother was the granddaughter of Thomas Arnold of Rugby, the famous educator, and the niece of Matthew Arnold, the poet and critic. Her father was Thomas Arnold, the Anglican clergyman, who, scandalously, twice converted to Catholicism, and her sister became Mrs. Humphry Ward, the celebrated novelist. Despite the care of her four children — Julian, Trevenen, Aldous, and Margaret — Mrs. Huxley found time to establish and serve as headmistress of a girls' school, Prior's Field.[5]

Two noteworthy literary thematic influences can be traced to the maternal side of Huxley's family. The struggle for certainty in the late Victorian world of religious doubt is evident from the poetry of Matthew Arnold. In "Dover Beach," for example, Arnold poignantly symbolized declining faith in the form of the desolate seashore scene and the retreating tide. This loss would lead to a world of human misery where ignorant armies will battle in the night. The poet's only solution was a call for personal love and fidelity.

Matthew Arnold, as an educator and social commentator, was to write criticism on literary, social, religious, and political themes — subjects that were to concern Huxley throughout his later literary career. Most noteworthy among Arnold's books is *Culture and Anarchy*, in which he prophetically warns that cultures cannot be produced by the machine. He saw industrialization not as an end but rather as a means to improve the human condition, a theme later explored by his nephew.

Huxley's aunt, Mrs. Humphry Ward, was another possible influence, especially through her literary themes on the conflict of faith and social reform. Her most popular novel, *Robert Elsmere*, depicts a young Anglican clergyman who abandons his calling to be of practical service to the poor. The central character may have been drawn from her own father's struggle to come to terms with his proper vocation as a clergyman. Her advocacy of Christianity grounded in social service rather than theology raised a public controversy in her time. Her other novels assailing social injustice and criticizing national indifference exemplify a literary attitude that was not lost on the young Huxley. Her nephew Aldous was to spend considerable time with his aunt after the death of his mother, and especially a period of convalescence following his temporary blindness. In 1912, when his friend Charles Harman came to stay with Huxley at Mrs. Ward's home, Harman remarked that there was a complete collection of Mrs. Ward's novels in almost every room of the house.[6]

His grandfather's devotion to science and his other remarkable forebears' passion for social reform influenced the sensitive young mind of Aldous Huxley. Here may be found the roots of his mature views on the scientific world of the 20th century. The ambivalent results of applied science or technology as it affected lives in the late 19th century were directly observed and experienced by this family of writers. England, at the center of the Industrial Revolution in the immense British Empire, had witnessed an improved standard of living and some social reform at the cost of overcrowded cities, ugly factories, and a downtrodden working class that suffered great economic insecurity. Charles Dickens had attacked the plight of the poor in his novels, and Karl Marx, then living in England, had called for a proletarian revolution. There was, however, little public understanding of the root of the problem — the connection between technology and the human condition. This understanding would come later.

An Altered Destiny

Born in the last decades of the Victorian Age into a European culture obsessed with technological progress, the young Huxley would presumably follow the family tradition in some scientific field, such as biology or medicine. He was attracted to science through his omnivorous reading, but personal tragedies would radically alter his attitude and eventual destiny. It was at Eton, as a King's Scholar, that two traumatic events were to alter the young man's outlook. The first was the death of his mother in 1908, a death that left a great void. "It was to Aldous the irreparable loss; a betrayal of his faith in life ... he never got over it," writes Juliette Huxley about the impact of Julia Huxley's death on her impressionable son.[7] Mrs. Huxley died of cancer at home under the loving care of her family. The drama of a dying patient suffering physically while the conscious mind questions the meaning of life is a theme repeated by Huxley, in one form or another, in several of his fictional works.

At the age of seventeen, while a promising young Eton scholar, Huxley was diagnosed with incipient blindness. In the spring of 1911, a medical doctor, Uncle Henry Huxley, told the family that the eye damage was already severe and there was little hope that Aldous would ever recover his eyesight. Overwork at Eton, depression over the loss of his mother, or a bout of influenza were possible causes, but Ernest Clarke, a prominent eye surgeon, soon confirmed a diagnosis that *staphylococcus aureus*, a bacterial infection, resulted in *keratitis punctata* or an inflammation of the cornea. With no antibiotics available at the time, permanent eye damage was unavoidable. Weekly injections of serum under home care were Aldous's medical treatment for the next year.[8] Never complaining, Huxley accepted his lot and went on with his education, teaching himself to play the piano and to read Braille.[9] He would suffer from near blindness for the rest of his life, and in some ways, his weak physical sight was befitting a man who was perpetually seeking an inner vision of reality. Through his own untiring quest for knowledge and with a succession of tutors, no time was lost in Huxley's continuing education.

His brother Julian regarded Aldous's blindness as a blessing in disguise, since he could not picture him as a routine family doctor, and he thought that his true genius would have been wasted in medicine.[10] Two ironies are evident in this misfortune. While Aldous Huxley's poor eyesight would have made medicine problematic, his lifelong dedication to reading and writing would prove even more taxing on his sight. Moreover, Aldous Huxley's gradual distrust of technological progress and his spiritual awakening both fly in the face of the dominant scientific attitudes of his time.

By 1913, Aldous's vision was partially restored. For the next 25 years, however, one eye was capable of only vague perception, and his good eye required spectacles of great magnification, as well as regular doses of atropine to dilate the pupil. He would later learn eye exercises to improve his sight, and he was to become known as exceptionally well informed in all fields of knowledge. The desire to see in a new way, a possibility ignored or denied by the average person, became an important discipline in Huxley's life. The very fact that he could consciously improve his physical sight was later to become a motive for deeper insight into the ultimate purpose of life.

With his father remarried, Aldous spent the spring and summer of 1913 at Oxford, staying with his brother Trevenen in preparation for university entrance in the fall. In October he was to enter Balliol College. He threw himself into his studies, and he quickly made a tremendous impression on faculty and colleagues as extremely intelligent and well read.[11] Fluent in French by this time, Huxley's capacity for knowledge was extraordinary. He was compared in learning to the *Encyclopædia Britannica*, volumes that he carried with him on his trip around the world in 1925.[12] In August 1914, however, a third tragedy was to strike his young life with lasting consequences.

While Grandfather T.H. Huxley had demonstrated an iron will vigor, some of his descendants were extremely sensitive and high-strung in temperament. Julian suffered from nervous breakdowns, and Trevenen, regarded as the most outgoing of the Huxley brothers, suffered from severe depression after a failed love affair and a disappointing performance in his studies.[13] While Aldous and his family were on vacation in Scotland, Trevenen left the nursing home grounds and hanged himself from a nearby tree. In a letter to a friend, Jelly d'Aranyi, the shaken Aldous spoke of his grief-stricken father, reminisced of the happy time that he and Trevenen had together and concluded: "It's a selfish grief perhaps, but oh Jelly, you know what he was to me."[14] The inevitability of suffering and the existential imperative to accept one's fate were to resonate in Huxley's steady awareness of life's tragedies.

Huxley responded to personal grief through the resources that were always a comfort to him: his books and his friends. In 1915, he indulged in the pleasant upper-class custom of extended weekends at country estates; he accepted the first of many invitations to participate in gatherings at Garsington Manor House, where intellectuals and artists were often the guests of society hostess Lady Ottoline Morrell. Bertrand Russell, Virginia Woolf, T.S. Eliot, and D. H. Lawrence were frequently among the notables in attendance.[15] Through intimate discussions with these literary figures, Huxley's sophisticated insights on the contemporary social world were to be nurtured. Here, also, he met Maria Nys, a young Belgian girl and World War I refugee whom the Morrells sheltered. In 1919, Maria was to become Huxley's first wife.

According to T.S. Eliot, many of these famous country house visitors were portrayed under disguises in Huxley's first novel, *Crome Yellow*.[16] Among the wartime guests were a number of pacifists who were classified as conscientious objectors. Aldous's poor eyesight led to his rejection by the Army, a status in line with the philosophical anti-war sentiment of this group. The argument of these conscientious opponents of armed combat was to remain with Huxley throughout his life and would find its way into many of his writings. After graduating from Oxford in 1916, Huxley stayed for a brief time at Garsington Manor before accepting a position as a teacher at his old school, Eton. The tedious classroom experience bears some resemblance to the brief academic career of Theodore Gumbril, the central character in Huxley's second novel, *Antic Hay*.

During this period, he published several collections of poems, but Huxley first had difficulty gaining recognition. He held a series of office jobs, and he edited and wrote literary reviews for *The Athenaeum* while contributing articles to several other periodicals. By the 1920s Huxley began to establish himself both as a critically acclaimed novelist and an essayist. He lived for a time in Italy and traveled worldwide before settling in California in 1937, where he was to remain until his death in 1963. While in Hollywood he was occasionally commissioned to write screenplays, generating an income that would provide a stable livelihood during the lean war years.

Huxley defined his long writing career simply: "My life has been uneventful, and I can speak only in terms of being and becoming, not of doing and happening."[17] Being and becoming is an ideal summation of the inner pursuit of this creative thinker. In retrospect, however, his was a productive life filled with the diverse achievements of a literary artist that included not only the novels, short stories, and essays for which he is best known, but also a mass of book reviews, introductions, biographies, travel books, articles, and even screenplays that were transformed into classic movies. Of these many writings, his eleven novels selected for examination demonstrate the range and development of his interests and talent.

Huxley's Development as a Novelist

Huxley frequently used satire as the chief tool in writing social criticism. It became his primary means of linkage between the narrative and the message. So biting at times was his satire, however, that he was accused of having a mean streak in exposing the ridiculous or pretentious. The master of satire whom Huxley admired and imitated was Jonathan Swift. As Swift acidly explained, satire was "a sort of Glass, wherein Beholders do generally discover everybody's Face but their Own."[18] This is the main reason, according to Swift, that satire is so popular a genre and why no one is offended by it. When, for example, his hero Gulliver sums up the common customs, mores, and manners found in English society of his day, the king of Brobdingnag is horrified and determines: "I cannot but conclude that the bulk of your natives to be the most pernicious race of little odious vermin that nature ever suffered to crawl upon the surface of the earth."[19] In contrast to Swift's indictment, Huxley may be considered more tolerant of mankind's foibles, but his satiric intent is equally strong.

Huxley exposes the folly of human ways in the settings, events, and actions of his fictional characters. In his early novels (*Crome Yellow, Antic Hay, Those Barren Leaves* and *Point Counter Point*), he satirizes a shameless world of frivolous pleasure seekers. In *Eyeless in Gaza, After Many a Summer Dies the Swan,* and *Time Must Have a Stop*, he ridicules the absurdity of materialism; in *The Genius and the Goddess*, he scoffs at the combative duplicity of human nature. Finally, the whole system of thoughts, values, and purpose of human civilization are satirically questioned in Huxley's worlds of future possibilities as depicted in *Brave New World, Ape and Essence,* and *Island*. Aldous Huxley's ability to blend a realistic portrait of humanity with clever parodies and satiric wit would become one of his most enduring achievements.

It is also important to note how accurately successive novels by Huxley reflect the social and intellectual crosscurrent of the times. At first, in the 1920s, Huxley was to write satiric novels of social criticism that depicted the long-range social and moral effects of World War I. These stories revealed how the loss of faith and idealism results in a self-centered culture seeking only material pleasures. Indifferent to any responsible role that they might play in their own destiny, people accepted years of financial depression and tolerated a government with no interest in social reform.

In the 1930s and 1940s, however, a progressive awareness of the possibility of spiritual enlightenment was to affect key characters in Huxley's fiction. These works demonstrate a radical change in character, a new attitude that was to reflect the deeper degree of spirituality that the author also experienced at this period of his life. This evolution began with recognition of human illusions, such as utopian dreams that technological marvels will be the salvation of mankind. Finally, in Huxley's last work of utopian fiction, a tone of cautious optimism suggests that humanity, free from crass materialism, can lead a balanced life by employing only selective technologies that will advance human development.

In the opening lines of Huxley's novel *The Genius and the Goddess* (1955), the hero complains: "The trouble with fiction ... is that it makes too much sense. Reality never makes sense."[20] The lament echoed Huxley's artistic dilemma throughout his prolific career: how to blend the appropriate mixture of exposition and narration so that it reflects a reality that makes sense. Although critics may attack Huxley's novels for didacticism, his overall literary and moral impact continued strong with his readers. In an early essay, "Sincerity in Art," Huxley asserted, "All literature, all art, best seller or worst, must be sincere, if it is to be successful."[21] He further states:

> The truth is that sincerity in art is not an affair of will, of a moral choice between honesty and dishonesty. It is mainly an affair of talent. A man may desire with all his soul to write a sincere, a genuine book but lack the talent to do it. In spite of all his sincere intentions, the book turns out to be unreal, false and conventional ... in matters of art "being sincere" is synonymous with "possessing the gifts of psychological understanding and expression."[22]

The eleven novels that comprise Huxley's venture into longer fiction will be evaluated on the basis of his own defined talent for "psychological understanding and expression." Transcending time, Huxley's ideas remain both instructive and relevant to the modern world. His first four novels (*Crome Yellow, Antic Hay, Those Barren Leaves,* and *Point Counter Point*) were all written in the 1920s. Similar in form, they are classified as works of social satire. Labels, however, do not do them justice. Iconoclastic for their time, Huxley probes the psyche of human nature through the eyes of amused, and somewhat detached, young men searching for meaning in a meaningless world — the world of the lost generation following World War I. And so this study begins with *Crome Yellow.*

TWO

The Four Social Satires

Crome Yellow

The Framework and Characters
in Huxley's First Novel

"I am working hard on my Peacockian novel, which I have pledged to finish by the end of July," Huxley writes to his father in June 1921, while he, along with his wife Maria and son Matthew, resided in a small, four-room house in Forte dei Marmi, Italy.[1] Inspired by the sparkling beauty of the Mediterranean Sea and the transcendent sunlight, he poured himself into his work and the writing flowed for some five to six hours each day. He completed the manuscript in just two months, almost the entire duration of his stay in this small village located some 20 miles north of Pisa.[2] He referred to it as entertainment and was pleased with "the fireworks of ideas, the erudite digressions, [and] the mild human ironies."[3] Whether meant seriously or tongue in cheek, he shared his mindset with H.L. Mencken when he wrote that he lacked the courage and patience to write a realistic work, and so he opted to create a "comic novel" in an "agreeable form" modeled essentially after Peacock requiring a "houseful of oddities."[4] To his brother Julian he was to write, "I hope it will amuse a little when it appears."[5] And so it both amused and outraged readers on both sides of the Atlantic after its publication. Published in November of 1921, Bedford calls its appearance for the writer "the end of the beginning," for from this point forward, Huxley had made a name for himself.[6]

Reminiscent of his time spent at Garsington Manor, Huxley brings us to the country estate of Henry and Pricilla Wimbush by way of a guest, Denis Stone, who has come for an extended stay during the hot and humid days of summer. Denis is just 23 — an aspiring poet who loves words, but often fails to find the right ones to fit the mood. He frequently desires to state something meaningful, amusing, or profound, but either misses the opportunity — as in his overtures of love for Anne — or is continuously cut short by the overreaching self-centered speech of another. Even in his arrival, no one seems to be present to greet him, and Pricilla Wimbush even states that she forgot he was coming. The house is filled with guests — Huxley's skillful plot device for bringing an eccentric assembly together under one roof at the same time. The characterizations are cleverly developed as we witness the guests either together as a single assembly interacting with one another, or separately in smaller, more intimate numbers.

The gathering consists of the intelligent, the witty and the dull. Henry Wimbush, the host, has just finished writing a history of the Crome estate, a study that, in addition to the recent excavation of artifacts like drainpipes on the property, has occupied the better part of the past 30 years of his life. Wimbush reads several passages aloud; these imaginative tales are skillfully woven into the novel with one about the dwarf, Sir Hercules, being especially memorable since it resembles satirically the inverted world in Swift's *Gulliver's Travels*. Henry comes to life only in the recitation of these tales and has little to any interest in contemporary affairs. His wife, the hostess of Crome — described by Denis as being very masculine — uses the horoscope to place her wagers on horses and dallies in spirituality, the reason for her invitation to Mr. Barbecue-Smith who provides an amusing anecdote about the lot of the writer in his advice to Denis on the pivotal need for inspiration. Anne, a niece of the Wimbushes, is four years older than Denis and, on that ground alone, rejects his overtures of love. But he is not alone — she also dismisses the more aggressive and lustful advances of Gombauld — a successful artist for whom she poses. Mary Bracegirdle — here Huxley unabashedly is having fun with the name chosen — has read Freud and sees within her "repressions" (i.e., a euphemism for sexual compulsions), an instinctual need that must be satisfied. And satisfied it is in one of the towers of the estate with Ivor, the handsome, Roman Catholic rogue who seduces her and then abandons Crome. Mr. Scogan is the epitome of the well-read, well-educated man of the world who engages at the drop of a hat in the lengthiest passages of the novel, discoursing on his view of art and life. In one noteworthy passage he foreshadows the very framework of Huxley's futuristic narrative written a decade later, namely *Brave New World*. Finally, there is Jenny who is deaf — silently she views the scene and records satirically in her sketchbook all of the outrageous, trivial, and scandalous vagaries of English society she witnesses at Crome.

In harsh contrast to the worldly delights of the assembly is Mr. Bodiham, the local vicar who is described as having features of iron — he rigidly sits in his rectory after delivering his Sunday sermon with fury. Re-reading the wonders of his sermon delivered four years earlier during the war — an event he utilized within the sermon to signal prophetically the Second Coming — he sits dejectedly since England is now at peace, the sun is shining and the people of Crome "were as wicked and indifferent as ever."[7] "Disgusting" is his wife's comment as they view the swimmers in the pond at the Crome fair, and Mr. Bodiham looks up at the sky and asks "How Long?" The presence of this character, the contents of his sermon, and his reaction to the escapades of Crome's residents are placed within the context of the players at Crome to provide an ironic and satiric contrast between the ways of the flesh and the rigid fundamentalism of a Christian creed. Very much the iconoclast, Huxley — at least in his novel — makes no judgment, but the outrageous juxtaposition is crafted to amuse and to fly in the face of post–Victorian sensibilities. While Huxley's depiction may have proved amusing to the secular and offensive to the pious, it is in his unconventional and flagrant regard for matters of sexuality that the novel proved to be controversial.

For here then is Ivor who takes Mary up to the tower and has his way with her; here is a woman, Mary Bracegirdle, who discusses with Anne which of two men — Denis or Scogan — she should solicit to satisfy her "repressions." Here also is a disagreeable moment between Anne and Gombauld over matters of the flesh. Anne accuses Gombauld of the same trait she sees in all male "savages" who blame their lustful desires on the women who allure them. Gombauld frustratingly replies that Anne was playing the same game with Denis and asks that she "leave that wretched young man in peace."[8] These scenes and conversations had not occupied the pages of a Peacockian novel or a romance narrative of the period, and albeit very mild by today's standards, they were shocking to some of Huxley's audience.

Among the array of eccentrics to weave in and out of the rooms of Crome, Denis is the connecting thread — we arrive and depart Crome with him. Unfortunately, Denis finds himself often unhappy and miserable, both in his unrequited love for Anne, and his fear of displaying any inadequacy. He often listens to others and fails to express an opinion. He even apologizes when Anne criticizes his tendency to quote others without providing the source or the context. The description of his lengthy contemplation over what to wear displays his superficial desire to ever please the public. Frequently cut short before he is able to answer a question or engage in a conversation, Denis repeatedly thinks noble, eloquent thoughts but does not vocalize them. Accused by Anne of being like the academic Scogan, she asks him why he cannot be more spontaneous and just enjoy things as they come along. Denis — in a moment of unusual personal revelation — admits that he cannot because he needs to analyze everything or else he cannot achieve any enjoyment. He admits that this is a folly. Touching on relationships between the sexes, Anne suggests that Denis needs a nice wife, a good income, and a regular job. Once more Denis thinks, "What I need is you," but cannot say it. He keeps fighting his shyness and wonders why she cannot see what he is thinking. On the brink of stating these words, Anne rises and says she will go and bathe. Once more, for Denis, "the opportunity had passed."[9]

Denis acknowledges — at least inwardly — that his love for Anne is hopeless and unattainable. He is seen locked in his room in a state of melancholy referred to as "accidie."[10] Denis's inability to help himself, Anne's daily presence in his life, as well as what he perceives as her romantic relationship with Gombauld, drives him to inexpressible jealousy and attendant despair. On rare occasions when he tries to seize the opportunity, his actions often emulate those of a buffoon. In this regard, for example, when Anne falls and twists her ankle, he finally gets the courage to kiss her only to receive her protestations; he then tries a cavalier act — to carry her back to the house — only to drop her and provoke her laughter. Even his words, "I love you," that escaped his strangled voice, solicited Anne's response, "My poor Denis."[11]

Gombauld — his chief rival — is better than him, Stone muses, on all counts: his looks, his humor, his confidence and his accomplishments. Denis, on the other hand, is merely an intelligent man with potential. Scogan — the erudite — tries to move Denis out of his reverie, but is cruel rather than kind. He tells Denis that he may never — like himself— amount to anything because he is a rational man and only madness gets anything done. Men of intelligence, he declares, must attain power by harnessing the insanities of the world to create a Rational State.[12] Denis still listens but is far too deep into his personal misery to appreciate Scogan's satiric pronouncements. In this shocking discourse, Scogan foreshadows the very structure of Huxley's dystopian achievement, *Brave New World*. In this case, Scogan explains, the Rational State of the future will dictate, by testing children at birth, an education proportionate to ability, thereby placing each person logically into an adult role suitable to intelligence. Denis dismisses his need for power to accomplish great things, but earnestly asks Scogan what his place would be within this Rational State. And poor Denis — much to the amusement of the reader — is told that he would fit nowhere. Satirically stated, Scogan indicates: "No, I can see no place for you; only the lethal chamber."[13] And then, in a twist of social mockery, Scogan says that he and Stone should be grateful for their lot, for the masses are toiling in the fields to allow them to speak of "Polynesia." Of course, "leisure and culture had to be paid for," he observes, but it is not the leisured and the cultured — like he and Denis — who are picking up the tab.[14]

If there is no place for Denis in the Rational State, is there any place for him in the irrational milieu of Crome? Despite his painful inadequacies in matters of the heart and the fact that he was his own worst critic, Denis Stone still did see himself as above others. When he went to Piccadilly Circus, he imagined himself to be the one conscious individual among the masses. Could there actually be a world outside himself as complete as the one he experienced within? Occasionally, this outer world did come into sharp focus as when he opened Jenny's private notebook and found a caricature of himself with Anne and Gombauld dancing in the background. The caption said it all: "Fable of the Wallflower and the Sour Grapes.[15] He ruminated on this for some time.

Ironically, Denis concludes that his worst fault is his lack of decisive action. Depressed after seeing Gombauld and Anne embracing, he ascends the stairs to the tower and gazes below contemplating suicide. Whether he would have gone through with the act is questionable for he is interrupted by Mary Bracegirdle who has been sleeping in the tower ever since her night of passion spent there with Ivor. For the first time, Denis opens up to another person and recounts to Mary his tale of woe: his love for Anne, his jealousy when seeing her with Gombauld, and his thoughts of suicide. Mary, in turn, recounts her own romantic pain and devises a plan for Denis. He must leave immediately. She even awakens him out of his slumber in the early morning so that he might go to the station to send himself a telegram: he must leave Crome immediately due to family urgent business.

Caught up in the plan, Denis accedes but regrets his decision especially when Anne states she does not want to see him go. Ironically, the reader knows that Anne was never intimate with Gombauld — she rebuffs his embrace and advances and scolds him. Mary, however, certain that Anne had also given in to her "repressions," tells Denis with certitude that it must have happened and that his only course of action is to leave. Denis swiftly departs, taking passage in what he describes as a hearse, not knowing what he is to do with himself when he returns to London having cut short his vacation, and promises that he "never again would do anything decisive."[16]

Crome Yellow: The Satiric Episodes

And so *Crome Yellow* concludes, but within its pages are cleverly narrated, irreverent scenes, satiric ploys, and dynamic characterizations that sparkle like the "chrome yellow" pigment from which Huxley tweaked the name. Denis Stone may have the capability of becoming a gem in time, but his duration at Crome provides the reader with many witty scenes by which Huxley holds up the Swiftian satiric mirror to his world. The plot of *Crome Yellow* is not filled with a great conflict leading to a riveting climax. Rather, the clever interfacing of scenes is played out by both engaging and eccentric characters who entertain the reader, principally by parading before him the parodies of life.

Even in its ending, there is an ironic twist — Denis fails to realize that he has been duped by Mary into action when she is incapable of doing the same. She works out a plan and forces him to follow through to his own detriment. He forgets her earlier revelation to him that concluded with Denis being ignored. As a matter of fact, Mary heard the gong of the lunch bell and left Denis in mid-sentence, neither apologetic nor at all concerned about his need to communicate. Moments earlier, she related, in all seriousness, how Ivor, after taking away her virginity — one she freely abandoned — left Crome and sometime later sent her a postcard with a four-line poem of passion. The note made a request: Could she ask one of the housemaids to send the razor blades he had left behind. While giving up her repressions had not provided the peace she sought, she realizes that she could never do without Ivor, but he certainly could do without her.

Despite Mary's tale exposing Ivor's crassness, the reader cannot help but be amused. This was the same woman who was aggressively seeking intimacy for its own sake, yet was now equating her one-night stand with Ivor as love. She had even sought Anne's advice in determining whom she should choose as a sexual partner to relieve her *repressions* — a word that Anne initially mistakes for *depressions*. In an amusing dialogue that cleverly interfaces rational objectivity with sensual underpinnings, Mary bravely announces that she cannot continue to keep dreaming of falling down wells. While Anne advises that she should wait until she is in love (or even married) to relieve her *repressions*, Mary insists that if she continues in her present state, "one may become a nymphomaniac if one is not careful."[17] She seeks "knowledge" — a euphemism for experience — and decides that her two choices are Denis and Gombauld, with Denis having the edge because he is more "civilized," thereby giving the word a new meaning.

That such a subject was not perceived to be the topic of polite conversation between two women of the era is a given; that Anne and Mary speak in a language that hints at but never states its true purpose is evidence of Huxley's satiric craft. Mary departs Anne's bedchamber stating that she will go to bed to think about it. Still in fear of her repeated dream of falling down a well, Anne replies — perhaps from personal experience venturing into Gombauld's studio — it is better than dreaming of falling down ladders. Later, bent on a course of action with Denis that will lead to a loss of *repressions*, Mary confronts the man who cannot stand her. Asking him which of the contemporary poets he likes the best, Denis, in a fury to rid himself of this woman's presence replies, "Blight, Mildew, and Smut," thinking of the three diseases of wheat."[18] Dismissing her, Mary was to muse for some time about not hearing or understanding Denis accurately, for surely these were not contemporary poets whom she had not read.

Then again there is the debate between Mary and Scogan. The latter sees sex as a laughing matter but Mary — with her *repressions* — sees it as a serious affair. Scogan explains that in sex one may find laughter and pleasure that surmounts the pain and misery of life. Shortly thereafter, following moments of silence, Ivor leaps into the room and Scogan solicits his response to the question: Is amour serious? Ivor answers that it is, to which Mary speaks of her triumph on the issue, but her glee is only momentary. Scogan asks in what sense it is serious, and Ivor announces that it is only serious when it is an occupation since "one can go on with it without being bored."[19]

After her lover departs, Mary presumably commiserates with Denis about her tragic romantic experience. It becomes obvious, however, that her commiseration is one-sided. Concluding that intimacy must always lead to suffering — a conclusion drawn from a single night's experience — she does not allow Denis to tell his tale of woe; cutting him short in mid-sentence, she does not hear nor heed his personal evaluation that often people fail to see others beyond themselves. Perhaps this is the one underlying satire that pervades *Crome* — no one in residence can think about anyone but oneself — narcissism reigns in this microcosmic world.

The slim, earthy division between Crome's guests and the animal kingdom is comically presented in a scene that concludes with Scogan's aforementioned prophecy. Mr. Wimbush has taken his guests to view the home farm. Six of them are viewing the pigsty when Mr. Wimbush announces proudly that his sow had a litter of 14. He continues that the sow next to it only delivered five. If she is not successful, given one more chance at greater productivity, she will be fattened and killed. Pointing to the boar and indicating that he may see the same fate since he is beyond his prime, these proclamations incite horror, delight and amazement among those assembled. Watching the army of piglets greedily fight each other to get to the mother's dug for nourishment, Mary fascinatingly counts the 14, Anne declares that farming is both indecent and cruel, and Scogan philosophically concludes that in this farm there is the perfect model of a sensible paternal order: breed them, work them, and then when they can no longer produce, butcher them.

Juxtaposed at this moment is Denis with a walking stick scratching the back of a boar. The hog moves closer and grunts at the pleasurable sensation that has all of the trappings of sexual foreplay. Denis declares that he is receiving as much pleasure in scratching the pig as the recipient. Later, in this farmland tour, Gombauld equates the fertility of these animals to human reproduction. He declares, "Everything ought to increase and multiply as hard as it can."[20] Pointing with his walking stick and thumping the bull's flanks, he continues that Anne, Mary, and Denis, and even Scogan ought to pass on their genetic talents to a bevy of children — it is a sin against life not to produce. Scogan is the one to respond to Gombauld's bold discourse. He, for one, looks optimistically to the future when Applied Science has gifted the world with another achievement, namely the dissociation of love from propagation. No longer will Eros struggle with Lucina. Free from the constraints that love can place on sexual desire, he once more foreshadows the sexual promiscuity that is an essential aspect of the world order in *Brave New World*. Scogan says that he envisions a future world in which people will be incubated in bottles with the family system destroyed. Anne — ever the irreverent one — replies that "it sounds lovely," to which Scogan sardonically concludes, "the distant future always does."[21]

In yet another satiric episode, Mr. Barbecue-Smith provides absurd advice to Denis regarding the craft of writing. Perhaps Huxley was having fun with the prolific writers of his time, or maybe he was recalling how swiftly he wrote *Crome Yellow*. But Barbecue-Smith states that between five and seven-thirty that evening he was able to write some 3,800 words. How? He put himself into a hypnotic trance, a trick he learned that he shares with Stone. He advises Denis to seek Inspiration and the writing will flow. At 38 years of age, he proclaims, he was struggling and poor, but now at 50 — with this method — he is highly successful at producing works in the blink of an eye.[22]

There is another scene — equally sardonic — when Denis is asked what he is writing. The high-brow society of Crome regarded poetry as the only serious contribution of the literary artist. When Denis admits that he is about to embark on verse and prose, Mr. Scogan — horrified at the possibility of a novel — decries the plot centered on Little Percy. He states that this young man, who moves from public school to the university, finds himself in London in a state of melancholy. Surrounded by bohemian artists, he writes a brilliant novel, engages in amorous affairs, and walks away at the end, into the future. Denis blushes at this recitation. He makes an effort to laugh and tell Scogan that he is wrong, but in his heart he is shocked that the man had described the actual storyline of his novel in precise detail. The overused plot of Denis's future novel may be both Huxley's humorous attempt at self-reproach, since he also had moved from poetry to the novel, but also a swipe at the predictable plots of many of his contemporary artists.

A whimsical series of scenes are depicted when the residents of Crome are occupied with the yearly Crome fair, a frivolous event organized by Mr. Wimbush. Each person is given a role: Anne is to man the tea tent; Mary will look after the children's sports; Gombauld will be painting portraits in five minutes for a shilling; and Mr. Scogan volunteers to tell fortunes, a role he takes on with gusto as he comically dresses as a woman and provides outrageous auguries to the unlearned and gullible townspeople. Denis is to write a poem — one that only sells three copies — and is to act as a steward to the event, a function that allows the reader to see much along with him. Once more, Mary, bent on one single subject, breathlessly recounts to Denis that there is a woman at the fair who has had three children in 31 months. Denis is counting in his head as Mary declares that she needs to tell her about the Malthusian League. And so it is, after hours of dancing, that Gombauld makes his advances on Anne, which Denis perceives as reciprocal, concluding his, and our, stay at Crome.

Crome Yellow: The Publication's Aftermath

Every writer reaches into his or her bag of experiences from which to create both the plot and the characterizations fashioned in a work of fiction. And it was no different with Huxley. While his sister Margaret was to write about Crome Yellow (and his other works) that she saw an "unkindness of attitude" that she never observed in her brother, the public, on the basis of the novel, was to regard Huxley as a cynic.[23] Huxley was very much taken aback at how many of his friends and associates saw themselves within characters in *Crome Yellow* and were quite offended by the portrait. Lady Ottoline was very upset by what she saw as an unfair and reprehensible depiction of her Garsington Manor; Philip Morrell reacted negatively to Huxley's depiction of him as Henry Wimbush; and Bertrand Russell likewise as Mr. Scogan. Ironically, although in appearance Scogan's description resembles Russell, it has been widely viewed that his opinions match those of Mencken.[24] Huxley argued that these were not meant as realistic portrayals, but comical and absurd representations in a work of literature. The Morrells, however, remained insulted, and Aldous and Maria were genuinely upset over their reaction.

Crome Yellow was a success critically and sold quite well, providing Huxley and his family for the first time with a decent living and the luxury of precious time to devote exclusively to writing. Huxley wrote it quickly with the intent of providing witty, satiric entertainment to his reader — there appears to be no underlying message as was to be present in future novels frequently labeled as those of ideas. F. Scott Fitzgerald — his American compatriot — hailed it as "the highest point so far attained by Anglo-Saxon sophistication."[25] The gathering of the idle rich, as well as the parasites who spend leisure time with them engaged in trivial pastimes, would be a source of critical humor for Huxley in the genus of his social satires. The aristocracy of England, and the nobility of the world for that matter, was dissipating — and so were the Wimbushes. It is not that the inhabitants of Crome gathered together for a summer holiday are without valid ideas, but often it is in their self-centered, materialistic meanderings, far removed from worldly concerns, that Huxley finds the meat of his satire.

Huxley's satiric skill and cunning portrait of a vanishing breed of the sophisticated English upper-class proved to be both shocking and entertaining to his contemporary audience. His insights into human nature, however, and his portrait of a select few, do transcend time and place. As the first in his subsequent full-length fiction, it is loaded with the wit, the clever dialogue, and satiric twists that were to be Huxley's trademark throughout the body of his work in the decade of the 1920s. While Huxley's intent was to entertain and satirically delight his reader, one may discern even within the pages of his first venture into the genre of the novel, a mind and a pen parenthetically searching for an intangible truth.

Looking closely, one may discover within the shadow of a Denis Stone the glimmer of a divided soul who is neither fully comfortable nor equipped to pursue any realm beyond oneself. It is posited that even in *Crome Yellow*, his first novel, Huxley wanted to say something meaningful in the midst of a seemingly otherwise meaningless world. This, then, was his first attempt to journey into the world of ideologies to penetrate the essence of what it means to be human in a world far less concerned with humane virtues. While Denis Stone experiences no growth but is only self-absorbed at the conclusion of the novel — as is true of all the residents at Crome — the satire serves to represent the need for him to supplant materialistic pursuits with something that has more purpose. Vicariously, the same may apply to both reader and author. Subtle in his approach, and assiduously never impinging on the development of story, Huxley was even then experiencing a need to journey into a realm that he would more actively pursue in his forthcoming novels. Here was the promise and potential for future literary success — a forecast that was to be achieved brilliantly.

Antic Hay

The Setting

Along with most of his generation, Huxley saw World War I as a terrible catastrophe that threatened the fate of Western Civilization. While earlier world epochs had caused deep pessimism, he could claim that "in no other century have the disillusionments followed on one another's heels with such un-intermitted rapidity; ... in no century has change been so rapid and profound."[26] In a contemporary essay, Huxley described the psychological sickness called *acedia*, or *accidie*, which is associated with early medical theory. This mental weakness is described as a profound hopelessness that paralyzes the will. Boredom, apathy, and despair are common symptoms. Huxley states that in the 1920s his generation had a right to suffer from an *accidie* that was forced upon them by fate.[27]

The pervasive sense of universal disillusionment characteristic of Europe in the early 1920s is the dominant tone of *Antic Hay*, and Huxley explains that the wave of human hopelessness was reflected in much of the art and literature of the time. Tracing examples of how the earlier impact of technology had profoundly affected humanity, Huxley cites the failure of the ideals of the French Revolution, the industrial progress that only increased social evils, and the urban slums as sources of human misery.[28] Europeans experienced ultimate disillusionment in World War I, but the following years of acute social and financial failures were to exacerbate this general sense of malaise.[29] This mood embodied Huxley's portrait of postwar London life in *Antic Hay*.

The title of the novel refers to an ancient country dance, and the epigraph from Christopher Marlowe's play *Edward II* reflects Huxley's satiric theme: "My men, like satyrs grazing on the lawns, shall with their goat-feet dance an antic hay."[30] Satyrs in Greek mythology were riotous woodland creatures whose physical features — goat's ears, legs, and horns — indicate that they shared human and animal traits. For Huxley, the city of London was filled with satyr-like residents — a pleasure-driven social class living idle lives fulfilling little human purpose and ignoring moral responsibilities.

The hero of the novel is Theodore Gumbril, who was to become the typical Huxleyan protagonist — an innocent eye through whom the reader both objectively and subjectively interacts with his world. Gumbril is a young schoolmaster who is to become involved in a sophisticated but questionable social milieu. The opening scene finds him sitting at a chapel service in his school, bored by a sermon that he believes to be nonsense. In his reverie, he is struck by the inspiration of a novel invention by which he could make his fortune. In short order, he resigns his post and joins an aimless band of his London friends in their meaningless pursuit of sensate pleasures on the road to nowhere.

Gumbril's father is an architect engaged in visionary social planning to whom his son reveals his distaste for teaching and his plans to amass a great fortune. The height of unabashed satire is evident in Gumbril's absurd design for trousers with an inflatable seat that will provide great comfort when sitting for lengthy periods of time. The concept attracts the attention of a clever but ruthless entrepreneur, who will use the modern technology of advertising to convince consumers to buy the dubious product. Boldero, the advertising manager, lays out the particulars of his crafty campaign. Speaking like a marketing expert, Boldero explains that they must first appeal to the customer's lust for comfort and craving for health and well being — both physical and spiritual. The sense of snobbery must also be appealed to by making the trousers a necessity without which a man would feel incomplete and inferior. An attractive slogan will stress the great advantages of these special pneumatic trousers over the ordinary outmoded kind.

On the London scene, Gumbril serves as an impressionable observer who describes for the reader the contemporary life and characters he encounters. His companions include Lypiatt, a third-rate poet and artist who recites his verse before the noisy revelers at a pub. Exposing the pivotal thematic intent early in the novel, Gumbril reacts vehemently to the poet's use of the word *dream*: "You can't possibly say 'dream,' you know ... not in this year of grace, nineteen twenty-two."[31] The disenchanted young man explains that modern people can have no dreams, no hopes, and no goals or, for that matter, any purpose to their lives: "After you've accepted the war, swallowed the Russian famine ... Dreams!" he exclaims.[32]

The literary argument initiates a spirited dialogue on ideals and values, a technique that was to become a characteristic of Huxley's novels. All action halts while the central characters, with great verve and penetrating wit, debate some burning issue of the times. Despite some critics who regard such arguments as a distraction, these intellectual exchanges are often the high points of the story. Gumbril is to encounter a number of diverse contemporaries in his travels about town, including the pompous Mercaptan, a literary critic whose lofty ideals do not prevent him from seducing Rose Shearwater, the demure wife of a friend. Rose is married to a scientist who is so consumed with his research that he has no time for her or a personal existence. Hence, she engages in an endless series of affairs with men in the novel, including Gumbril who pursues her while wearing a disguise. The popular fad of assuming disguises to emulate famous personalities underscores further the ineffectual lives of most of the characters.

The loose morals and the frantic search for pleasure are epitomized in Myra Viveash, a wealthy socialite who was probably patterned after Nancy Cunard, an extravagant and often scandalous aristocrat. Biographer Sybille Bedford indicates that Huxley fell in love with Cunard in 1922, the year he wrote *Antic Hay*, but the affair lasted only a few months.[33] Myra Viveash is fearful of old age and loneliness, and shamelessly has affairs with several of the characters, including Gumbril, while remaining an openly discontented and insatiable spirit. Her name is an intentional oxymoron: she is alive but has been burnt to an ash. She ignites passion in the men she meets, but cannot respond herself. She has sworn never to love again after the loss of her only true love in the war, and now she settles for the erotic pleasure procured in the chase.

One of Myra's more challenging conquests is the scientist James Shearwater, who typifies the theoretical specialist so absorbed in experiments that he cannot interact with the real world. Analogous to Mary Shelley's characterization of Victor Frankenstein, he locks himself away from the real world, absorbed in his scientific exploration at his own personal expense. Shearwater is unaware of his own wife's infidelity and does not know how to deal with the temptress Viveash. When she and Gumbril come to visit him at his laboratory, he screams and turns away from the glass through which they view him. His visitors leave realizing that they should not take the scientist away from his work, but Shearwater actually believes that by working harder he can exorcise the illusion.[34]

Immorality and cynicism destroy all sense of human values among the characters in *Antic Hay*, but Huxley does provide a chance for Gumbril's redemption through his tender feelings for Emily, a young woman with whom he has a platonic relationship. She evokes strong emotions in him, as well as a sense of terror analogous to when one shuts out the noisy world and is drawn deeper into an unfamiliar, calming silence. Gumbril, however, finds this atmosphere so alien that he cries out for the deafening music and frivolity of his world of thoughtless pleasures. He knows that a meditative, reflective attitude is impossible to maintain in this context, and so he runs away from the tangible healing possibilities of the real world back into a comfortable, careless cocoon.

The simple and warm-hearted Emily does temporarily free Gumbril from his false persona, and he acts less pretentious around her. The poignant scene is Huxley's attempt to dramatically promote an integration of self— both intellectually and emotionally. This was to become a dominant focus in Huxley's other novels of the 1920s. This integration, however, is not the ultimate goal for Gumbril and the other residents of *Antic Hay*— a point that Huxley drives home by way of contrast. To Huxley, the complete person was one who was capable of embracing the contradictions inherent in human nature, but tragically this concept is missed by Gumbril and his friends.[35]

Hence, Theodore Gumbril remains an incomplete creature of instinct. Convinced that old-fashioned ideals were passé in a postwar world where beauty and goodness are no longer acceptable standards, he resorts to the only model available — irresponsibility. Later, however, Gumbril regrets allowing Myra Viveash to force his breakup with Emily, but this betrayal was his escape from his genuine self, and he is left a divided being. He painfully concludes: "And here am I left in the vacuum." To which Myra replies, speaking for herself and all of the players in *Antic Hay*: "We're all in the vacuum."[36]

Gumbril's father concludes that the human race cannot learn by experience and that suffering, war, and poverty are inevitable:

Several million people were killed in a recent war and half the world ruined; but we all busily go on in courses that make another event of the same sort inevitable. *Experientia docet?* [Experience teaches?] *Experientia* doesn't [Experience does not teach]. And that is why we must not be too hard on these honest citizens of London who, fully appreciating the inconveniences of darkness, disorder and dirt, manfully resisted any attempt to alter conditions which they have been taught from childhood onwards to consider as necessary, right and belonging inevitably to the order of things.[37]

There are moments in *Antic Hay* where the characters' aimless conversations are so undifferentiated that it is difficult for the reader to identify who is speaking. This sense of anonymity may have been Huxley's method of emphasizing the general spirit of futility. The various personalities in a frantic pursuit of false values search in vain and only find more confusion. Given this intent, the author's literary impressionism reveals the consciousness of the age in a style unequaled by most of his contemporaries.

Antic Hay: Theme, Influences and Characters

In a 1923 letter to his father, Aldous Huxley expresses regret that his father found the novel *Antic Hay* distasteful. Huxley points out that the novel was written by a member of the war generation for his peers. The novel was deliberately meant to reflect "the life and opinions of an age which has seen the violent disruption of almost all of the standards, conventions and values current in the previous epoch."[38] He insists that the book is serious since it takes the various aspects of life — tragic, comic, fantastic, realistic — and combines them into a single whole.[39] This new style of narration may be distasteful at first reading, but the praise of his contemporaries was sufficient proof of the relative merit of the work. In this letter, Huxley does take offense at his father's accusation that he exploited his own mother's early death in the scene when Gumbril recalls his dying mother and her deathbed counsel. This same somber remembrance of the loss of his mother at an early age was to find its place in several later novels by Huxley.

Of primary interest in this letter is Huxley's analysis of the novel's theme — a reflection of the lives and attitudes of those who had witnessed the violent disruption of all of the mores, customs, and values of the previous age. The social, political, and economic upheaval that transfixed the European scene following World War I was unprecedented. While the working class suffered the severest hardships, the more privileged class found themselves estranged from ancestral values and moral purpose. In his novel's depiction of aimless men and women, Huxley was, in a sense, joining the Lost Generation of literary writers. T.S. Eliot, Fitzgerald, Hemingway, and other postwar figures developed a similar theme — the dehumanizing aftermath of total warfare, and the uncertainty of a young generation unable to come to terms with the moral collapse and economic insecurity of a new age.

T.S. Eliot's poem *The Hollow Men* (1925) declares that people are "hollow" and "stuffed." Eliot's modernistic view is that of a postwar world filled with vacant people who have no convictions, ideals, or vision to sustain them. Struggling to complete the words from the *Lord's Prayer*, the poet reflects a society that cannot articulate a relationship to God. This is a world that will end "not with a bang but a whimper." This same sense of disillusionment and a hunger for spiritual revitalization are reinforced in what has come to be regarded as Eliot's greatest work, *The Waste Land*. In this long interior monologue, the poet follows the journey of a soul struggling for redemption. *The Waste Land* represents Europe in 1922, a civilization heading for an even greater collapse during World War II. This superstitious world now seeks its spiritual truth from a clairvoyant. Romantic love is dead, and humanity, in the decaying twilight, faces a bleak future.

T.S. Eliot was to have a significant influence on Huxley. Jerome Meckier writes that the impact of Eliot's searing poetry on the satiric novels of the 1920s and 1930s has not been adequately stressed. He offers as examples Waugh's *A Handful of Dust* (a title taken from Eliot's *The Waste Land*), Fitzgerald's *The Great Gatsby*, and Huxley's *Antic Hay* as evidence of the anguished mood expressed in Eliot's verse. These works also reflect the diminishing moral significance of human life in modern times.[40]

In 1965, Eliot wrote a brief remembrance of his meetings with Huxley, first at Oxford and later at a weekend house party. Eliot candidly reveals his less than favorable response to one of Huxley's youthful volumes of verse. Over the years, however, recognizing a kindred critic in the essayist, Eliot also admired Huxley's skillful development of the satiric novel. He was confident that Huxley's place in English literature would remain both unique and assured.[41]

On the American literary scene, F. Scott Fitzgerald's novel *The Great Gatsby* (1925) is a parallel story of a young man seeking his fortune against the backdrop of a dissolute, materialistic society. The mysterious Jay Gatsby denies his shadowy past and takes on the persona of a sophisticated financier and war hero to win his socialite ideal, Daisy Buchanan. The aimless, frivolous existence of the nouveau riche contrasts to the toiling masses of the American poor, and Gatsby's material success cannot hide his flawed character. A cruel twist of fate ultimately destroys the hero and the myth of celebrity that he worked so hard to maintain.

Ernest Hemingway was to develop a similar theme in *The Sun Also Rises*, the 1926 novel that some critics regard as his finest work. Here, a lost generation of alienated expatriates wanders aimlessly through Spain. The narrator, Jake Barnes, is sexually impotent from a war wound, while other characters are symbolically impotent in their inability to achieve a purpose in life. Critics have observed a strong similarity between Myra Viveash, the socialite character in *Antic Hay*, and the sophisticated Bret Ashley in Hemingway's story. The futile conflicts likewise remain unresolved at the conclusion of the novel, and the reader is left with the powerful impression of sad, rootless characters. The mood of indifference and boredom evident in Hemingway's narrative with its thematic futility of sensate pleasures could be superimposed over *Antic Hay*, a novel equally emblematic of an era.

In a 1923 essay published the same year as *Antic Hay*, Huxley was to write on the subject of modern pleasure that only led to boredom. He argues that the greatest menace to society in the 1920s was not war but the low state of pleasurable activities. Unlike the distractions of the past, which demanded some intellectual faculty or human initiative, he claimed that vast organizations now provided pleasure that required no participation on the part of the recipients. Huxley sees the passive submission to pleasure as poisoning the higher faculties, and he wonders whether the coming generation might not decline into premature senility. The combination of an unused mind that is almost atrophied, incapable of entertaining itself, and wearily uninterested in the available distractions may result in a future civilization subject to chronic boredom.[42] This analysis applies to Huxley's description of the society characterized by Theodore Gumbril and his associates.

The social hostess Myra Viveash is a victim of this chronic boredom. As a dissolute member of the privileged class, she fears growing old and reflects that she has never made anyone happy — except possibly her lover, Tony, who was killed in the war.[43] Critic Harold H. Watts observes that "Myra fears that she will be overwhelmed by nothingness, by a lack of essential meaning in her life."[44] The anguish of an alienated society secure neither with itself nor with its future is expressed in the final scene when Gumbril and Viveash tour in her limousine through London at night. The new electrical advertisements have turned the city into a technological fairyland, but the poor and homeless masses still huddle in the dark streets of the slums.

The privileged class thus continues to chase its petty pursuits, lured to their material cravings by the new technology of advertising. Huxley's satiric wit is evident in Gumbril's plans to market his trousers with an inflatable seat that will enable gentlemen of distinction to sit in comfort for long periods of time. In an essay on the fine art of advertising published shortly before the novel, Huxley wrote: "And now I have discovered the most exciting, most arduous literary form of all, the most difficult to master, the most pregnant in curious possibilities. I mean the advertisement."[45] Huxley recognized the modern advertisement as a form of technology or "applied literature."[46] He claims that writing a sonnet is child's play compared to preparing advertising copy. Huxley insists, tongue-in-cheek, that an advertisement must be intelligible and emotionally moving, much the same qualities that are required of good drama. He continues:

> What infinite pains must be taken to fashion every phrase into a barbed hook that shall stick in the reader's mind and draw from its hiding-place within his pocket the reluctant coin! One's style and ideas must be lucid and simple enough to be understood by all; but, at the same time, they must not be vulgar. Elegance and an economical distinction are required; but any trace of literariness in an advertisement is fatal to its success.[47]

The depiction of the advertising campaign that Gumbril's agency prepares — one that will persuade gullible consumers that their life will be incomplete unless they purchase a new pair of Gumbril's inflatable trousers — resonates as strongly in the world of modern marketing as it did at the time it was written.

In his description of the scientist, James Shearwater, Huxley was to describe a modern version of one of the theoretical but impractical residents of Laputa as satirized by Jonathan Swift in the 18th century. Huxley objected to any technology that separated mankind from its intellectual and spiritual pursuits, that fostered a climate of mediocrity, or that led to the destructive horrors of war.[48] He was to argue further in his essays that human beings are not machines, and that they cannot be subjected to machine-like efficiency without suffering the loss of imaginative creativity and honest emotion.[49] Shearwater represents the one-dimensional, soulless product of an exaggerated emphasis on science that is divorced from human values. He can run an expert experiment and collect data, but he has lost all sense of empathy and passion because he has forfeited his essential human nature.

Evelyn Waugh, the English satirical novelist, offered in a contemporary review of *Antic Hay* a typical criticism of the author. He pointed out that "the story is told richly and elegantly with few of the interruptions which, despite their intrinsic interest, mar so much of Mr. Huxley's story-telling."[50] Waugh explains that the novel is really an examination of two falterers — Gumbril and Viveash — in their quest for happiness.[51] He notes that throughout the story, however, there is an insistent undertone suggesting that true happiness is achievable despite the failings of the central characters.[52] As with much of modern fiction, there is no neat resolution at the end of *Antic Hay*, but this bleak world is not tragic. Like Waugh, Huxley was mocking the foolish, amoral, and ultimately meaningless social whirl of his times.

Antic Hay: A Novel of Social Criticism

The *angst* of a lost generation is posited on three distinct but related levels in *Antic Hay*: loathing for the past, blindness to potential in the present, and an illusory trust in the inevitability of a happier future. On the first level is the dehumanizing and destructive aftermath of modern mechanized war that has left the younger generation cynical and shorn of ideals. Alexander Henderson sums up the mood of the novel as a reflection of the times:

> Of certain sides of London during those years it gives an unsurpassed picture. The feeling of the pointlessness of everything, the intentionally senseless diversions, ridiculous games like "Beaver," the headlong rush to jazz and drink — anything to forget the war — the whole uneasy movement of the time symbolized so perfectly in the "Last Ride" ... of Mrs. Viveash and Gumbril.[53]

The more compelling and devastating effects of war can be found in the plight of the common citizens who suffered from the long financial depression. In one scene of the novel, for example, Gumbril gazes through the railings at the penetrating darkness of the park and observes legless soldiers who are grinding barrel organs, hawkers of toys standing with holes in their boots in the gutters, and an old woman who holds a stained handkerchief to her eye. Gumbril ponders what is wrong with the woman's eye. Then he recalls reading in the newspapers of lovers who ended it all by turning on the gas, and the ruined shopkeepers who did the same by leaping in front of trains. He asks if one had the right to be content and well fed, if one had the right to all of these luxuries while others are suffering so much[54]

The physical tragedy of a crushed humanity — crippled, dispossessed of home and livelihood, living in poverty and distress with little hope of economic relief— is briefly treated by Huxley. This would be in keeping with the cynical or selfish attitude of the new generation who tended to ignore the problems of the poor and unfortunate. The striking disparity, however, between the terrible conditions of the less fortunate and Gumbril's circle of purposeless and privileged companions discreetly drives home the point.

Huxley masterfully juxtaposes the frivolous talk of several upper-class characters as they walk through a poverty-stricken area. The deep misery expressed by one slum dweller contrasts to the foolish chatter of the rich visitors. A poor cart driver argues with a policeman who insists that his old horse must be put to sleep because it is lame. The horse is the man's sole means of earning a living, and without the animal, he and his wife, Florrie, who is described as a "black bundle," can find no employment. That day they had walked for miles to apply for a job, but there were only three vacancies and over 200 applicants. Gumbril is a solitary voice when he empathizes with these wretched souls. His well-born companion, however, responds with abhorrence and repeats the refrain of a song that he learned as a child, a refrain that curses the lower classes. His friends are not shocked but rather concur with his sentiments, and one concludes that the song expressed what they all were feeling but lacked the courage to articulate.

The class prejudice that long dominated English life is seen by a socialist companion of Gumbril as the real cause of popular discontent. Huxley's upbringing in a class-bound pre-war England may have contributed to his keen insights here, as well as his graphic portrayal of the caste system dictated by technology in his futuristic novel *Brave New World*. Gumbril's associate claims that the revolution that is certain to come will not be caused by wealth but class distinctions. The irony here is that this would-be socialist is part of the scheme to develop the inflatable trousers that Gumbril hopes will make him a millionaire. The division between the social classes and the callous attitude toward the poor as depicted here would, however, precipitate England's shift toward socialistic ideologies following World War II.

On the second level, the dismal poverty, discrimination, and sense of insecurity caused by past failures have so affected people's lives that they are unable to recognize their present potential. The 1920s upper-class, aimless generation depicted cannot empathize with the poor, and they are often angry that such degradation should even intrude on their pleasant lives. The intellectual class may have felt some sympathy for the poor, but they were bitter or frustrated over their inability to affect any social reforms. The young veterans among them who fought in the trenches and saw the slaughter felt that their sacrifices had been in vain.

This general mood of alienation is strong in the novel. Early in the story, one of the cynics observes to his companion: "Does it occur to you ... that at this moment, we are walking through the midst of seven million distinct and separate individuals, each with distinct and separate lives and all completely indifferent to our existence?"[55] On receiving no reply, the questioner taps on the pavement as if he were searching for some crack that would reveal the secret of their lives.

These lives are not only alienated but also devoid of meaning. When Gumbril allows Myra Viveash to draw him away from his rendezvous with his friend Emily, they dance at a cabaret to the latest popular song, "What's He to Hecuba?" The oft-repeated refrain borrowed from Shakespeare's *Hamlet* is answered by the trite, "Nothing at all." The lyrics are repeated by Gumbril and Viveash as they glide across the dance floor: "I am nothing to you. You are nothing to me." Myra confesses that she adores the tune. The novel's narrator explains that the tune fills up space, kills time, and gives one a sense of being alive.[56]

Myra inquires of Gumbril where all the young people are, and he openly replies that he is not responsible for them—for that matter, he is not even responsible for himself.[57] The scene of Myra Viveash and Theodore Gumbril, dancing across a floor, singing a song about nothing is riveting. In many ways it anticipates the shallow happiness shared by two futile characters, Lenina Crowne and Henry Foster, as they dance to synthetic music projected 600 years into the future in Huxley's *Brave New World*.

This cabaret scene continues with the staging of a play, a pretentious avant-garde allegory that opens with a man's lament over the loss of his wife in childbirth. The child, described as a monster, is cursed to live without love, in dirt and impurity. Passionately in love with a self-absorbed young woman, the creature is rejected and later locked in an institution where he ultimately dies. Mrs. Viveash is glad when the play is over, and she returns to the dance floor with Gumbril, both of them coldly unaffected by what they have observed.[58] Huxley, in a 1923 essay entitled "On Deviating into Sense," relates how striking the wrong key on his typewriter once produced a title that epitomized the contemporary human condition: "The Human Vomedy." He found this accident produced a biting criticism of modern life.[59] This title might aptly apply to the cabaret scene in *Antic Hay*.

On the third level, the hope that technological progress will produce a better civilization in the future is all but destroyed in the novel. At the conclusion, the reader is left with the image of Myra Viveash and Gumbril on a perpetual pilgrimage, moving from one social event to another, fully conscious that all of their tomorrows will be as terrible as today.[60] Apparently, Myra Viveash recalls Robert Browning's poem when she exclaims, "The Last Ride Again," as she and Gumbril drive to Golgotha Hospital, the name associated with the site of Christ's crucifixion.[61] The belief that the future holds no more hope of happiness than present circumstances is a certainty accepted by Huxley's characters as a philosophical truism.

One of the earliest critics to observe that Huxley's novel exploited the cynical possibilities of science and technology was Joseph Wood Krutch. In his 1923 review of *Antic Hay*, he cited the remark of the Restoration playwright Congreve that he could not look on a cage of monkeys without experiencing some vague embarrassment. There is something of this sense of discomfort on the part of the reader as he accompanies Gumbril and his friends on their journey to nowhere. The war exacted its toll in the form of continued human deficiencies, and these are painfully examined in the narrative.

Among the other characters in *Antic Hay*, Lypiatt, the failed artist, retreats into the darkness of his apartment and refuses to answer the door to Viveash and Gumbril when they visit. He is alone with his pistol and his suicide note, and the reader never learns whether he takes his own life. In the final analysis, it is insignificant, for he has already died to his true self even if physically he survives. Meanwhile, Gumbril's architect father, wise to the excesses and shallowness of modern existence, nevertheless can only gaze at the scale model of the ideal city he had carefully planned but may never see built in the real but imperfect world.

The remaining characters, indifferent to the horrors of the city that surrounds them and fearful of any renunciation demanded by any idealistic challenge, continue to drift in a world in which inevitable progress is the only creed. Their plight is dramatically rendered when a group exits the restaurant with no purpose in mind: "One after another, they engaged themselves in the revolving doors of the restaurant, trotted around in the moving cage of glass and ejected themselves into the coolness and darkness of the street."[62] The scene of a mass of wanderers, segregated in cages of glass, not touching but projecting those before them into the dark is an arresting concept.

Antic Hay is a brilliant reflection of the intellectual perplexity of the period when it was written, a perplexity symbolically rendered in the delusion of its characters.[63] Gumbril's penchant for disguise may be the more obvious illusion. In attempting to delude others, however, Gumbril ultimately deludes himself.[64] As a prototype of the mentally rigid scientist, Shearwater is another example of self-delusion in his obsession with statistics gathered from his research and the abstract generalities he obtains.[65] To these victims of delusion may be added the minor literary critic who never writes an important article, and the would-be artist with lofty ideals but little talent. The seductress role of Circe can be applied to Myra Viveash, whose glamour sets a pattern of deception. All of the men in the novel are bewitched by her, and each foolishly believes that he can win her love.[66] In George Woodcock's laconic words: "Myra brings the meaning of the book, as stated by Huxley, into focus since she is the character who most of all embodies the inner death of disillusionment that is the result of war."[67]

The plot of the novel may be considered to resemble a wheel that is constantly turning. At the beginning of the story, Gumbril stands at the edge of the wheel, and occasionally he reaches the center of life and glimpses reality, but he quickly slips to the outer edge once more. The sequence of events deliberately finds the three chapters on ideals and Gumbril's possible fulfillment of happiness with Emily at the center of the work. It is questionable, however, whether Gumbril will ever return to the center — to reality — since the novel ends with his taxi-ride to nowhere with Viveash.[68]

A complex work like *Antic Hay* that reflects the unhappy human condition in the 1920s is not without wit. Huxley was skillful in blending satire with realism. The dialogue is often witty and the situations satirically drawn, but the problems of the microcosmic world of London society visited in the novel remained real and serious. Although social and economic concerns continued to be key issues, Huxley, nevertheless, points out that people take progress for granted:

> The experience of technological and even of human progress is seldom continuous and enduring. Human beings have an enormous capacity for taking things for granted. In a few months, even in a few days, the newly invented gadget, the new political or economic privileges, come to be regarded as parts of the existing order of things. We do not spend our time comparing present happiness with past misery; rather we accept it as our right and become bitterly resentful if we are even temporarily deprived of it.[69]

Huxley saw no solution to social ills at this time, but his own journey toward a conscious awareness of meaningful human progress would be recorded in the fiction that followed.

Antic Hay is the work of a young novelist who vividly portrays the lost generation in Europe following World War I. While the satiric portrait of the pointless existence of Gumbril and his circle is a telling reflection of the times, it also represents a vivid example of the human cost of scientific and industrial progress. As a member of the war generation, Huxley knew this world and his direct impressions may also be vividly found in his essays and letters written during the era. The sense of universal boredom and despair was, according to Huxley, the result of both war and the technological changes that affected all lives.

Gumbril, however, even more than Stone before him in *Crome Yellow*, realizes his potential for something more than the idle existence of his friends and associates. Yet when he comes in contact with Emily and the possibility of meaningfulness, he runs away and retreats back into a life of pointless pursuits. Once again Huxley is parenthetically pursuing the essence of purpose and the need to journey further into the realm of meaningful reality. As with Stone, Huxley vicariously journeys to the base of the mountain, yet proceeds no further. He would begin the ascent with Calamy in the novel to follow.

As a sensitive, talented writer, with a gifted family background and concern for the human condition, Huxley would write four novels of social criticism in the 1920s — *Antic Hay* was his second. In them may be found his tendency to satirically portray shallow, one-dimensional characters who only occasionally suggest a potential to attain a sensible maturity. In the other two novels of this era, however, Huxley begins to develop — in his characterizations and narration — a hopeful perception while continuing to employ biting satire to critique a philistine society. And so the evolution continues in *Those Barren Leaves*.

Those Barren Leaves

Background and Structure

Huxley and his family were to spend the better part of four serene and productive years in Italy. In the spring and summer of 1924, he was to complete his third novel of social criticism. It is a disservice, however, to label it as such without the qualifications that it is far more than the masterful satiric portrait of the post-war idle rich, but it is also Huxley's movement into self-examination. Many pages are filled with deep questions about life, reality, love, and an individual's relationship to the world, as well as an initial venture into the compelling realm of mysticism. The witty repartee of the characters is present, and they are certainly well drawn and superior to his two previous outings in terms of full development; the satiric barb is skillfully employed, albeit not with so much of a sting as in previous ventures; the appreciation and depth of knowledge about Italian art is comprehensive and reflects Huxley's many travels throughout Italy; the telling of a story with five interlocking parts is cleverly done; and the vivid descriptions enticing as one moves throughout Italy with Lilian's entourage. But within the pages of *Those Barren Leaves* lies Huxley's own initial search for deeper meaning that was to become more transparent in his later novels of transformation (i.e., *Eyeless in Gaza*, *After Many a Summer Dies the Swan*, and *Time Must Have a Stop*).

It is with this novel that one may question the separation of fiction from a philosophical tract. Huxley was to write to his father in April 1924 that "the mere business of telling a story interests me less and less."[70] The division between the temporal and the mystical—between the worldly and the other worldly—ultimately takes the character of Calamy to the lofty slopes to meditate in silence. One cannot help but accompany him, along with Huxley, to the summit to understand the meaning and purpose of existence. For, as Huxley continues in this same letter to his father, he had come to realize that "the only really and permanently absorbing things are attitudes toward life and the relation of man to the world."[71]

This is not to say that Huxley had abandoned the craft that made him an instant success in the literary domain. The remnants of the Peacockian novel are still present with an assembly of eccentric personages, sometimes comically drawn, engaging in a variety of topics at Mrs. Alkwinkle's palace. The first section embraces strictly "An Evening at Mrs. Aldwinkle's," in which most of the characters are explicitly revealed as they spend one night with the dowager queen of the arts in her castle. Following this narrative, however, we have a departure from the customary format. There is the unusual movement of the guests to locations other than the primary setting, and even a shift in the narrative voice from omniscient to autobiographical. At least in the opening of Part II ("Fragments from The Autobiography of Francis Chelifer"), one is unsure what connection there may be between this man and the other guests assembled in the opening section, but Huxley soon brings the two together and ingenuously takes us back to the palace with the autobiographer in tow.

In Part III, Huxley cleverly takes the reader into the intimate conversations of romantically inclined couples. The intensification of their relationships — or, as in the case of Lilian Aldwinkle and Francis Chelifer, the impotence of their relationship — is progressively drawn in "The Loves of the Parallels." Parallel in time and space are: Calamy (the poet) and Mary Thriplow (the novelist); Irene (Lilian Aldwinkle's niece) and Lord Hovenden (a "student" of Mr. Falx); Cardan (the sycophant and inheritance-grubbing rogue) and Grace Elver (his mentally deficient match); and the aforementioned Lilian and Francis. Huxley ingeniously moves the reader from one pair to another, even providing an enlightening and amusing soiree into lower-class life in the small dwelling inhabited by the Elvers. But the parallel view of these lovers hints at Huxley's parallel view of a life lived and a life pondered.

It is in "The Journey" (Part IV) that the train moves from the Palace of Cybo Malaspina to Rome, wherein Huxley not only provides the reader with a bird's eye view of the eternal art surrounding the city, but advances what was to become the platform for Huxley's insatiable thirst for the *more*— the insatiable need to examine oneself and therein to find the real, the true, and the beautiful. In passages riveted with questions about reality, love, and death, the story gradually becomes secondary to the philosophical underpinnings to the point that in Part V, the lion's share of the passage is the debate between Cardan and Calamy about reality and the course of action to "see" it clearly. Calamy expands on the theme that humanity spends most of its time on the surface without taking the time to think deeply and locate what is real behind what one erroneously sees as real. Huxley was embarking, with Calamy, into a mystical sight that comes from insight.

Huxley must have spent most of time in the development of these dialogues, and while he writes that the novel "cuts more ice, I think, than the others and is more explicit and to the point," he contradicts that by stating that it may have been "off the point."[72] Here, then, was an intellect in search of who he was, no longer finding satisfaction purely in the development of a good plot or satiric portrait. In many ways — albeit some critics may have seen this as a departure from the pure narrative form — *Those Barren Leaves* becomes an amalgamation of the various parts that divided Huxley's world view. In structure, form and presentation, it is far superior to what he had produced earlier, but Huxley was his worst critic both artistically and personally. While earlier he wished that he had the time to do nothing but write, he wished now that he could take time to *not* write and just to think.[73]

Like Calamy, Huxley was on his own journey to the mountain top to cultivate meditation in search of a deeper meaning.

Those Barren Leaves: Characters and Their Dilemmas

The characters in *Those Barren Leaves* may metaphorically symbolize the leaves of Wordsworth's poem from which Huxley derived the title. They may constitute people whose lives are fading away like the leaves of a tree whose fragrance remains after its death—much like the fragrance that remains on the leaf that Mary Thriplow removes from the bay tree. So it is with Mary at the opening of the novel who receives the telegram announcing Mr. Calamy's arrival before Mrs. Aldwinkle and her guests return from the baths. Mary treasures the fact that she will be able to spend some time with the man alone. Having heard from Lilian Aldwinkle that Mr. Calamy was young, handsome, rich and amorist, Mary dressed for the occasion accordingly. It was true that Mr. Calamy had abandoned his professional success to travel, but Mr. Calamy's pursuits for meaning were far more serious than she expected. Fearful that she was on the verge of presenting herself in a disapproving light (creating a "floater," as she dubbed it), she craftily finds a way of removing her expensive jewelry unnoticed and stuffing it within the opening behind the cushion of the sofa upon which she is seated.

All through dinner Mary is apprehensive about saying anything that will offend anyone. At thirty, and working on her latest novel, she is very much a chameleon adjusting her image according to the pleasure of whomever she is with. When she says anything that Mrs. Aldwinkle finds disagreeable, she corrects what she has said so that it fits in with the other's opinion. Mary pines for the one true love of her life, her cousin Jim, who has died, and for whom she writes letters of love and reminisces about the past when they were together. In one poignant scene, she recalls the scent of the barber shop where Jim had his hair cut. When she grasps a leaf off a tree while taking a stroll, she smells it and it brings to mind her beloved Jim. Mary's recollections of conversations and shared experiences are noted for possible use in her next fictional narrative. While she hopes for a romantic interlude with Mr. Calamy—one that comes to fruition—she does not anticipate falling in love with him as she does. Stoically, she tries to comprehend her complex lover's words when he uses his hand as a symbol of reality beyond what one sees, and ultimately has no choice but to release him to the hermitage. After letting Calamy go, Mary retreats back into her letters to Jim, to thoughts she believes to be more mystical, and finally even to sounds that remind her of a dentist's drill. Our last image of her is when, with joy, she has decided to write a story about a dentist who falls in love with one of his patients, a thought that she carries with her as she is lulled into a deep sleep.

Mr. Calamy posits in a conversation with Mr. Cardan that, while people may initially think that emancipation is good, in the end what they get is boredom. Relating a generality that applies specifically to him, it is clear early on that this very serious gentleman of the world finds life dull and is seeking far more than the triviality with which he is far too frequently acquainted. Musing in conversation with the other men of the house that he sometimes wishes that he were not "externally free," he relates that if he were not then he would justifiably have something to grumble about.[74] When asked by Cardan if he knows what he likes, Calamy responds with a list of what he does not like, including wasting time, engaging in fruitless social functions, or chasing women. Yet he finds himself doing the very things that he feels to be useless. He concludes that "it is an obscure sort of insanity."[75]

And so he continues with his insanity for he does not desire, nor does he want to pursue intimacy with anyone, especially Mary Thriplow — although he does find her attractive and sensually desirable. As a true divided soul, he is disappointed in himself when he does the very thing that he knows, deep down, he should not do. He pursues her and captures her and makes her love him. Unable to say that he truly loves her, he holds back, and then when she chides him or proposes that they separate, he becomes the romantic dilettante. Even when Mary speaks of love, he thinks that this is a waste of time; he should be thinking of other things, but "what were they" he did not know.[76] Ultimately, Calamy's need to find some deeper meaning or the answer to whatever else he should be thinking, compels him to seek the contemplative life; his conversation with Cardan and Chelifer — the gist of the final section of the novel — reflects much of Huxley's initial search for the mystical. At least Calamy, dissatisfied with the ordinary things of life, seeks an answer and is willing to experiment with allowing the mind to go beyond in the undisturbed silence of contemplation. Less can be said for his disillusioned counterpart in Francis Chelifer.

Juxtaposed to these two outward and inward seekers of pleasure and wisdom is the ancient Mr. Falx. In another time and place he would have been a prophet, but instead is a defender of all laborers of the world. When others find delight in the marvels of Rome, he argues that tens of thousands of slaves were used to create it and asks if it is worth it. His interjected comments on the degrading manners of the assembly, and his cries to not drive so fast when Lord Hovenden is at the wheel of his Velox, provide amusement within chosen scenes. He is outraged by Mrs. Aldwinkle's perspectives on life and what he perceives as the immoral attitudes and actions of her guests, and fears that they may contaminate his charge, the unspoiled Lord Hovenden. Unfortunately for Mr. Falx, his fears become reality when Lord Hovenden falls madly in love with Irene.

Irene is only 18 and is a highly impressionable young girl who admires everything that her Aunt Lilian says. Brushing her aunt's hair each evening, Lilian is the one who encourages Irene not to be cold and to fall under the spell of love, citing Lord Hovenden as a prime object. Irene — the "Natural Woman" who still enjoys the worldly work of stitching undergarments — was remolded by her aunt into the "Unnatural Woman" who spends her time in appreciation of the arts. To Irene, underclothing is the flesh, while poetry and painting are the spirit. Trying to prove that her aunt was wrong when she said Irene lacked passion, she heeds her aunt's advice and, in time, falls in love with the dashing lord. When she finally has the nerve to inform her aunt that she will marry him, Lilian is beside herself with anguish, stating that Irene does not love her, everyone is abandoning her, and in desperation, asserts that her niece is too young to marry. This reaction was precipitated by Lilian's inability to seduce Francis Chelifer no matter how hard she tried. Wisely, Irene, at first thinking that she will give up Lord Hovenden for her aunt, pulls back and tries to comfort her with the words that they will always be together and that she can visit them frequently.

Lord Hovenden, her love, is young, handsome and rich. Mispronouncing "th" as a "v," his statements sometimes lift off the page with an aura of comic relief. He admired Mr. Falx and considered him a mentor of sorts but did not enjoy their frequent attendance at boring labor symposiums. It is, therefore, at Hovendon's insistence that they initially accept Mrs. Aldwinkle's invitation, and it is his excuse of ill health and the doctor's order to leave the city that enables their return to the Aldwinkle estate and his love, Irene.

The young lord aggressively pursues Irene from the start, and is reasonably upset when she initially spends so much time with him — encouraged by her aunt — and then appears to evade him. Her elusive behavior makes him jealous as he believes that she may be interested in the newly arrived Chelifer; Irene is unable to tell him the truth that her aunt has charged her to find out where Francis Chelifer hides when he cannot be located. Strengthened when he is behind the wheel of the Velox on their journey to Rome, Hovenden first takes the wrong turn, and then keeps driving around and around Lake Trasimene, stating that he will continue to do so until Irene accepts his proposal of marriage.

Mrs. Aldwinkle is a woman, perhaps in her fifties, who is described as handsome, with wide shoulders and a childish head that appears as if her body was engineered in two parts. She had feared that the fates had schemed against her for some time to keep her away from those places where exciting things happen, so that now she avariciously encroaches on every conversation or circumstance on the chance she should miss something of importance. Firmly believing that "through art man comes closest to being a god," she tries to encourage all around her to follow the same creed.[77]

Lilian has had a series of amorous affairs that she delights in gratuitously recalling with embellishment. The only relationship she cannot embellish is her former lover Henry Cardan since he is still present at her palace and knows the truth. Many people have come and gone from her lavish dwelling; she cannot resist regarding herself as a princess "surrounded by a court of poets, philosophers, and artists."[78] Lilian Aldwinkle very much epitomizes the saying that those who can, do, and those who cannot, teach; she loves art in all of its forms and encourages it in her niece Irene and all who surround her, but Lilian herself is incapable of writing a poem, painting a portrait, or playing a musical instrument. Instead she supplants her inability by surrounding herself with those who can. And over the years there have been many. One of her greatest fears as she grows older — in addition to becoming unattractive — is that the bevy of people whom she cajoles to join her will stop. She fears that she will either run out of interesting people or they will cease to arrive at her door, and the absence of imaginative artisans to stimulate her senses would be tantamount to a death march.

Ever the one in control, she stays outdoors, viewing the stars long after others have taken refuge within, despises saying "good night," and even insists that her guests retire when she does. Upon everyone's arrival, she must conduct a historical tour of her mansion, much to the repeated dismay of her guests who had been through this many times before. Yet the sycophants obey and follow, for it is Mrs. Aldwinkle who is the patron paying for all the comforts that they receive.

The young, handsome, and talented Francis Chelifer arrives at her castle by mystical means — she conceives that she has saved his life after a sail-boat strikes him and has rendered him unconscious as he floated upon the waters of the Mediterranean. Like others before him, she would make him love her. Finally, one evening, after doing everything she could to the point of suffocating the man with her constant presence, she enters his bed chamber and pleads for his love, only to be interrupted by the shouts of others when Grace Elver becomes violently ill. While Chelifer stoically does not react at all to her protestations, he is equally unresponsive to just about everything else in life.

An entire section is devoted to Francis Chelifer's life before he enters Mrs. Aldwinkle's abode. This is done in a clever manner. While Mr. Chelifer floats upon a raft in the warm Mediterranean awaiting his mother's arrival for a trip to Rome, he nostalgically and amusingly recalls incidents from his youth, his past and his present by way of fragments from his autobiography. Within Chelifer's philosophical musings is the heart of a sad, perplexed, and tormented soul, who may very well be Calamy's foil since he remains static and fails to take any definitive action to remedy his insufferable state. Writing at Cog's court — in the heart of London — he recollects in his narrative his father's love of Wordsworth, whom he quoted frequently; his mother's pleasure in playing the harmonium at their home in Oxford; the droll state of affairs at Miss Carruther's boardinghouse where Miss Fluffy and Mr. Brimestone reside; and, finally, his idealized love for Barbara Waters.

In the latter, Chelifer's divided soul very much resembles, in fragments, Mr. Calamy's. For Francis Chelifer first met Barbara when at a water picnic when he was fourteen, and instantly her face became his image of perfection, a distinction in the flesh that could never be attained. All through his adolescence and young adult life he imagined her, saving himself for he knew not what, disappointed when he faltered and gave into affairs of the flesh that never satisfied his need for something higher and nobler. He met her several times but was incapable of telling her how he felt, until the war came, and from France he pours out his heart in a missive that he believes she would never receive since he sent it to an old address. But she did get it, and upon their meeting there was a rapid movement into intimacy, a move that he resisted at first because he knew full well that once their relationship was consummated, she would lose the romanticized aura he held for her. As in all self-fulfilling prophecies, it comes true.

Ironically, Chelifer had rejected a previous invitation from Mrs. Aldwinkle when Prince Papadiamantopoulos visited (again Huxley having fun with a name), but declined, so Mrs. Aldwinkle is delighted when she finally meets this promising poet. But Francis is discontent with his poetry and feels that he really has nothing to say. Earning his livelihood as editor of *The Rabbit Fanciers' Gazette*, a publication noteworthy for offering tips on the breeding of rabbits, he uses the publication to write philosophical articles reflecting on life, much to the dismay of the directors. While Chelifer's narrative sparkles with wit, it is in the wanderings of his psyche that we gain a glimpse of the divided soul who becomes a centerpiece for many of Huxley's future protagonists. In the final analysis, here is a soul unable to find fulfillment in being attached to life while intellectually tugged toward the realm of detachment. In a series of questions and answers, he reflects on man's lot in working at a job that provides no soulful fulfillment; he knows with Mary he needed to live in the moment, but the all-consuming sphere of thought overwhelms him. He finds himself in love with the idea of love but not with its physical substance. So when the "Chinese lantern lady" (aka Mrs. Aldwinkle) captures him, he submits and willingly is transported to her abode in body, but resists in mind, because he fears that there is no escape. Yet he finds a way of removing himself from this woman who threatens his soul by ascending the 232 steps to the tower where he could physically — and sensitively — remove himself from the material world. Sadly, at the conclusion of the novel, when he and Cardan visit Calamy, he indicates that "three days hence ... I shall be at my office again."[79] Unlike Calamy, Chelifer continues to live the very life he disdains.

Mr. Cardan (the Scogan of *Crome Yellow*) is one of Mrs. Aldwinkle's semi-permanent parasites, albeit he declares that he has never been a successful one. A hedonist at heart, he takes a journey on foot to the home of the brother of the butcher with the prospect of gaining a work of art that he may purchase cheaply and then sell for a great profit. But the journey is long and tedious and the statue is a tombstone that is worthless. But he does meet Grace Elver and her brother, and when her brother reveals to Cardan that Grace is worth 25,000 pounds (since she inherited it from her hideous godmother upon her death), Mr. Cardan's mind begins to work up a scheme to collect that fortune. But, alas, his plan goes awry when Grace insists one evening to dine on fish, the very food that proves to be noxious. Ironically, Mr. Cardan must pay the priest for his services at her funeral, and gains nothing from his time with Grace since the marriage never took place.

Grace is mentally challenged and is brought to Italy by her brother in the hopes that she will get malaria and die, thereby giving him her inheritance. Elver reveals all in a drunken stupor to Mr. Cardan. Grace is enraptured by Chelifer's mother, a charitable creature who feeds the stray cats of Rome and takes Grace under her wing in teaching her proper etiquette. Grace marvels at all that she sees, and can be seen, handkerchief flying in the air, calling to everyone as they travel to Rome. Ironically, Mr. Cardan does Grace's brother a favor in whisking her away with him, for it is on their journey that she succumbs, thereby allowing her brother to escape the endless bonds of poverty.

Those Barren Leaves: Analytical Reflections on Life

In his letters, Huxley was to reveal three critical aspects of his third novel: the characters are more rounded and fully developed; it is more to the point; and it exposes Huxley's desire to write not just a story, but provide pictures of different aspects of life.[80] Far superior in form, development of story, characterization, and meaningful theme, the novel marks a turn in the road of Huxley's fiction — as the critics were to see it — a turn toward the fiction that would allow him to integrate story with idea.

No one character — except for Chelifer's autobiographical entry — dominates the story, nor is there a penetrating spotlight on one character for any extended period of time. The transitions in time and space between the various characters dovetail each other. Several topics are presented conversationally and thoughts expressed both outwardly and inwardly by way of the omniscient narrator. One topic — concerning the writer — could very well be considered Huxley's personal view of his accomplishments and the public and critical treatment of his novels.

In a discussion with Mary Thriplow, Mr. Cardan suggests that most readers do not read every word an author writes. They read casually or even skim the words that the writer has spilled his blood and tears over in creating. She, therefore, should not be offended if she is misunderstood. Calamy pokes even further. Miss Thriplow should be delighted that she is misunderstood. After all, one can get upset with the "imbeciles" who cannot understand the obvious; one may be hurt because they surmise that you are as "vulgar" as they; or sense failure because of misinterpretation. On the contrary, imagine being completely understood, revealing oneself totally to be at the mercy of those to whom you have opened up your soul. No, Calamy concludes, Mary should congratulate herself for she has an adoring public who likes what she writes but for the wrong reasons; she is safe from their reach and may maintain herself intact. [81] Is Huxley toying with his audience and his critics by speaking satirically through the mouths of his characters?

But there are far more serious subjects explored in this narrative. Mr. Cardan meditates on the possible maladies of his future. Repeatedly trying to keep his mind off this fixation and wishing there was someone with whom to talk, he looks through the spyglass of the limited time he has left after his sixty-fifth birthday and fears what is to come. The prospect of diabetes or arthritis or gout or losing one's mind leads him to wonder who would look after him. Alone with the doctor or the nurse and the possible generous brief visits of friends, he would gasp for air in the throes of inevitable suffering and death. Fortuitously, it seems, he would provide some happiness for Grace Elver in return for her wealth that would sustain him in his old age. [82] But there he was in the empty church before her funeral, the coffin and its occupant not counting for company. And once more Mr. Cardan views the inevitable visage of death.

He thinks back to his beloved Angora cat who ate too many beetles and died ignominiously coughing up its vitals. A person may not fear that death, he thinks, but what of one from poisoned fish like Grace? It was a horrendous death. And now the worms await her. "The tragedy of bodily suffering and extinction has no catharsis," he ruminates. [83] Time swiftly takes the body on its course to extinction. Only the spirit can provide freedom, but even it dies when the body ceases to be. To Cardan, there is only the body. It is beautiful and healthy in youth and decays across the years, leading to ultimate extermination. Comparing the spirit to the stunning feathers on a bird's head, feathers that die with the bird, so also does the spirit die with the body. Cardan wonders once more how he will die. Reflecting that the wise man does not think of death, but its ugly head cannot help but intrude on life, and when it is forced upon the mind, it renders one difficult to find delight in anything. Such a pronounced denunciation of a life devoid of meaning, presented by a hedonist, is placed deliberately before the major insights of the novel presented by Calamy: first in his dialogue with Mary, and then in his conversation with Cardan and Chelifer. Both discourses are uplifting in comparison to Cardan's dismal forecast.

In the first scene, Calamy and Mary are discussing the subject of love, and he tells her that one can resent love because of what it interferes with. Flippantly, she retorts that she apologizes for interfering with such important pursuits as his thinking about his hand. Frustrated by her inability to get him to tell her what he was thinking about, she bites that hand. Ultimately he conveys to her the results of his deeper thoughts, illustrating them with the use of that very hand. He posits that when one begins to think of the different ways of viewing the tangible, it becomes more and more intangible, obscure and mysterious. Yet if one works very hard at it, one may come out on the other end of the obscurity and see it in a new light.

He uses his hand as an example and holds it up to the window. As a child, one may see it as just a shape blocking the light; but what of a physicist's view? He sees an electromagnetic field that permits only certain waves to hit the eye. Then, what of the chemist? He sees atoms building up into molecules. Now if he were to put his hand into the fire, it would be withdrawn — intentionally or involuntarily — and begin to repair itself as seen by the biologist. Furthermore, the same hand that killed a man has helped others; the hand that has written words has touched a beloved. With that, he touches Mary's breast and indicates that when he touches her body, he touches her mind. Therefore, as this one hand may be seen in a multitude of ways, so it is capable of constituting a variety of realities. Yet what is the connection between these various realities? Calamy concludes that he does not know, but it may be possible to ascertain the connection if one is truly free to do so: for the mind to be totally open and undisturbed by the irrelevant. Thus, his decision to pursue the journey into the unknown is through the medium of a silenced, undisturbed, contemplative mind.[84]

In the second scene he meets with Cardan and Chelifer upon the hill near his humble abode. When he learns of Grace's death and Cardan reiterates in brief his synopsis of the body/spirit connection and the death of both at the conclusion of life, Calamy asks that he be forgiven the use of a quotation, namely: "The Kingdom of God is within." His conviction is that salvation is not in a life to come, but in the here and now. Furthermore, it is the ultimate goal of salvation to conquer that kingdom. To be upset about the spirit rotting with the body, to Calamy, is "mediaeval."[85]

Yet Cardan objects. How does this knowledge help him in the agony of old age? What good does salvation do when he gets old and dies? Calamy responds that the mind has created time and space and matter, but what if there is a reality beyond which the mind has not explored? And how is man to use words he has invented to describe something that is beyond human understanding? Therein rests the need to take the time to breathe deeply, to think openly, and to enter the mystical world beyond a known reality.

Chelifer, disturbed by what he hears, pounces on Calamy's words and argues that one does not have a right to run away — it is the coward who runs away. If one runs away from life because one views a reality different than the masses — the masses who have lived a superficial existence — one must plunge into that world and live as the majority of mankind has lived to know what human life is all about. Calamy calls him a sentimentalist in reverse: while the ordinary citizen sees life as so much better than it is, it is the Chelifers of the world who see things differently and gloat over the agony they experience in dealing with daily existence. The debate continues between the two. In some ways, Chelifer cherishes his dismay at the practices of those who skate across the surface and never think of what is below. Yet he insists that he must remain a part of that very world. And yet it is he who shouts in the "mist of whiskey," "Nothing so richly increases the significance of a statement as to hear it uttered by one's own voice, in solitude."[86] Chelifer may find it more comforting to cherish solitude in a world where the vast majority — of which he is included — refrain from self-examination, yet he censures those who engage in any enterprise of a non-secular nature. Hence, he continues to work at *The Rabbit Fancier's Gazette* while writing poetry and impractical articles; romanticizes the ideal of love but cannot consummate it; seeks refuge in the tower but will not leave Mrs. Aldwinkle's palace; and denounces Calamy's path while finding his own disagreeable.

Calamy continues that it may be possible that there is a reality totally different than the one that is known, operating at the same time as the known reality — basically running parallel to each other. Perhaps a change in environment or a movement beyond bodily restrictions would enable a person to witness that other reality. Perhaps if a person thinks deep enough he may find that what he viewed as real was just an illusion. And beyond it is what is real. The call to mysticism is derided by both men to whom he speaks, but they are coming to an understanding of the man's validation of the mystical path. While Chelifer feels that it is only the sentimental imbeciles who pursue causes beyond the real world, Calamy objects that it is often those of superior intellect who seek another path, persons such as Buddha, Jesus, Lao-tze, and Boehme. The fools are those who do not attempt to reach below the surface of their reality and treat with contempt anyone who dares to do otherwise.

Chelifer feels that a person has no right to run away from what 99 out of 100 people perceive as real. But Calamy believes he or she has every right: why should a special mind not have the right to be discontent with surface appearances? While he describes Chelifer as a sentimentalist inside-out, no offense is taken and the three part company with Cardan promising to check back with Calamy in six months to see where he stands and if he has changed his views.

Huxley touched upon the concept of freedom in *Antic Hay*; his fascination with the existence of parallel worlds was ever on his mind: "How he adored the *extraordinary*," writes the biographer Sybille Bedford.[87] The desire to explore the mysterious boundaries of life through the mind would become more and more the centerpiece of Huxley's writings, both in fiction and nonfiction. Calamy's struggle and Chelifer's negated exploration can be summed up in Huxley's voice that penetrates chapter six of the opening section of the novel. In an introduction to the amusing choices of Irene between writing poetry or sewing undergarments, much may be said about Huxley's own personal struggle with the dueling forces of being.

The narrator states that almost every person is torn between divided allegiances: to the flesh or the spirit; to love or duty; to reason or prejudice. These diametrical forces are pulling humanity in one way or another — toward good or toward evil — and occupy the conflict in most dramas. The theme of the divided soul at odds with itself occupied Huxley's treatment of Gumbril in *Antic* Hay; it is explored more fully in *Those Barren Leaves*, and would receive even greater treatment in the novels to come. The very essence of the divided soul can be said of Huxley himself who desired to write what others would read, but suffered the pangs of not always being understood. It is the same force pulling Huxley in a direction that would later prove less and less popular, especially as he embarked on his own journey for self discovery through the very medium that was his handicraft. Huxley succinctly states the unity of his intended theme when he writes that it is "the undercutting of everything by a sort of despairing sceptisim and then the undercutting of that by mysticism."[88] The pairing of these two entities progresses through the pages of his third novel.

As another forecast of the future seminal work of his life, *Brave New World*, the narrator continues in this same section to entertain the possibility that the conflict of duality — one that has occupied man's psyche unceasingly — will be eliminated in time as science advances and all beings are created to occupy their rightful place within an ordered world. Perhaps then, *joy* will replace suffering and all art will cease. At present, while the author may spend just a few paragraphs describing the protagonist's happiness, he will go on and on for twenty pages about his misery. Therefore, when suffering comes to an end, he will have nothing to write about. And Huxley concludes that "perhaps it will be all for the best."[89]

Of course, his projection does come true in *Brave New World*, but for Huxley, the misery of one unable or unwilling to dig deeper into the mysteries of life would forever provide the material for literary examination. While Chelifer may find his times repugnant, Calamy sees them as an opportunity for growth when all things are made possible. Lord Hovenden agrees as he looks out on the panorama of Perugia and declares, "I like vis [i.e., this] place." Standing with Irene on a parapet looking down upon the roofs of the city, the two lovers absorb the vastness of the sky, blended with the noises of the city which "served but to intensify the quiet, to make the listener more conscious of its immensity in comparison with the trivial clatter at its heart." Once more, Hovenden reiterates what Huxley was feeling when he wrote these words, "I like vis place."[90]

Those Barren Leaves comes to a halt without resolution, for Calamy's journey, like Huxley's, cannot anticipate an answer to the mysterious secret of the universe. It is simply in the willingness to open one's mind to the possibilities that the divided soul may be fulfilled. Calamy certainly is in a better place than the other *barren leaves* (beings) that he leaves behind: Mary with her thoughts of Jim; Cardan at the mercy of his hostess; Mrs. Aldwinkle off to Monte Carlo; Irene and Hovenden in the throes of passionate love; and Chelifer skeptical of the cosmos. Standing alone is the prophetic figure of Calamy, a figure whose ideas would be expanded into a multiplicity of form in Huxley's next novel, *Point Counter Point*.

Point Counter Point

"The Musicalization of Fiction"

Point Counter Point (1928), until the arrival of *Brave New World* (1932), was recognized as Huxley's most famous — and successful — work of fiction.[91] Structured, as its title intimates, as a musical composition in words, it takes the best of his three other novels of social criticism and weaves them together into one melodious whole. There is certainly an abundance of characters representing the strata of English society in amusing ways, as was evident in *Crome Yellow*. The gathering at Tantamount House, listening to the music of Bach, resembles the Peacockian influence present in his first three novels. Reflecting English society in the late 1920s, the ennui-ridden, tragic figures of *Antic Hay* are not absent. But Huxley wanted more than to sit in a satirical posture as he did in his previous three novels. He brings with him what he began to explore with Calamy in *Those Barren Leaves*— the desire to see reality in its various forms. Not sticking with the contemplative mode of the latter, Huxley found within his own life experience people and ideas that could be expounded in fictional form. Walking the sometimes treacherous tightrope between essayist and novelist, he places within the mouths, the minds, the actions and the very notebooks of his characters a multiplicity of perceptions transitioned, one into the other, like the movements in a symphony by Bach or Beethoven.

Philip Quarles is a successful writer detached from life by a massive intellect. It is in his notebook entries scattered within the novel that the reader gains insights not only into his character, but the structure of the novel, its theme, and perhaps implicitly into the mind of Huxley. In one of his entries, Philip writes that, while at Lucy Tantamount's home, he was "a victim of a very odd association of ideas" that would become the ingredients of his next novel. Much like the "musicalization of fiction," he continues, he would weave a work akin to a musical composition with abrupt transitions in mood. Of course, he would need a satisfactory supply of characters engaged in "parallel, contrapuntal plots" with the god-like author considering the various aspects of life.[92]

On a ship bound for England from India — a country that Huxley had visited on his trip around the world two years earlier — Elinor Quarles discusses with her husband, Philip, his desire to experiment with a new way of looking at things. She finds it rather "queer," but encourages Philip to explain himself. Sounding much like Calamy, who used his hand to explain the multiplicity of reality, Philip states that he wants to explore the same "multiplicity of eyes and multiplicity of aspects seen." He catalogues those who see reality differently from the biologist to the chemist, from the physicist to the historian, from the religionist to the economist.[93] Elinor wishes that for once Philip would write a simple story of love gained, lost, and finally regained, but Philip knows, as Burlap (an art critic in the novel) acutely appraises his work, he cannot write a book from the heart. Since Philip's entries clearly reflect the structure and intent of *Point Counter Point*, one cannot help but question whether Huxley was really writing about himself.

In the fully developed description of Philip Quarles and his later journal entries, Bedford believes that the answer is "yes"— there is much of Huxley, albeit selective, in Philip's characterization.[94] For Quarles, like Huxley, could be both a cynic and a mystic, a humanitarian and a misanthrope, all dependent on the opinions or lifestyles of others at any given time. Yet he would always be true to the essence of his mutability. If there was one under-lying way of life that Quarles could always believe in, it was "the mixture of pyrrhonism and stoicism ... an enquiring schoolboy among the philoso-phers."[95] Although the description seems to fit, it would be unfair to accept all of Philip Quarles's traits as those of Huxley. In this regard, D.H. Lawrence, a writer with whom Huxley had a lasting friendship, was to write in a let-ter after reading Huxley's novel that "there are many men in a man," and that the man who wrote *Point Counter Point* is only one of the Aldouses.[96] While Philip Quarles may not translate into a fully developed Aldous Hux-ley, certainly his desire to write about the multiplicity of reality does but-tress Huxley's intent in contrapuntal form.

Hence, the characters and their perception of the world parade before us. Lord Edward Tantamount refrains from the world of the living and sees reality only under a microscope, while Lady Edward plunges fully into the reservoir of life, viewing its absurdities with relish; Lucy Tantamount, their daughter, finds life a bore and enjoys playing with men's feelings in her pow-erful role of femme fatale, while Walter Bidlake, her pawn, sees life merely as a defendant on trial, ravaged between a guilt for Marjorie, his mistress, and a irrational lust for Lucy; John Bidlake sees life as a painting in which he is the consistent recipient of a lady's virginity, while Burlap hypocritically bemoans the promiscuity of his age, and writes about the mystics while sur-reptitiously doing all that he states he loathes. And so the contrapuntal dramatis personae display their lives in multifarious forms.

Elinor Quarles, Philip's wife and daughter of John Bidlake, sees her role in life as one to provide the heart to her husband's cold, passionless intel-lect, yet she finds herself yearning for the passion that is so barren in her own soul. Ironically, she withholds the needed intimacy from the distin-guished leader of the British Freemen, Everard Webley, until it is too late — he is murdered by a pair who hates both his person and his politics. Upon closer examination, one might wonder what would have happened if Elinor had consummated her relationship with Webley. Might the intellectual Philip — narrowly living in a detached world — have been wounded by her infidelity? Might he not realize until then the happy, contented state he has occupied with the woman he loves as his counterpart? Could he have been shattered in the same way that Spandrell is shattered when his mother remar-ries? All of this is pure speculation since neither he nor his wife is able to be unfaithful in an attempt to experiment with their emotions.

Meanwhile, Sidney Quarles, Philip's father, is an impotent businessman whose wife is the epitome of savvy in all areas that he is not. He is left to spend his mornings doing crossword puzzles while pretending, for years, to do noteworthy research on a volume about democracy that will never see the light of day. To feel superior in at least one pursuit, he engages in discreet, parsimonious affairs, only to be exposed by an angry courtesan (Gladys Helmsley) who claims she is pregnant with his child.

The contrapuntal plot moves in and out, back and forth, from person to person in time and space, until the loose connectors are brought together in one crescendo at the conclusion of the novel. At the centerpiece of all of these movements is a twofold duality: the intricacies of the human condition, especially in matters of the heart, and the philosophical underpinnings in a quest for the meaning of life.

> O wearisome condition of humanity,
> Born under one law, to another bound;
> Vainly begot, and yet forbidden vanity,
> Created sick, commanded to be sound.
> What meaneth Nature by these diverse laws?
> Passion and reason self-division's cause.
> — Fulke Greville, 1st Baron Brooke[97]

These lines from Greville prompted Huxley to request of C.H.C. Prentice, his publisher, that the title of his novel be changed to *Diverse Laws*, since he believed that title better served the theme of the work. Although it was not changed, the lines do reveal an aspect of humanity that is consistently explored in *Point Counter Point*— a humanity torn between two forces. It would be so simple to call it the struggle between the forces of good and evil, for that would fit nicely into the mold of epics from time immemorial. But life is not that simple, and to be human is far more complex. Like Chelifer before him, Spandrell cannot find happiness and yet continues to do the very things that make him unhappy; like Calamy before him, Burlap believes that he is pursuing the mystic path despite the fact that he daily does the very things that are of the flesh and not the spirit. Walter promises Marjorie that he will give up his affair with Lucy, and at the moment, with full resolve, means it, until Lucy beckons him to her, and then he falls once more under her spell. Elinor knows that an affair with Webley is a misplaced consummation of the passionate love she feels for Philip — a love that will never be reciprocated — and yet she finds herself on the verge of doing what she knows she will later regret. And Philip, try as he might, wants to express to Elinor his love and devotion, but after a failed attempt at passion with a desirable Molly d'Exergillod—a woman who bores him with her incessant talking—he tries, but cannot say the words, only to bury his face in a scientific treatise. Spandrell was to describe these torn allegiances as "a curious sort of manure-heap" wherein reality is both attractive and disappointing.[98] Why is humanity doomed to do the very things that do not bring it happiness?

In the opening of the novel the answer lies in Huxley's satiric wit as Walter makes his way to Tantamount House, with its Roman façade, listening to a symphonic performance of Bach's suites. Providing an historical background to both the house and its guests, Lord Edward, the proprietor, has inherited the wealth of his family but is discontent with his lot in life. Contemplating the best method to commit suicide, he has an epiphany when he reads the words in an article, "The life of the animal is only a fragment of the total life of the universe."[99] Aware of solidarity and his place in the world for the first time, he is resolved to dedicate his life to science. Shortly thereafter he falls in love with one Hilda Sutton, a Canadian who rolls her "r's" and takes great delight in shocking her guests in the most indiscreet manner. She is aware of the tongues that wag behind her back, and she consciously provides them with plentiful ammunition. In a carefree manner, she feels self-assured in the affirmation that with position comes power.

The eccentricity of power and manner is depicted in the person of Lord Edward, who works only by night and sleeps by day; his love for Hilda is like his relationship with the laboratory organisms he dissects. Unable to make any serious human contact, he takes delight in frivolous and cruel experimentation; his latest dissection is to remove the tail of a newt in order to attach it to its amputated foreleg. Suddenly, in the midst of this experiment, he is physically moved by the music of Bach emanating from his wife's soiree below. He descends the many steps from his laboratory into the palatial music room where the guests are gathered. Embarrassed by the realization that he is in full view of the assemblage, he nervously places his smoking pipe in his jacket pocket. When the music stops, he tries to immediately make his escape, but he is assaulted by the young Everard Webley who tries to convince him to join the cause of the British Freemen.

Edward objects and then vehemently engages in a tirade against politicians who spend their time on useless things that they label progress—they should be concerned with more worthwhile endeavors like preventing the extinction of phosphorous. Most of the guests are bewildered by the ranting of the proprietor. After his vocal pronouncement, he swiftly retreats. So out of touch with reality is Lord Edward that one day he calls for his daughter to visit him in his laboratory. His daughter, a widow, has been engaging in a series of amorous liaisons for years, yet Edward can only speak objectively to her about the fact that he has heard that she has been known to kiss gentlemen in conservatories. He is the blunt of humor as Lady Tantamont — his daughter — relates this farce to her friends. Lord Edward adheres to a boring, fastidious menu of foods; his schedule never deviates from day to day; and, appropriately, is seen in a stately pose walking with his brother at Gaddenden Park, the latter a cripple who is fittingly pulled by an ass, a symbol of both men and their position in life.

The other quests are equally worthy of the same title. There is Lady Edward, who seeks her passionate pleasures in the arms of other men, including John Bidlake. They were lovers for years and now maintain a civil friendship. Mrs. Mary Betterton — also a former lover of Bidlake — is overheard speaking about the boredom and cynicism of youth. Her reason for their discontent? They are spoiled from birth and given so many freedoms and pleasures that they fail to appreciate life. She had not seen the inside of a theater herself before she was eighteen. Molly d'Exergillod, another guest, is described as one who does not sleep with her husbands but only talks to them; Polly Logan is humiliated when Lady Edward overhears her "floater" disdainfully indicating that the woman is Canadian; and into Lucy's mouth Huxley places a summation of the gathering at Tantamount House when she states that she hates nothing more than "the noise of cultured, respectable, eminent people."[100] The history behind these assembled few and the contrast between what is seen and what is real is explored with minor transitions between them. Thus begins the contrapuntal structure of the novel that flourishes and splinters into multiple parts removed from the Tantamount House setting.

Within these parts is Philip's mother, Rachel Quarles, who believes that the unhappiness of humanity rests in an ill-chosen path away from God. For her, all of life is a struggle on the cross that must be embraced — her Christianity is her salvation. Imagination, as she describes it, is always far better than reality. She even convinces Marjorie — the poor, mistreated one whose drunkard husband abused her and whose love for the unfaithful Walter diminishes her — to see reality in a new way, as the way of all means to God. In her newfound religiosity, Marjorie is converted and finds peace — or at least has persuaded herself that she has.

Then there is Frank Illidge — a member of the working poor who received his education by chance on a scholarship. Illidge works for "Old Man" Tantamount, and despises all of the upper class with whom he is acquainted — a class he believes Webley's politics will perpetuate. Embarrassed by his entrance into the gala when he tripped on a step, Lady Edward adds to his scorn by deliberately introducing him to his nemesis, Webley, by the wrong name — she calls him Mr. Babbage. Illidge recalls the destitute conditions of his youth, the inability to provide for his brother, and the hopeless existence of his mother doing hard manual labor each day of her life. Now, his brother stands eight hours a day before a milling machine so that he might produce coats for the privileged class. Someday, Illidge hoped that the nobility would be cursed to work as his mother, much as had happened in Tsarist Russia. All of these thoughts justify in his mind his participation in the destruction of their leader, Webley, the golden-tongued promoter of a Fascist regime (or at least that's how Illidge and Spandrell view it).

Everard Webley has it all — fame, fortune, good looks, and a devoted following as leader of the British Freemen. In Philip Quarles's notebook, he describes how Webley sat on his white horse and mesmerized the crowd with his words of freedom and equality, the same words that thrilled and impressed his Elinor, the woman that Webley woos. Everard even pictures Elinor with him, married, and pursuing their dreams together. He offers her a passionate love, and although it is never consummated, there is little doubt that Webley will not satisfy his and her appetites. It is during Webley's speech that Illidge is removed and given a black eye when he demonstrates against the man. Thereafter, Spandrell uses Illidge's hatred of Webley to incite him into a murderous scheme. It is ironic that Webley is killed in anticipation of a consummated union with Elinor in her very home. Spandrell has conveniently been privy to Elinor's abrupt departure and requests that he provide apologies to Webley for canceling their dinner date. He and Illidge, therefore, lie in wait for the unsuspecting victim. Parenthetically, the Huxleys were very concerned about the Fascist movement and the loss of liberties in their much loved Italy while he was writing *Point Counter Point*.

It is in the character of Maurice Spandrell that we have the saddest indictment of the human soul in a tug of war against the very fiber of its being until it collapses. The man reminisces about the last time he knew true happiness when he and his mother were on a ski trip when he was 15. He knew even then that moment of happiness was precious, and in his mode of prophecy, fulfilled the subsequent downward spiral when she remarried

General Knoyle. From that point forward, he did all that he could to violate their love, to torment her with his debauchery, all the while suffering miserably from the betrayal of self to wanton ways. He lives in squalor and his station bruises her heart when she visits him. He turns away from her when she kisses him, and he is only willing to take from her the money he needs to survive.

Spandrell explains to Illidge and Philip Quarles at the latter's club that when the war came, he thought he might contribute something noble and worthwhile. But his ability to speak three languages and ties to his stepfather — a general — placed him away from the front lines and in a safe position of Intelligence. He did not want his life saved; his one promised venture into the world of hope brought him back to the prophetic plight from which he suffered since. "So it became a kind of point of honor to do the opposite of what I'd desired," he concludes.[101] Finding pleasure in his boastful description of innocent Harriet's destruction for amusement, he is habitually lazy, and engages knowingly in vice to such an extent that he has become amoral. Spandrell meets with a diverse band of artists at Sbisa's, the afterhours local watering hole, and therein finds dialogical diversions into the mysteries of life.

At Sbisa's, the Rampions, Burlap, Quarles, Spandrell, Lucy Tantamount, Walter, Willie Weaver, Cuthbert Arkwright and others, meet — on various occasions — to discuss matters of the human condition. Mark and Mary Rampion appear to have the only healthy marriage among all of the couples in the novel. Mary, falling madly in love with Rampion, gives up her life of gentility and follows him in his artistic pursuits as both a writer and a sketch artist. Mark and Mary's relationship is founded on mutual respect, passion and intellectual equality. Not born a noble savage, Mark Rampion learns from Mary to sublimate his Puritan tendencies for hard work and to accept her perception of life as something that comes naturally and easily. She was to keep house and care for her husband and their children modestly, even after his success. Never realizing the breadth of his talent, Mark is not averse to giving sketches away free of charge to the likes of the greedy and penny-pinching Burlap simply because he likes him. To Spandrell's gloating rendition of his conquest of Harriet as an experiment, Rampion declares that he not only hates women but that he hates sex — better yet — he even hates himself. And he may not be far off the mark. Rampion and Spandrell continue in their debate using art and literature as a basis for understanding the human condition. Rampion believes in a revolution in favor of life and wholeness — not in an either/or path of promiscuity or asceticism. And both of these divergent aspects are present in the lives of Denis Burlap and Beatrice Gilray.

Beatrice has just put Peter Slipe out of her house because he dared to cross the line — she has never made love and found the mere touch of a man revolting. Denis Burlap, on the other hand, is different: he is a man of culture. This sophisticated gentleman lives with Miss Gilray, as well as off her; suffering terribly from the loss of his wife, the beloved Susan, Beatrice has come to treat Denis like her child. Since he is neither a *pouncer* nor a *pawer*, she ruminates, Beatrice trusts him — a man more in love with the idea of love than love itself. As editor of *Literary World*— the periodical for which Walter Bidlake works — he writes uplifting articles about life and the lives of the saints, especially St. Francis upon whose life he is writing a treatise and whom he regards as a role model. Overcome with her adoration for the man, Beatrice even volunteers her time and money to the paper's success. Ever expressing his yearning for the mystical and the spiritual, what no one knows is that Denis Burlap has a dirty little secret — he is a lecher. He had tried unsuccessfully to move his professional and personal relationship with his secretary, Ethel Cobbett — a relationship initially based on a mutual love for the lost Susan — into the bedroom. Since that revelation, she now watches his every move, and laughs contemptuously when he gets his comeuppance after writing glowing letters of praise for the tripe of a Romola Saville, a woman whom he has not met and hopes will be his next sexual conquest. Romola Saville turns out to be *two* women who arrive at his office amusingly disbelieving that he fell for the nonsense they wrote collaboratively. Patience does pay off when finally Beatrice, rubbing his chest with camphorated oil due to a cough, succumbs to his physical advances.

John Bidlake is an aging artist and connoisseur of life. A major successful artist in his time, it appears, according to the critics that he has lost much of his fire and has become somewhat of a cynic. In looking at the reviews of his latest exhibit, he ponders that the sole difference between a favorable and an unfavorable one is that one states brutally what the other only implies with condescending praise.[102] Taken ill at the Tantamount soiree, he cannot help ridiculing the assembled guests much to his former lover's delight, Lady Edward. Blaming the caviar, John Bidlake avoids calling the doctor because he fears the truth that he may be dying. With Rose — his first wife — he had fallen in love at the tender age of 23. But children — two sons — and the offensiveness of responsible living got in the way. He had affairs with his models, ignored Rose, and drove her away with the children. His oldest son was to die of cancer of the intestines — a disease that obsesses John. And the other son from this marriage was to be seen recently by Elinor as a striking military figure (50 years old) with a pronounced mustache. John Bidlake cannot accept that he has a son of 50 and that he is 73. A second marriage was brief (two years) and John still cannot think about the deceased Isabel, whom he adored. A third marriage of convenience with Janet — he could come and go at will — produced a daughter, Elinor, and a son, Walter, both of whom he sees irregularly.

John does return home to Mrs. Janet Bidlake on the occasion of his latest illness. But this time it is serious and terminal. He takes no delight in his art, and sometimes finds some pleasure in his grandson Philip. He is a man of the world who cannot face the travails of aging. If ill-health did not get in his way, he would have gone on as a hedonist indefinitely. The cancer makes him feel vulnerable and mortal, two aspects of life he has repeatedly avoided. And Elinor with Philip — as well as the triangle of Walter, Marjorie, and Lucy — represent the very aspects of life that he so successfully was able to avoid.

Marjorie Carling was enthralled by the young, handsome, talented Walter Bidlake, but did not seek an affair from her husband who drank too much and treated her poorly. She was busy with her partnership in a decorator shop, and was devoted to Mrs. Cole, her partner. But Walter swept her off her feet — he was different, the odd mixture of both man and woman in his sensitivity, understanding and passionate love for her. She peruses his many letters wherein he was far more eloquent than in speech. He was shy in person but bold in his love letters. He promised her passion, and security, and protection. So she left her husband who would not give her a divorce, and became Walter's devoted, and later pregnant, mistress. The sterile description of the cell that multiplied and grows within her to form a life resembles Huxley's description of the Bokanovsky test tube creations in *Brave New World*.[103] Marjorie knows this is a dead end relationship, but she unpacks the very bags she had just packed because she has nowhere to go, and knows she cannot live without Walter. On Walter's part, now that he has conquered poor Marjorie and made her into a one-dimensional dedicated spouse, he despises her and yearns for his freedom.

Walter repeatedly asks inwardly — never outwardly — why Marjorie cannot just accept things as they are. Why could she not have just remained with her husband and not moved in with him? Walter even justifies his anger by looking back at their idyllic months at the cabin as romantically embellished and not real. Because she loves him and demands fidelity, he hates her, and irrationally pursues a woman who is the very essence of all that he abhors, Lucy Tantamount. Spandrell was to ask Lucy why she torments Walter, and she answers that he deserves it — he wants to be a victim and she is very willing to play the game and oblige his instincts. Spandrell and Lucy had been lovers some time earlier in Paris, and she finds the man dangerous and interesting. Walter, meanwhile, waits patiently during a prolonged evening hoping he will have some time with Lucy alone, but she enjoys the company of others until the wee hours of the morning. Lucy will not speak of love with Walter; twice he is frustrated when the moment was right for a consummation of their union, but they are humorously interrupted, first by a cockatoo and then a visitor, Frank Illidge. Finally, Walter has his way with her, tenderly impressing Lucy, but later facing Marjorie's tears that torment him out of a sense of decency, making him vow an allegiance that he knows he cannot keep. The resolution is short lived when Lucy calls him back to her lair.

Walter is meek and shy when it comes to the matters of life as when he asks for a raise from his stingy boss Burlap. Yet the dichotomous side of his nature shows up in the brutal literary criticism that he imposes on submitted manuscripts he reads as assistant editor of the *Literary World*. Walter keeps hearing his brother-in-law's words that he needed to be true to his instincts. But he keeps resisting them out of a sense of nobility of action, thereby holding his breath and refusing to move when a foul-smelling tramp sits next to him on the train, and wiping his hand on his coat as he is repulsed in memory by the dying touch of Wetherington, a man he visited with his mother in his youth. When Lucy Tantamount leaves England for France and promises to meet Walter in Madrid, he has all of the lies prepared for their rendezvous. But then she whimsically changes her mind. Angry, he vents his protestations in writing to which she provides both admonishment and a gleeful account of her latest sexual conquest, an Italian with whom she goes to bed upon their first meeting. While Lucy plays her game and Walter is miserable, Marjorie tries to find an escape in the spiritual exercises practiced by Mrs. Rachel Quarles.

Philip and Elinor Quarles are in many respects the central characters in the contrapuntal plot. The height of Philip's detachment is visible when in India a dog is run over and he responds with only a psychological generalization about the incident. No sentiment — no feeling is evoked. Elinor realizes that she must be the one to make contact with people because Philip is so intellectually detached. She must be the heart for both of them. Elinor is willing to sublimate her own passionate instincts for the love of a man who is without passion. She wants him to succeed, but fears that he may never be able to write something meaningful because he has not experienced anything meaningful, including his love for her.

Philip explains in a journal entry that what he envisions is a frame story within which there are many others stories within each other — one subplot leads to another. And in *Point Counter Point*, the novel, is the very structure that Philip describes. For from Philip we have the philosophical observations about life, and the subplots of his father and mother as well as Elinor. From her we have the yearning of a heart in love but dissatisfied, and the likened subplots of Webley, Spandrell, and Illidge, in turn, and their relationship/contrast to Rampion; from Walter, the subplots of Marjorie, John Bidlake, Lucy Tantamount, Lord and Lady Edward, and Burlap, et al. The subplots transition in any and all directions from one another, ever blending into a contrapuntal whole.

And it is from the union of Philip and Elinor that we have the sad and often misunderstood story of little Philip. Here is a young boy — probably dyslexic — who is enthralled with the return of his parents from India after their absence of ten months; he seeks his mother's love which is reciprocated, but is able to evoke only disinterest in the stoicism of his father, the erratic behavior of his grandfather, and the steady but sometimes bewildering hand of his governess, Mrs. Fulkes. Little Phil becomes the enigma resulting from the separated head and heart of his parents. Falling ill from meningitis, his comatose being foreshadows impending death. But Philip revives and requests food because he is hungry; Elinor is delighted to oblige her son despite his apparent deafness, pleased with signs that his vision has returned. Philip's father is only pleased because his wife is no longer distressed and there is peace in the home. Shortly thereafter, however, little Philip experiences convulsions and dies. Maria Huxley was very distressed over her husband's all too realistic portrayal of the child's death.[104] Some have questioned why this was necessary. But the question that is better asked is: *why not?* Was not Huxley trying to display all views of life, and far too often in reality the innocent suffer the pain inflicted by indiscriminate Nature and the brutally civilized manners of others?

The story of young Philip's death swiftly follows upon the murder of Webley and is juxtaposed before Spandrell's assisted suicide. Conflicted by his hedonistic exploits and the desire to achieve mystical experience — to find the God who hides — Spandrell wished to live the conversion that "nothing happens to a man except what's like him."[105] He truly believed that since the age of 15 he had been doing the very things that are an integral part of a self-fulfilling prophecy. He plays his last card, sending a postcard to Illidge, and a note to the Secretary General of the British Freemen, announcing that Webley's murderer — armed and dangerous — can be found at 5:00 P.M. the following day at his own flat. The Rampions accept Spandrell's animated invitation to listen to a movement of Beethoven on his gramophone — a movement that Spandrell declares proves the existence of the Divine. As Rampion and Mary are listening to the music, there is a knock on the door, followed by a shout, an explosion and then another explosion. Spandrell lies dead on the floor with a revolver near his hand; the three men in green uniforms look on, and then one of them declares that Spandrell shot first. In a style that anticipates the Savage's hanging body at the end of *Brave New World*, the music ends and all that could be heard is the needle scratching on the disc.

In his typically irreverent style, Huxley moves to the final scene with the hypocritical Burlap. He walks home after an enchanting luncheon embellished with praise and paid for by Mrs. Betterton. Why should he not be happy? His book has sold, he has a series of lectures scheduled, and he is rid of Ethel Cobbett — whom Beatrice despised. Of course, he did not fire her in person — he had the business manager send her a letter stating that due to financial reasons they were reducing the office help. Whistling "On the Wings of Song," he does not think that Ethel so loved him that she could not go on living without him, nor could he foresee that she would put her head in the oven and turn on the gas. Without a shred of remorse, he knows that life goes on. He is so happy that he and Beatrice pretend to be children and bathe together. Huxley satirically concludes, "Of such is the Kingdom of Heaven."[106]

Point Counter Point:
A Closer Look at the Ideas in a Novel of Ideas

Philip Quarles, in another notebook entry, writes about the novel of ideas, a label given to many of Huxley's fictional works. Quarles writes that the novel must be populated by characters who serve as realistic mouthpieces for the ideologies they express. The interfacing of thought with action, of idea with characterization, is no easy task, especially since the character must have something significant to say, and only one one-hundredth of the human race have any ideas at all (the latter being Huxley's satiric observation). Adding that the congenital novelist does not write such books, Quarles adds that he has never pretended to be a congenital artist. Huxley's own admission of the defect of such a work as written by Quarles is that it is fiction, and it is often difficult to make the characters real people as opposed to monsters.[107] It is in the latter case that D.H. Lawrence was to write that he wished to smack Lucy across the mouth, and that Rampion was "the most boring character in the book — a gas bag," this coming from the very man that some critics have identified as Rampion's source.[108]

Rampion advocates, almost existentially, that "existence precedes essence." In his art, he displays his philosophy — the symbolic struggle of the human soul for wholeness — a wholeness that may be equivalent to a godliness in a spiritual/mystical sense and not a religious one. While Spandrell asserts that a man does all that he can to fulfill what he sees as his destiny, Rampion argues that Spandrell resists life and thereby its possibilities for redemption. Rampion affirms his faith in life while Spandrell denies it. In essence, Spandrell acts as Rampion's foil, for "Spandrell's determination to be either a demon or an angel has made him waste his chance to exist, Rampion would say, as a man."[109] Spandrell conveniently executes his ultimate denial of life at the very moment that Rampion and his wife affirm it while listening to Beethoven. Rampion may fear that humanity's progress may be headed to a bottomless pit, but he nevertheless calls once more for balance: eight hours out of 24 as an industrialized worker and a real human all the others.[110] Philip Quarles, in another journal entry, writes that Rampion takes in all of the facts whereas others hide from them or pretend they do not exist. Hence, Rampion makes his life fit the facts rather than the other way around.[111] Philip continues that his problem, unlike Rampion, is his inability to transform his detached intellectual skepticism into a congruent whole.

Philip Quarles provides the philosophical musings of the human mind in his journal entries. Like Chelifer in *Those Barren Leaves*, we read his accounts, but Chelifer despises his lot while Quarles accepts it; Chelifer writes of irrelevant, self-centered interests while Quarles expands on an exploration beyond self. The Rampions are somewhat like Calamy in Huxley's previous novel in that they are the only ones that provide an element of hope in a world laden with the dismal waste of an inoperative populace.

Morality, religion, politics, and mores are all on display side by side in striking relief of one another in *Point Counter Point*. It would appear that all are frauds — the hypocrisy of Burlap, the lecherous and deceptive actions of Mr. Quarles, the puffed up political pretense of Everard Webley, the romantic notions of the dissatisfied Walter Bidlake — all are shams presenting a false façade for the world to see but behaving in a manner contrary to themselves. With satiric brilliance in some cases and brutal honesty in others, Huxley passes no judgment but acts as a camera capturing the various images without a caption. In the end, Rampion's ability to live a virtuous life fully cognizant of the dichotomy present in all beings is a vindication of the journey to wholeness. It is possible. The senseless murder of Webley and Spandrell's ultimate denial of life — his inability to embrace what he knows to be true — is a vision of the tragedy of hopelessness. Perhaps the cruel but human sensualist, Lucy Tantamount, may say it all when she relates to Walter the words that would be repeated in many of Huxley's novels: "But you can't get something for nothing."[112]

If one is looking for resolution in *Point Counter Point*, there is none. How can there be resolution when Huxley's intent is to present life in its varied forms. In striking contrast to each other, character after character is presented with a unity only in the familial or societal ties they share. The author's attitude toward different characters becomes the godlike privilege that Quarles writes about in his journal.[113] If Rampion — and to a lesser degree his wife — becomes the sole hope for the future of humanity, in this regard Huxley was moving his narratives in the direction of balance in the journey toward wholeness. This same journey was to take on more mystical channels in his later novels of transformation.

Point Counter Point: Final Observations

If Aldous Huxley's career came to an abrupt halt with the publication of *Point Counter Point*, it would be considered his crowning achievement in the realm of fiction. It was to be supplanted by his first venture into dystopian literature four years later with *Brave New World*. Within the pages of *Point Counter Point*, however, is to be found the persona of a man in his multifarious forms speaking through the characters he created. For here may be found the supreme intellectual, detached from the world he observes, colorfully depicting what he sees with the eye of an eagle. He is able to write of the world while not being a part of it, much like the "Lady of Shallot" in Tennyson's poem. Here also is the misanthrope, cynically observing the triviality of the idle rich, looking with disdain at the materialism that surrounds him yet never needing to seriously worry about his own sustenance. The artist is also present, painting in words the symbolic meaning of life from the perspective of the varied eyes of the beholder while the reader looks over his shoulder, seeing on the canvas what he has portrayed. Here is the struggle of all humanity torn between two masters and not always choosing the path to happiness. The mystic is also found — or at least the rudimentary form of a mystic — betrayed by his own self-centered needs. And finally, here is the man seeking a balance — seeking the wholeness of life — yet realizing there may never be any unity but just the ability to be the young child among many philosophers.

Quarles and Spandrell and Rampion and the others, including even Burlap, integrate together to provide a synthesis of contrapuntal parts; they may not always make for a pleasing musical piece to the ear, but certainly they are reflections of reality in its limitless form. Is Huxley successful? The critical praise and popularity of the novel seem to respond positively. The struggles of the characters and their philosophical musings do bear the markings of universality and transcendence to our contemporary world. Are the characters real? One may argue that the balance Huxley sought between the essayist and the novelist weighs at times more heavily in one direction than the other, but it would appear that the overall results do equate to a balance.

Ever the consummate artist, Huxley would have preferred spending far more time in the development of his narrative, but deadlines had to be met. He writes to his brother Julian that he wished, like Flaubert, he could spend four to five years on a book, then he could make it rather good.[114] He even offered that his publisher reduce his compensation due to his delay in submission; the writing just took far longer than anticipated especially when it weighed heavily on him and produced a period of writer's block.[115] But Huxley took some time away from the novel to write a collection of essays (*Proper Studies*), and one wonders if the transition and transference from one genre to another was the sticking point in the creation of his final product.

Whatever the case, the intellectual prowess of the man, his ability to convey varied ideas within the context of fiction, his craft in the development of plot and character as well as his superlative command of the English language blend together in one cacophonous whole sustaining the contrapuntal essence of its theme. Huxley was to repeat this contrapuntal structure in the abrupt transitions between Lenina, Marx, Mond, Foster, Fanny and the voice of hypnopaedic slogans in *Brave New World*. D.H. Lawrence was to write to Huxley, admiring the courage that it took to write such a truthful narrative. He indicated that it took far more courage to write *Point Counter Point* than it took for him to write *Lady Chatterley's Lover*. He concludes that "if the public knew *what* it was reading, it would throw a hundred stones at you, to one at me."[116]

Point Counter Point is a very complex book and not all of the intricacies of its plot are examined here. At times in the reading, one may feel ill equipped to comprehend all that Huxley has to say. But in the end, even the time taken to contemplate what he has presented is the reader's own journey to self-discovery. Huxley was to write after the book's publication, "I have at last written a rather good, but also rather a frightful, novel...."[117]

"Rather good." Was not Huxley ever the master of understatement?

THREE

Three Novels of Transformation

There may have been an element of justifiable outrage when Aldous Huxley, the master of social criticism, sexual emancipation, and denunciator of Victorian sensibilities expressed a distaste for the sensual triviality of life and sought a path to enlightenment — a path through a pacifism of mind, heart and body to achieve a unity of purpose in the love of mankind. Critically, one could understand that indignation only within the context of a reader who did not perceive within Huxley's novels a progression of the author toward this end. While *Crome Yellow* was his first socially satiric venture and *Antic Hay* continued in that vein viewing the frivolities of a lost generation post–World War I, *Those Barren Leaves* and *Point Counter Point* both reflected Huxley's weariness to continue in the same genre, as well as his struggle to write novels within which views of life — or philosophical ideas about life — are acutely explored. Blending novels and interfacing characters, Chelifer of *Those Barren Leaves* may be Huxley's expository view in *Crome Yellow;* Anthony Beavis in *Eyeless in Gaza* may be one step further on the road to self-awareness as compared to Rampion in *Point Counter Point.* Did not Calamy (*Those Barren Leaves*) leave the comforts of Mrs. Aldwinkle's mansion and his sensual love for Mary to experiment with a meditative path; likewise, did not Rampion (*Point Counter Point*) — the antithesis of Spandrell — provide the body, as well as the mind, of Philip Quarles in the unity of purpose reflected symbolically in his paintings? Why should Anthony Beavis in *Eyeless in Gaza* not further the journey of self-discovery that Huxley himself was surveying?

The argument against this may hold a three-fold interrogative premise: first, should fictional literature be meant only as a work of art and not a reflection of its creator; second, should not imaginative literature be just that and not be required to posit a truth; and third, how can one speak of a progression of the author when *Brave New World*— arguably his masterpiece — stands between *Point Counter Point* and *Eyeless in Gaza*? The latter novel—the first sequentially of these transformative works—will be used to answer these queries.

In response to the first inquiry, Huxley's letters and biographical material are enlightening. He relates that the writing of both *Point Counter Point* and *Eyeless in Gaza* caused him great anguish, accompanied by insomnia, a loss of appetite, and significant writer's block, especially in the penning of the latter novel.[1] These same materials indicate, during the writing of his first transformative novel, that he was reading books on dreams, pamphlets on pacifism, writing a brochure for the peace movement, ruminating on the need for relaxation and meditation, and spending more and more time in exercise and gardening.[2] He describes to E. McKnight Kauffer a physical remedy which, in its details, sounds exactly like what the fictional Miller suggests to Beavis when they first meet in Mexico.[3] Furthermore, war was more than a threat while he was writing *Eyeless in Gaza*, "and the prospects look to me worse than ever," he corresponds to Julian.[4] He spoke against military action on a B.B.C. broadcast in 1934,[5] and delivered a series of lectures on the topic.[6] The only hope for Huxley regarding the sorry state of affairs was that the pacifists would succeed over the militarists.[7] With Fascism and Communism on the rise, Huxley even envisioned the possibility of a pacifist conference to gather world leaders together to express their grievances as a means to peace.[8] Later, Huxley was to write about the many forms of meditation in a letter to T.S. Eliot, suggesting that he hinted at such in his pacifist 32 page pamphlet.[9] All of these are identifiable elements developed within the framework of *Eyeless in Gaza*.

Additionally, how can one not view as less than coincidental that Anthony Beavis, like Huxley, loses his mother at a young age, attends the same school as Huxley, reads the same books, lost a best friend to suicide (analogous to Huxley's brother Trevenan), and shared the concept of intellectual freedom?[10] If all of this is not enough proof that Beavis's and Huxley's experiences are similar, there is Huxley's essay written in December 1936, entitled, "How to Improve the World," wherein the same advice is given that Miller gives to Beavis: start with one's diet and seek the road to self-knowledge. Miller was modeled after F.M. Alexander, a therapist and author, who greatly influenced Huxley during the writing of the novel, and he is even mentioned by him in one of Anthony Beavis's journal entries. Maria, Huxley's wife, writes in her letter to Eugene Saxton, that she hated *Eyeless in Gaza* for all of the personal upheaval it caused, but Aldous was markedly changed because he saw Alexander each day and has made an "essential discovery." Aldous, she continues, is a changed man physically, mentally and morally: the change "comes [out] in the novel."[11] Finally, in his letter to Rosalind Huxley, Aldous discusses at length that the novel's characters were often derived from real life. This source precipitated great distress when the characterizations were clearly recognizable, which was particularly evident when his father identified himself in the novel.[12]

Huxley provides the answer to the second objection in a journal entry of Anthony Beavis, dated October 30, 1934. The topic is imaginative literature. Mark Staithes, while at dinner, remarks that he finds that imaginative literature is not true to life because it assumes that human beings live by reason and organized sentiments when in fact they do not. Beavis writes that he agreed with Staithes because if literature were to show human beings as they really are, they would either kill one another or hang themselves. Imaginative literature was not doing its job. What should it do? Huxley's answer is that it needed to "bring the facts home to the whole mind ... a complete expression ... leading to complete knowledge ... of complete truth."[13] Hence Huxley's desire to not just tell a story but, if possible, to expose a truth about life.

Finally, in response to the third objection, Huxley did make a departure from the social novel to the world of dystopian literature, and therein that shift may account for a temporary lapse in the progression to self-discovery. But in that vein, one may go afoul. For Mustapha Mond's explanation of how the Utopian world came into existence — an explanation occupying three central chapters — is fundamentally the antithesis of what Huxley was trying to get across. John the Savage yearns for the path to self-discovery and truth, but cannot find it in the world of mindless, sensual pleasures. Being outnumbered, he takes the path that Brian Foxe chooses because he, like the latter, cannot live separated from humanity and still be a free individual.

The following novels, therefore, exhibit Huxley's journey into the world of spirituality where the mind, body, and spirit become one. Never choosing a religious path, he was to choose a Buddhistic view of life, seeking an ultimate *nirvana*. Living in a world where the individual is constantly struggling with noble virtues fighting against sensual pleasures — knowing what one should do versus what one actually does — Huxley presents souls dissatisfied with what they see and with what they do, who are searching for the more noble path to self-discovery and fulfillment. *Eyeless in Gaza* is Huxley's watershed moment in which the novel of ideas moves profoundly towards a perennial philosophy of life.

Eyeless in Gaza

Blindness Begets Insight

The title of the novel comes from Milton's account of the Biblical story of Samson in *Samson Agonistes*. The mighty Samson reveals to Delilah the source of his strength — his hair. Betrayed, he is taken captive by the Philistines, and with a shorn head is reduced to grinding grain, a job reserved for oxen, in the city of Gaza. Blinded so as to render him further harmless, Samson is converted in Milton's account to free Israel from the Philistine yoke: "Ask for the great deliverer now, and find him / Eyeless in Gaza at the mill with slaves." [14] Samson, with hair re-grown, is paraded before the assembly on a festive day. In turn, he tears down the pillars of the temple, crunching Israel's enemy and killing himself in the process.

The concept of one needing to die in order to be free is the contradictory but profoundly spiritual basis of most of the eminent religions of the world. Christianity has used the symbol of the Cross as an affirmation of death that is followed by the resurrection — the birth of a new life after shedding the trappings of the old. The Buddhist Four Noble Truths affirm human suffering, but direct one to the path of full liberation seeking *nirvana*— the state of freedom from suffering through a rebirth. The Eightfold Path is offered as a means to salvation of the human spirit. By Samson's death, he frees the Israelites from the control of the Philistines; his own freedom comes about through the denial of a separated self and the embracement of a unified humanity. Samson's ability to become aware of his calling through a physical blindness gains him the insight to see the proper path. Taking the story of Samson as a figurative and not literal embodiment of his theme, Huxley uses the story and Milton's words to express the novel's essence.

The theme of the novel, therefore, is freedom — not only from without, but especially freedom from within. Authentic freedom, however, may cause a vacuum. In Huxley's earlier works, it was okay for the satiric cynic to just describe the vacuum and leave it at that. But for the Huxley who stated at Oxford, "I think the good will win at the end," he needed to provide some closure.[15] In his latest fictional effort, he needed to go further than he had in *Point Counter Point*. If he had not found a resolution to his own dilemma, how could he possibly find one for his protagonist, Anthony Beavis, in *Eyeless in Gaza*? His answer lies in the haunting struggle of all humanity between the virtuous path and the cowardly one for self-preservation.

Anthony Beavis is preparing for a lecture on pacifism but knows he is threatened by an anonymous telegram that states that, if he speaks, it will be his last. What does he do? We identify with Beavis's desire to escape so that he will not "feel" the blow and be asked to withstand the punishment — even death — without even a feeble attempt at retaliation. His old self seeks to run and avoid confrontation — just enjoy the pleasures of life. But his new awareness will not allow the old self to be victorious. So the reader hears Beavis's final proclamation of awareness that "whatever it might be, he knew now that all will be well."[16]

How did Beavis achieve this moment? It did not happen overnight, but in the process of his life experiences. At 43 (almost Huxley's age at the time of the writing), Beavis has come to appreciate his place in the universe and moves forward with a supreme, but constantly tested, sense of inner peace. To achieve this end, Huxley, along with Beavis, needed to process what would bring this man to this stage. Repeatedly, in his many correspondences, Huxley writes about what a strain it was in writing the novel, and his need to bring it to a satisfactory resolution. The Huxleys were in a bit of a financial squeeze with the delay of its publication, and Aldous was unable to sustain the two-books-a-year deal he made with Chattos. He wished, as he stated with *Point Counter Point*, that he had more time to devote to it, but "wolves at [the] doors imposed immediate publication."[17]

The case remained: how would Huxley tell Beavis's tale? The answer comes in the form of dated entries in non-chronological order. Much like the contrapuntal arrangement of *Point Counter Point*, Huxley creates a thinking man's plot arrangement wherein the reader must sort through the non-sequential pieces to come to the synergistic conclusion. While Joyce may have been a model in concept, he is certainly not in structure. It begins 18 months before the conclusion of the novel. Playing out like a Greek or Shakespearean tragedy, the reader knows the *what* but not the *how* of the story. The journal writings of Beavis intermingle with the various threads of the plot. If one were to untangle the threads and place them in chronological order, it would look something like this.

Untangling the Threads: The Plot in Chronological Order with Analytical Postscripts

1902–1904: Anthony Beavis's mother has died; he is described by his father John as a "poor motherless child." He and his father and uncle ride the train to his mother's funeral, and he hears the sound of the wheels repeating "dead-a-dead-a-dead" over and over; in his mind, he wills the refrain to become "to stop the train, pull down the chain."[18] His father is an etymologist who speaks in brief colloquialisms; he misses Maisie (his wife) and in short order introduces Anthony to his stepmother, Pauline Bennett, a plump lady who enjoys culinary pleasures. Uncle James despises all women, loves the sound of words, and is later revealed to be a closeted homosexual. At Mrs. Foxe's home — the home of Brian, his closest friend from school — we first meet Mary (Champernowne) Amberley and her husband Roger. Brian's father, present at the funeral, undergoes a lengthy illness and leaves a lucrative estate to his widow upon his death. Anthony loves spending time with the Foxes on holidays, even though Mrs. Foxe is constantly engaged in the charity of bringing in the crippled and orphaned, to Anthony's discomfort. The narrator inserts a commentary that sometimes in life one may come across those whose deformity is in the form of communicative ability, as was the case with Anthony's father, John Beavis. Despite his uneasiness with Mrs. Foxe's avocation, Anthony's time at the Foxe home is joyful, and he and Brian develop a strong bond.

At Bulstrode (the boarding school), Brian and Anthony share a visionary moment looking up at the stars as they sail a whittled boat with paper sails across the imaginary ocean in the gutter outside their room. Overcome with emotion, Brian cries for Beavis at the loss of his mother, projecting what it would be like if he lost his own. Anthony's other classmates are sympathetic, to such a degree that even Mark Staithes, the bully and distinguished athlete at school, invites Anthony (called Benger) to participate with the others in embarrassing the "buffoon, " Hugh (Goggler) Ledwidge, whom they spied upon on as he was privately masturbating. Brian Foxe (called Horse Face) defends Goggler because it is the decent thing to do, and makes Benger feel inferior as he is cajoled to throw a slipper at the humiliated target.

Analytical Note: Anthony Beavis, in this early entry, is revealed to be a divided soul who sees within Brian the very essence of goodness that he desires but refrains from trying to attain. Needing the affirmation of his friends, he does the very things that Brian — the more noble and sensitive one — refuses to be bullied into doing. The bewilderment of youth faced with ultimate tragedy at the loss of his mother, Beavis is confused and seemingly desensitized by the circumstances surrounding him. All is a preamble to a child who will become father of the man.

1912–1914: Anthony and Brian are at Oxford. Brian has fallen in love with Joan Thursley, the daughter of a disgruntled minister and a mother of definitive manners. Spending some time with Joan at her uncle's house, Brian is assured of her love and their mutual interest in birds. Introducing Joan to his mother, Anthony, and Beavis's parents, Brian demonstrates that he cares deeply for her. Mrs. Foxe is a widow of refinement with solid Christian values — values that she bestowed and burdened upon Brian in an act of possessive love. Anthony is uncomfortable being around her for fear that she will not only disapprove of his point of view, but give voice to a contrary spiritual perception that he did not want to acknowledge. Mary Amberley — recently divorced — is to join them for lunch, much to Anthony's pleasure. At the end of the day, all go in different directions, leaving Anthony and Mary Amberley alone to begin the young man's first sexual liaison with an experienced and sensual creature ten years his elder.

Brian deems that he should pass the summer in Germany but cycles several miles to Joan's home to see her before his departure. There, the patient Mrs. Thursley is continuously interrupted by the minister who complains about the noise in the house while he is trying to write his sermon. Brian gets Joan alone for a few moments and, suddenly, while on their walk in the woods, he kisses her and then withdraws because he knows what he feels and is conflicted. They write to each other, and in September he is surprised to see her waiting for him at the station, an act that creates great jealousy and displeasure in Mrs. Foxe, a displeasure that she tried, unsuccessfully, to hide.

After graduating from Oxford, Brian decides not to take his mother's money — Joan is forced to agree with him — and delays their marriage until he has established himself. He works day and night, to the point of physical exhaustion, at a newspaper in Manchester. He knows that Joan is to spend some time in London with her aunt, and writes to Anthony requesting that he meet with her to find out how she is doing in his absence. Anthony does just that and feels great sympathy for the girl who describes the fact that she deeply loves Brian, but that his austerity in matters of the heart makes her feel dirty, as though she were the perpetrator of coarse desires. She says that Brian's mother is possessive and obsessive and has probably made Brian set his sights too high. What would have been wrong with accepting her money and getting married? Anthony feels sorry for the girl, but makes an error in judgment by confiding what took place to his lover of two years, Mary Amberley. Mary demonstrates to Anthony what he should have done — what the girl really wanted — in an aggressive move of sensual pleasures. What is worse, she bets him to do just that — take Joan in his arms and kiss her.

Once more we have the case of a person knowing what he should do and doing just the opposite. Anthony meets with Joan, attends a performance of *Othello*, and carries her to a coach after she faints. There, impulsively, he kisses her and wins the wager. She, however, misinterprets the actions as love, which Brian will not reciprocate. To the silent Anthony, she declares that she will write Brian to call off their engagement. Anthony does not and will not tell the girl that his actions were merely a desire to win a bet. Instead, he has her promise that she will not write Brian until he has had a chance to speak to him.

On their weekend, during which they hike, read and converse as friends, Anthony thinks of every excuse not to tell the truth to Brian. He tells him that he met with Joan and that she was bewildered about their separation — he further states that his friend should face reality. However, Anthony manufactures all sorts of scenarios in his mind as to the manner in which he should tell his friend the truth — to take the blame on his shoulders, and make him realize that he is the one at fault, without revealing what really has transpired. He even thinks of running away and escaping. In this way, he would not have to face the complicated situation which could only end with hurting several people for whom he cared. Alas, after unsuccessfully composing a letter to Joan and posting one to Mary, whom he angrily but only half-heartedly decided not see again, he is determined to speak to Brain after his friend returns from his solitary trek.

Many hours after his departure, Anthony determines that Brian has probably taken the train to London. He goes upstairs to pack his bags when he sees in Brian's room three envelopes — two to be mailed and one without a post: one is addressed to Brian's mother, one to Joan, and the third to Anthony. Among the letters is Joan's note to Brian stating the very things that Anthony did not want his comrade to read, and Brian's letter of disappointment with the actions of his closest friend. Brian concludes that he is like a statue that has been broken into a heap of dust and fragments. He knows that he could not have done what his friend did, and cannot comprehend why he did it, knowing fully of his escapades with Mary Amberley. He wants to hate him, but cannot, and knows just as clearly that he cannot go on. He concludes with the words, "God Bless you."

Methodically, Anthony picks up the two sealed envelopes and places the envelope addressed to him with Joan's letter into his pocket. He proceeds downstairs and watches the sealed envelopes as they are consumed by the flames in the hearth. He then alerts the authorities. They search for several hours before finding Brian's contorted remains at the base of a cliff. Anthony comforts Mrs. Foxe, who now realizes that her love had been possessive, yet even now she asks that Anthony be Brian's replacement. Anthony writes to Joan that Brian's death was an accident, and lies that her letter to Brian had not reached the house until after her fiancé's departure; he will keep it for her. He questions if he may ever see Mary again after what has happened. He is inwardly angry with Mrs. Foxe and Mary and Joan and all who are to blame for his friend's death, but in his heart he knows that he is the one who is responsible — a responsibility that he is not willing to face.

Analytical Comment: The kind, sensitive soul that is Brian Foxe is so conflicted by both ethical and moral paradoxes that he becomes a martyr for what is noble and virtuous; the man who stutters as he speaks finds it difficult to express what is so deeply emblazoned in his heart. "Eyeless" in his own Gaza, he leaps off a cliff to free himself from the twisted world that others have created. Rejecting a life of comfort, love and security for what he believes to be a more righteous end, he flees from sensual yearnings, fails to grasp his mother's true possessiveness, and forgives the very selfish actions of his best friend. The memory of Brian will haunt Anthony Beavis all the days of his life, but not until much later will he fully come to see this tragic event as an epiphany along the road toward a discerning awareness of one's true self.

1926–1928: Helen Amberley announces to her sister Joyce, who will marry Colin Egerton, that she will steal something in each store that they visit, which she proceeds to do, much to her sister's horror and chagrin. The final item — a kidney in a butcher's shop — makes her playful and seductive mother howl with laughter as she relates her daughter's latest escapade to her delighted guests. With a voice described as both aphrodisiac and comic, it is the former that compels the handsome Gerry Watchett to take her to her room and have his way with her while the guests wonder where their hostess may be. Gerry is no longer rich — he has lost all of his income — and now shrewdly uses his charms to advise Mary on financial matters, and seduce poor innocent Helen after caring for her sick and dying kitten.

The dinner party at Mary Amberley's home resembles the Peacockian framework of old — an assembly of extraordinary and eccentric individuals discussing a variety of topics, both profound and mundane. There is the degenerate Beppo Bowles; the shyster Gerry Watchett; the uncomfortable archeologist, Hugh Ledwidge; the very militarily Colin Egerton; the discontented Mark Staithes (who arrives late); Joyce Amberley, the changeling who hangs on every word of her betrothed; Helen Amberley, the " hopelessly frivolous" one (by her own description); and Anthony Beavis, the now-published academician and intellectually detached observer.

Hugh Ledwidge is embarrassed because he cannot socialize, and fears both Mark and Anthony for they were privy to his terrible mortification at Bulstrode. He is only comfortable with books and his writings. He cannot express to Helen how he feels, and is awkwardly jealous as she glides across the floor with Gerry Watchet, dancing to the tune "Yes, Sir, That's My Baby." Later, filled with excitement, she accepts Hugh's list of books she should read, and impulsively kisses him several times while standing above him on the staircase. Hugh departs and writes a lengthy letter of admiration to Helen that he posts before midnight. In the meantime, upon Mark Staithes' arrival, Mary indicates the he is either impotent or a homosexual because he dismissed her advances eighteen months earlier.

Mark Staithes is an unusual fellow. Seemingly sexually ascetic for the greater good of personal superiority, he lives in a dingy flat despite the wealth of his privileged family of generals and stockbrokers. The family is outraged when he enlists during the war, refusing to take the lucrative job that his father has found for him, and snubs the gentry by journeying to Mexico to run a coffee plantation. At home, he distributes revolutionary literature, joins the party, and is ever hopeful to overthrow the leaders and transform humanity. Miss Pendle, an elderly woman who he has taken in, reveals the sensitive side of his otherwise hardened façade.

Mary Amberley has been swindled by her lover, Gerry Watchet, who has escaped to Canada; she is unable to cope with her dwindling funds, and has become addicted to morphine. She dwells in the world of the past and escapes from a reality that she cannot face. Helen struggles emotionally and physically with her addicted mother and the knowledge that Gerry has been a lover to both Amberley women — her and her mother — leaving her pregnant in the bargain. She tries to detach herself from the act of aborting her child, and mistakes Hugh's letter of protection for a proposal. She is distraught and yearns for a safeguard from the cruel world. She tells Hugh that she does not love him, but she will learn to be a responsible and good wife — the very qualities that he does not want in her. For Hugh idealizes the concept of love, but cannot feel it or give it. He is horrified that marriage will mean a larger flat, and what is to become of his housekeeper Mrs. Barton?

Analytical Comment: In sharp contrast to the other sections that revolve around Anthony Beavis, he is now only briefly mentioned as a detached observer on the scene. There is, however, a fundamental purpose to this. Anthony Beavis has come into adulthood as part and parcel of this social scene for a number of years. The gathering of self-absorbed individuals wrapped up in a world of sensate and meaningless pleasures becomes a backdrop for his detachment. These sightless ones have been blinded by their lust for life, and Beavis has counted himself among them. The contradictory impulses evident within their displaced and hedonistic lifestyle are the essence of what will later drive Beavis to seek an alternative path toward a new vision of reality.

1933–1935: The novel opens with Anthony viewing the photographs of people, events, and places past: his mother, Maisie, Mary Amberley at the beginning of their affair, and his days at Eton. He records in his notebook that progress is for historians but is never felt by those experiencing it — it is only a retrospective game. Helen Amberley, his present lover, enters — her face reflects the turmoil of her unhappy marriage to Hugh Ledwidge. Anthony is the ever-mindful and detached scientist — the sociologist — who can view the world objectively, including the one within which he is engaged. Helen remarks that he is all pretense — his handsome good looks entrap a person but there is nothing underneath: he is always "getting something for nothing."[19] The picture of Mary makes him ask about her mother whom Helen indicates is still addicted and doing miserably despite her time in a nursing home.

Helen and Anthony are sunbathing in the nude on the roof of a villa next to the blue Mediterranean. As he caresses her hand and begins the motions of lovemaking, his detached mind thinks of Brian: how he lived and for what purpose he died. Helen touches the scar that runs diagonally across Anthony's thigh — a scar left by a stupid recruit at a Bombing Instruction who threw a hand grenade short. Anthony remained in the hospital for ten months and six surgeries, thereby keeping him safe from the war. Sometimes, he reflects, he feels that he has been a bit too lucky.

Just then a plane sinks dangerously close to them, and hurled out of it is the body of a dog; blood splatters everywhere as the carcass lands ever so close to them. Helen begins to sob, but Anthony is revolted and detached. She leaves the roof, dresses, and announces that he is to leave her alone. She walks back to the hotel and Anthony decides to give her some time to process her feelings. He returns to the snapshots, cleans up the mess, and disposes of the carcass of the dog. After a brandy and a swim, he thinks of Helen and his fondness for her. He will go to the hotel to tell her that. When he arrives at her hotel, however, Helen has checked out. Since the train has already left, he wonders if he is not better enough in his newfound freedom. A letter from his broker informs him that it is a good time to sell some of the shares he inherited from his Uncle James. He ponders that he is better off than most during the Depression. The snapshots and memories of Brian's dead body spotted with flies — like the dog — at the base of a cliff, haunt him.

Helen arrives in Paris and must ring at her mother's flat several times before she answers the door. Disheveled and in dirty pajamas, her mother indicates that she had to take measures to prevent her maid from stealing her stockings. She had locked the bedroom door but lost the key; she had to use a flat-iron to smash an opening that she crawls through. The room was filthy, but Helen could do nothing but laugh as the two of them are forced to crawl on the floor through the narrow space into her mother's locked bedroom.

On the train to London three days later, Helen is amazed to read of the highly praised novel that her husband has written entitled *The Invisible Lover*, which offers an idealized version of their union — one that Hugh Ledwidge was never capable of attaining. Helen barges into their apartment and embarrasses Hugh with the reading of a note from Anthony that she has just received which proclaims his love for her. At that meeting is Ekki Gisebrecht, a flaxen-haired German revolutionary who becomes her next lover.

Escorting Ekki to Basel to meet the notorious communist leader Mach, Helen is barred from their meeting and arrives at the appointed place 15 minutes too early. She finds Ekki asleep on the bed, and then loses consciousness herself when she is struck on the chin by a stranger. Having been found several miles outside of town, she awakens in a hospital bed and recalls what has taken place as Ekki is already across the border in Germany.

In the meantime, Mark Staithes is dissatisfied with literature, music and art. Nothing provides him with pleasure; he seeks something more. The "something more" he advocates to Anthony is the ability to take a risk and feel that one is really alive. He solicits Anthony's participation in a journey to Mexico to assist Don Jorge in his revolutionary struggle. He recounts for Anthony the history of the man who was the only one to resist the revolutionaries attacking the landowners. His brothers were killed, and then his wife and sons. He went to work for another and stopped resisting, but became popular among the Indians who felt that they could trust him. Rising in the political realm, he was being attacked once more and asked Mark, who knew him when he was in Mexico, for his help. Anthony at first resists, but ultimately accedes to the proposition of his friend.

Anthony and Mark venture out to Mexico, traveling by sea and then many exhausting miles by land. Mark has a terrible fall while Anthony is lost in exhaustive reverie. Mark insists on continuing to travel, but his leg is infected. Anthony decides to leave Mark in the village and travel for medical assistance. A "miracle" happens when he comes across a Dr. James Miller. He not only amputates Mark's leg and saves his life, but the serenity of the man, his wisdom and his perception of reality speaks to the mind and heart of Anthony Beavis.

It is Miller's words and his doctrine of pacifism that invade the pages of the novel within Anthony's journal entries. This man believes that one must clean the body first, and then rid the mind of litter. To do this, one must detach oneself from the physical comforts of life, knowing that enlightenment is near at hand if one is willing to meditatively seek it. If one treats people as bugs — as Mark advocates — they will treat you as a bugs in return. But if one treats people as human beings, they will eventually treat you as one. If you are injured or die in the process, that is okay — others will carry on.

It is Miller who lived out his pacifism as he was repeatedly struck by one who disagreed with his philosophy at one of his lectures, yet he did not strike back. It is Miller who Helen despises until she comes to better understand the man, even to appreciate that Anthony desires asceticism not to imitate Mark, but to prevent separateness through sensuality. And it is Miller who leads Anthony Beavis to his conversion of body, mind and spirit, to read the spirituality of those of various faiths, and to take the time to ponder William Penn's words that "Force will subdue, but Love gains, and he who forgives first gains the laurel."[20] Reconciled with Helen and uncertain of where their relationship will go, Anthony prepares to deliver his lecture on pacifism with the threat of bodily harm transmitted by an anonymous telegram. Wrestling with the thought that he could be hurt or killed, and needing to not retaliate in a position of implemented non-violence, Anthony tells Helen that he is "happy" — for lack of a better word. For now "there is only this final peace, this consciousness of being no more separate, this illumination ... this unity of life ... demonstrated even in the destruction of one life by another."[21]

Analytical Comment: Within these years may be found a parade of characters seeking some semblance of peace and happiness but often misdirected in their approach. Standing among and apart from them is Anthony Beavis who comes to embrace a cause deemed to be in conflict with humanity's need for aggressive action. And so concludes the sequential arrangement of the novel. But it begs the question: Why did Huxley not arrange it in the same manner? The answer may be found in two approaches since Huxley never responded to the issue: First, in an analytical examination of the plot; and secondly, in an analysis of Anthony Beavis's journal entries that expound his meditative progression. In both cases, the central focus is Anthony Beavis — either in his actions, inactions, or the experiences of those around him. He is the central protagonist whose presence — or lack of presence — is the motivating thematic heart beating to the rhythm of freedom.

Eyeless in Gaza: An Analytical Examination of the Plot

What is the outcome of each character's experience? Helen, the frivolous one, gave her body to Gerry not knowing that the cad was also her mother's lover. Overcome with despair after her abortion, she seeks protection in the arms of a man she does not love and who is incapable of loving her or anyone else in return. The unhappy marriage leads her to Anthony Beavis, who is passionate but detached. In Ekki she finds a youthful mate whose political zeal she neither understands nor appreciates. With his departure, she somehow returns to Anthony, reconciles, and feebly attempts to comprehend his newfound freedom through his association with Miller.

Helen is a one-dimensional figure who epitomizes Anthony's self-centered interest. She steals for fun; kisses Hugh Ledwidge because she is heated after dancing; makes love to Gerry because of the sensitivity he gives her after her kitten's death; and turns to Ekki as a physical counterpart to the detached men she had encountered. In Helen is Anthony's own betrayal of self — a body without spirit, a shell with potential never realized.

In Brian Foxe, Anthony sees transparent goodness that uncomfortably reflects his own inadequacy. Brian stutters, but otherwise is a person of integrity, courage and comes closest to perfection. However, Brian's perfectionism is so pronounced that he can never measure up to the image he has projected. When Brian defends Goggler, refuses his mother's money, cares deeply for Joan but separates himself from her for fear of his carnal desire overcoming his virtue, and forgives Anthony in the end, he embodies the virtue Anthony seeks to attain, but also the lack of balance that must be avoided.

Mary Amberly is all heart and spirit but no mind — she ignores and dismisses reality at any cost. Living off a handsome allowance that evaporates due to the poor investments of her lover Gerry, she avoids reality because she can afford to do so. It is fitting that, when she loses most of her wealth, she escapes reality through a morphine addiction. Although she is Anthony's first truly passionate lover, she is a woman of the flesh that Anthony tires of— he no longer finds fulfillment in a mindless companion. The same may be said for Beppo Bowles, Gerry Watchet, and others of their ilk. Rubbing elbows with the rich and famous no longer satisfies Anthony. Mark Staithes, however, represents the passageway to self-discovery, even though he is not the guide.

Mark provides for Anthony a person of a contrary view and passionate intellect. It is Mark who ultimately convinces Anthony to risk everything — including life — for a cause. The cause does not matter, nor the outcome — it is the process that counts. Mark is an angry young man who defies all the sensibilities of his family and class. Anthony may not be as courageous as Mark, but he does provide for him a respite from the ennui of life. Once more it is symbolic that Mark loses his leg and becomes a cripple, for he is crippled of mind in much the same manner that Anthony's father was crippled in speech. Mark can go no further than to fight — to treat violence with violence. He is so intolerably angry and upset with Miller when the doctor speaks of pacifism, for Mark can only boldly treat humanity as bugs, showing them no fear, for example, when he wrestles with the insulted cowboy at the hotel bar in Tapatlan, Mexico. Mark represents a stagnant, violent tendency in speech and action that must be supplanted by the polar opposite virtue of pacifism. This may be a philosophy completely contrary to Mark's way of life, but it is vital in Miller's doctrine to achieve the inner peace that comes from being totally free — a detachment from violence that begets violence.

Through Mark and his need for medical attention, Anthony is able to find his "miracle" in Dr. James Miller. The doctor becomes Anthony's spiritual guide — it is the person that he has been looking for all of his life. Dr. Miller fortuitously appears when Anthony is ready to really listen and follow. At an earlier period, he would have done Beavis no good — he would have been dismissed as Anthony pursued the distraction that entertained him, be it wine, women, or song. As Miller states, Anthony was filled with negativity. Now, however, he sits at the foot of his Buddha, listening and questioning and pondering the words that he puts into meditative action.

Hence, all of the characters' lives blend into an amalgam of Anthony's journey, each the piece of a puzzle forming the complete picture. He has traveled for 43 years when he meets Miller, and he has been a part of the lives of Helen and Mary and Mark and Brian — each a signpost on his way to his personal *nirvana*. The non-sequential arrangement of his life interwoven with their own reflects the passage of time in the abstract, not the linear form. The progress of Anthony's journey to awareness can be measured in bits and pieces — in fragments of the past — each influencing, in their own way, the present.

Eyeless in Gaza: A Journey to Awareness

Expository Preamble: The journal entries of Anthony Beavis interspersed between the non-sequential plot sequences may be less than clear in reflecting his journey to awareness. Paraphrasing the personal accounts and presenting them in chronological order may render a more comprehensive delineation of his journey to awareness — a journey much on the mind of Huxley during this same period. (The date of each entry is noted in parenthesis at its conclusion).

At Oxford, Anthony Beavis' room is cluttered with books — so short a life and so many books to read, he ruminates. He ultimately settles on *The Way of Perfection of St. Teresa*. Even then as he awaits Brian's mother, his own father and stepmother, and Joan Thursley, he is inclined to look for a better path to the life he is living in the many books that he reads. He is a restless soul who enjoys devouring all the knowledge that is available (June 18, 1912).

Cogito Ergo Sum—"I think, therefore I am," he writes within his journal deliberating the ultimate conclusion to the Cartesian syllogism. Deeply involved in writing an article about personality, he asks: Does one inherit a personality or is it developed by those around him or her? He ponders the fact that Hamlet's problem was he knew too much — he probably would have been happier if he only knew as much as Polonius. In essence, Beavis concludes, Hamlet did not have a personality. He continues to wonder how one can define personality. He deduces personality as the totality of experience as well as that of the moment; hence, it is feeling and thought combined (December 8, 1926).

Beavis writes about Uncle James after his death. His uncle had converted to Catholicism in his later years. He contemplates an atheist who became a Roman Catholic. He considers his father who could not comprehend a brother who was a homosexual at a time when no one even acknowledged it as a feasible lifestyle. He recalls that Uncle James would visit him every day in the hospital bringing gifts to many of the young soldiers from whom he received delight. But when the war ended, so did his temporary paradise. The remembrance of his conversion precipitates Beavis' lengthy research on Anabaptists in the library. In the same narrative, he mentions that he learned from his father about Mrs. Foxe's stroke. However, instead of feeling sympathy, he experiences profound relief: she would have been the chief witness for the prosecution against him. She had written Beavis many times during the war, letters he neither read nor answered, yet he kept them. Suddenly he was compelled to open them, but was pleasantly interrupted by Mark Staithes' telephone call with an invitation to join him. He gladly accepted rather than sorting through the past (May 20, 1931).

Anthony Beavis meditates on the very duality that had often confounded Huxley: Every biography — every life story — can be summed up in the fact that human beings know what they ought to do, but continually do the opposite. As proof, this very day Beavis went to visit Beppo who was ill. He bought him some expensive food and lied that he had a committee meeting to attend — a means of escaping from an uncomfortable scene. Of course, there was no meeting, but he knew that he would not be able to tolerate listening to idle chatter about people and parties — at fifty he thinks that Beppo ought to not attach such importance to the material things of the world. Miller had told him about self-examination and how it will aid in an understanding of self. Beavis feels that he is taking the first step toward this goal by writing in his journal. This narrative procedure may allow him to process what he has done and said in an attempt to comprehend why he did it — hopefully, it will lead him to a better way through understanding. Beavis relates that Miller's way is pacifism and a non-theological form of mediation akin to F. M. Alexander's training in the use of self; the man who had become his mentor advocates that one begin with physical control, and through self-examination to manage impulses and feelings. After their discussion, Beavis contributed money to the cause and agreed to write and speak on its behalf (April 4, 1934).

Today Beavis had lunch with his father who acted like an old man. Pavlov and his conditioning research became a part of Beavis' reflection; he realized that if one behaved like an old man, the body would respond accordingly. He did, nonetheless, admire his father's sense of serenity that apparently comes with old age — he wished that he could combine that selfsame serenity of old age with the vitality of youth. He closes: To be dispassionate and not indifferent would be the ideal (April 8, 1934).

Beavis writes that Mark, who was present for the lecture, relished listening to his friend's harangue about the stupidity of his audience after his second speech that evening. After further contemplative reflection, Beavis realizes that if even one person got the message and changed accordingly, he had achieved something. He submits that he had worked on his notes for hours — it seemed natural and so easy to go back to the stance of the "Higher Lifer," namely the academician who can perpetuate the impractical and get others to accept his findings as invaluable (May 20, 1934).

In today's discussion with Dr. Miller, Beavis came to comprehend the following truths: (1) We are all capable of love; (2) we inflict limitations on that love; (3) we can choose to rise above these limitations; and most importantly, (4) love begets love just as hate begets hate. Consequently, hell is remaining stagnant in behaving as one always has (May 26, 1934).

Beavis writes that he saw Helen that day for the first time since his return from America. He realized and admitted that he wanted to be free in their relationship so he absorbed himself in his work to the detriment of their love. He further elaborates that Miller realizes that he is grasping the technique, for through it Beavis is becoming more consciously aware of the world around him. Centering oneself, discarding all bad behavior and self-centered interests, he has come to appreciate that one is able to turn the ordinary boring routine of life into the extraordinary (June 1, 1934).

Today Beavis writes that he was speaking to three or four about spirituality and the peace movement and Miller's "anthropological approach." He continued to explicate on the topics of courage, self-sacrifice and patience. He indicates that he spoke with such earnest intensity that he was overcome with himself and realized, for the first time, that he was filled with his own pomposity — what he was doing was shameful. He, therefore, apologized and sat down. He now notes that while it was wrong for him to be indifferent and detached and not make contacts, it is equally wrong to make those contacts and enjoy displaying his intelligence and power of articulation. He realizes that he now needs to mediate on those virtues that are the opposite of vanity and a lust for power (June 25, 1934).

Beavis acknowledges that he had just spent a revolting evening with

Helen and some of her friends. He relates that their concept of change is to liquidate all those who disagree with them. He regards this as "Revolting!" Repeating a phrase that would become part and parcel of the Huxley mantra, he writes: Man acts today like he was made for the Sabbath — and all things for that matter — rather than the other way around. He continues that one must learn to use the self and to direct the mind. He affirms that there is no short cut; it is a wearisome challenge to examine everything and yet not fall prey to idolizing the very things that one has created (August 4, 1934).

Beavis recounts his meeting with Helen that day when they spoke about the past and their relationship. She explained that she truly loved Ekki, and could have loved Beavis the same way. She declares that she believes that Beavis is trying to escape again into the idealism presented as pacifism by Miller, but he reassures her that he is not. In fact, he tells her that he is trying to face reality fully with all of its blemishes. He confirms that he is not involved with anyone at the present time. He continues that it was important for Helen to realize, and for him to vocalize, that the asceticism he was practicing was not out of the desire to be a separate, superior individual as Mark, but because he has come to accept that sensuality — namely, lust — gets in the way of pacifism; he feels that sex cannot be an end but a means to the unification of two separate individuals. Such would be the ideal! (August 10, 1934).

Miller's presentation of scientific films opened up a glorious world unknown to Beavis and others until a short time ago. He asked Miller what the effect of this new knowledge — unavailable until now — would have upon people, and he replied that it will have an effect to the degree that each person wants it to. Miller affirms that no longer can anyone who accepts this path pass the buck and blame others. Full responsibility of self is necessary to see the light (September 11, 1934).

Beavis reflected today on the words of William Penn: "Force may subdue, but love gains; and he who forgives first wins the laurel." Beautiful words to live by, he writes. He helped Helen that day entertain her sister and brother-in-law. It was unpleasant to be around such impatient, angry and bitter individuals, but he has come to realize that he cannot just use his mediation as a form of masturbation to escape reality. True meditation, he offers, will allow one to more meaningfully interact with people in the very streets of London (September 15, 1934).

Beavis notes profound remarks made by St. Teresa: "Let us look at our own faults and not at other people's." He ponders, however, that too much self-examination may be as bad as none at all. He ruminates that God may or may not exist, but contemplation of the Divine makes one realize goodness in one's life derived from a source that is superior to it. Reaching a spiritual epiphany akin to Huxley, he concludes that whether it is the Christian God or the Buddhist Mind, all interpretations are valid: one can either see senselessness or the potential for good — it is a matter of choice (September 21, 1934).

Beavis writes of his meeting with Miller and the large crowd that gathered — they were the dispossessed. He laments that pacifism seems to be a concept embraced in an inverse ratio to prosperity: Increased unemployment and disillusionment over the economy appears to support a greater acceptance of pacifism. He offers that this is not positive pacifism; it is a negative one. At these times of stress, the mind tends to hate a vacuum. Negative pacifism and skepticism, therefore, are simply holes in the mind needing to be filled. Beavis continues that they can be filled temporarily with Fascism or Communism or the golden articulation of a leader like Hitler. The major concomitant question follows: Do we have the time to fill the holes with positive pacifism; and if we have the time, do we have the ability? (September 21, 1934).

Beavis writes: Is God a person? He wonders: Would it give a person more power to recognize goodness by believing in a personal or an impersonal God? He concludes that the answer lies in one's perception since each mind works in a different way. Therefore, there is no right choice. It follows that it is essential to read about all of the spiritual approaches to meditation; in each may be found the nucleus to a better understanding. He definitively concludes, it can resolutely be stated that within mediation may be found the key to goodness (Christmas Day, 1934).

Expository Postscript: Anthony Beavis's journal entries conclude with the above. Three months later (23 February 1935) we find him ready to deliver a speech, conflicted once more with the duality of either doing what is right, or running away to safety — a safety of body, however, but not of spirit. Firmly dedicated to the cause of pacifism both in body and soul (as was Huxley), he knows in his heart that despite what takes place, all will be right in the end. With this image the novel concludes.

Eyeless in Gaza: Final Words

Huxley, through the character of Anthony Beavis, views the world around him and is disillusioned. The overture to World War II is beginning;

Fascism and Communism were temporary fixes in Europe that he knew would inevitably fail; mankind had from the beginning of time engaged in acts of violence that destroyed and divided, never built; and the craftsman was creating a work of imaginative fiction that he wanted to represent another way of perceiving reality. He may have rationally concluded: if humanity could not see the evil of its ways; if a conference could not be held for all world leaders to come together to understand one another; if the Great Depression was of the soul as well as the economy, then perhaps, if for no purpose than his own elucidation, he might be able to weave a personal conversion into a novel of ideas. Perhaps Huxley wrote the storyline in sequence and then took all 51 dated entries and shuffled them like a deck of cards, inserting between them Anthony Beavis's journey in the dark night of the soul. Maybe Huxley imagined where Beavis would be at a particular point in time in his journey and simply wrote a corresponding piece to a selection. It is uncertain what methodology he used, but the results are crystal clear: this is a novel of the transformative soul.

The talented writer uses his words as the conductor uses the notes of the various instruments in his orchestra to create a magnificent symphony. Structurally different than *Point Counter Point*, but stylistically similar, Huxley takes his character to a deeper point in time and place than in his former work. In essence, Anthony Beavis's journey to understanding is tantamount to a bildungsroman narrative on a spiritual plane. The disordered sequence speaks of Huxley's view that the human perception of time is untrustworthy; the true meaning of events can only be found in the conscious rearrangement and subsequent reassessment of them.[22] The disorganized arrangement of time may acutely resemble a screenplay with the Wordsworthian projection that the child is father of the man as its subtitle.[23] Huxley had been filled with Beavis's cynicism for the ways of the world that he reflected satirically in his four novels of social criticism; he would take a step beyond and attempt to fill the vacuum created by disillusionment with a mystical conversion. He would ever be conscious that we were "born under one law, to another bound," but he was untying the knot in the hopes of being truly free.[24]

In 1937 Huxley was to move to Hollywood, California, where the pleasant climate and the lucrative writing assignments were equally attractive. Distressed by deteriorating eyesight and the growing threat of another world war, Huxley lived a quiet life that was characterized by a spiritual search for the meaning of existence — a quest that was reflected in his future writings.

While Huxley never converted to a formal religion, he came to recognize a higher purpose to life to which mankind should aspire. Huxley's main focus in his three novels on this theme was to dramatize the contrast between individuals who attain spiritual enlightenment and those who remain trapped in their illusions. The latter are doomed to repeat their mistakes in the blind trust that material progress or Epicurean pleasures will provide genuine happiness.

After Many a Summer Dies the Swan

Huxley's break with Europe led to his permanent residence in the United States with his wife, Maria, and their son, Matthew. Upon his arrival, Huxley went on a lecture tour with the English writer Gerald Heard on the pressing issue of international peace. He also completed a philosophic study entitled *Ends and Means: An Inquiry into the Nature of Ideals and into the Methods Employed for their Realization.* Huxley and his family settled in Southern California because one of his film scenarios was accepted by a movie studio.[25] Writing screenplays would provide a supplementary income during the lean war years, but Huxley had no illusions about the intellectual shallowness of the movie industry. In writing the screenplay *Madame Curie* on the discovery of radium, however, he continued his family tradition of popularizing science for the masses.[26]

At this time he was still struggling with poor eyesight, but he found some success with the Bates method for improving vision, a natural exercise system he would describe later in *The Art of Seeing.* He also returned to fiction by writing a fantasy with a California locale, *After Many a Summer Dies the Swan,* which was published in 1939.[27] He had jotted down notes for the novel while working at a movie studio where the Hollywood atmosphere, the fascinating studio people, and the social crowd were a vivid source of local color. Huxley had passed through the United States on his earlier round-the-world tour, and he recorded his critical impression of Los Angeles, or what he called Joy City:

> The wealth of Joy City is unprecedentedly enormous. Its light-hearted people are unaware of War or pestilence or famine or revolution, have never in their safe and half-empty Eldorado known anything but prosperous peace, contentment, universal acceptance. The truest patriots, it may be, are those who pray for a national calamity.[28]

This view is close to the atmosphere of Huxley's first American novel. The plot of *After Many a Summer Dies the Swan* centers on an elderly millionaire, Jo Stoyte, who lives a life of luxury in a magnificent castle on a hill overlooking Hollywood. This clever, ruthless businessman is insanely jealous of his young mistress who shares with him his opulent lifestyle. He also fears death, and he maintains an unscrupulous doctor to provide him with full-time care. The doctor pacifies Stoyte by falsely assuring him that his research will uncover the secret to longevity.

A visiting Englishman, Jeremy Pordage, is the innocent eye who describes the scenes and characters. Pordage is a scholar hired to catalogue a set of ancient papers that Stoyte has recently purchased. Running parallel to Stoyte's story is a subplot that contrasts with the hedonistic lives of the castle's inhabitants. William Propter, a classmate of Stoyte's in his youth, is the wisdom figure who leads a simple life far below the castle. He expounds a mystical view of life to casual visitors, and he convinces Boone, a young employee of Stoyte, to turn away from the pleasure-crazed castle and to seek a higher way of life. The young man becomes an innocent victim of amorous intrigue. He is mistakenly shot by Stoyte, thinking he is a rival lover who had lured his mistress into a liaison. Stoyte's power and influence succeed in concealing the crime by false records claiming that the murder victim died of natural causes.

The novel reaches a melodramatic climax brought on by Stoyte's obsession with longevity. Through Pordage's research, an English nobleman is found who apparently has survived for hundreds of years on a steady diet of the raw intestines of carp. Stoyte and his party visit the earl in the basement of his castle where he has been kept alive, away from the sight of civilization. The earl is a disgusting sight, however, a living bundle of bones and tissue who has lost all his human faculties. Stoyte can only marvel at the possibility of living so long a life and escaping death — regardless of the ghastly fate this ensures.

The subplot discourse on spiritual enlightenment represents Huxley's ongoing venture into a mystical dimension. The contrast between Propter's exalted view of life and the selfish irresponsible ways of Stoyte and his followers is vividly realized. The California locale, incidents, and personages depicted in the novel are drawn to a degree from actual people and events that Huxley observed, and they are worthy of examination.

After Many a Summer Dies the Swan: Influences

While affiliated with the MGM studio, Huxley attended social gatherings that included Marion Davies, the movie actress and mistress of publisher William Randolph Hearst. A powerful newspaper tycoon, Hearst became for Huxley the perfect symbol of American capitalist ruthlessness. A decade earlier Huxley had written of a Hearst-like character and his simple-minded mistress in his short story "Chawdron." His earlier description of a monomaniac could easily apply to Jo Stoyte: "When you're totally uneducated and have amassed an enormous fortune by legal swindling, you can afford to believe in the illusoriness of matter, the non-existence of evil, the oneness of all diversity and the spirituality of everything."[29]

Frank Baldanza, in an essay on Huxley and Hearst, points out that in addition to modeling his central characters in the novel on Hearst and Davies, Huxley probably derived his impression of the vulgar materialism and the shallow, self-absorbed guests at Stoyte's castle from firsthand experience. He and his wife had visited Hearst's ostentatious mansion at San Simeon on at least one occasion. The name Obispo, Stoyte's lecherous physician, may be a derivation of San Luis Obispo County near San Simeon.[30] The caged baboons that Obispo and his assistant experiment with may have been suggested by the fact that Hearst kept a private collection of wild animals on his lavish estate. Jeremy Pordage, the scholarly, objective observer, may also be a satiric caricature of Huxley himself as an amazed visitor from England.[31]

In a letter to his publisher in 1939, Huxley wrote that he had abandoned writing a long and complex novel in favor of what he called a fantasy written in the manner of *Brave New World*. Although the novel is highly satirical with a fantastic climax, Huxley maintained that the book was based on realistic psychological conflicts. He refers to it as a "wild extravaganza, but with the quality of a most serious parable."[32] The frenetic Hollywood that Huxley observed in the late 1930s was both fascinating and disturbing. The rapid technological improvements associated with moviemaking helped to support an opulent lifestyle for film producers and screen stars. The fine line between the celluloid images and the real world often, however, became blurred. Illusion and reality were often indistinguishable for those caught up in this social world. Huxley's novel contrasts the extravagance and excess of the motion picture capital with the serious human need to find a spiritual response to the problems of existence.

Some critics call the novel an allegory while others are with Huxley in referring to it as a parable. Although both terms are associated with conveying a lesson, in a parable the emphasis is on a real story with moral significance — whereas in an allegory the symbolic abstractions and personifications convey the message.[33] Whatever the label, the novel was written to be appreciated on two distinct levels — the literal and the figurative. If the literal story seems beyond belief, one can discover the genesis of the plot in Huxley's private correspondence.

In 1949, he wrote to his son, Matthew, the account of an unidentified visitor to the home of William Randolph Hearst and Marion Davies. Hearst is described as an "old man, who is dying, emaciated almost to the vanishing point, but desperately clinging onto life." Hearst refuses to lie down but remains upright for fear he may never get up again, and Marion Davies is described as permanently drunk. She confesses to having been unfaithful to Hearst and worries about who will inherit his vast fortune. Huxley concludes: "The reality sounds infinitely more gruesome, and also more improbable, than the fictions of *After Many a Summer*."[34] On the figurative level, this is a morality tale of self-centered people desperately clinging to life, but who are not wise enough to listen to one who has acquired the right knowledge.[35]

The book's title is taken from Tennyson's poem *Tithonus*, which describes a mythical character who was granted immortality but longs for death:

> The woods decay, the woods decay and fall,
> The Vapors weep their burthen to the ground,
> Man comes and tills the field and lies beneath,
> And after many a summer dies the swan.[36]

As swans are believed to live to a very old age, so did Tithonus. He does, however, age physically despite his immortality because he did not ask the gods that he remain young and healthy. His aged life has become intolerable and he longs for death, a request denied him because, "The Gods themselves cannot recall their gifts."[37] In Huxley's novel, this is the tragic fate of the 18th century Earl of Gonister. He still lives in his English castle as a grotesque wretch — feeble and senile — but still alive. When Tithonus is released from the natural cycle of life, he finds that immortality, not death, is the real cruelty.

After Many a Summer Dies the Swan: Theme and Characters

The tragedy of Tithonus is witnessed in Huxley's novel by Jo Stoyte, the millionaire who lives in terror of dying. The world is on the brink of another world war, and nations are preparing to use modern technology for universal mass destruction. Selfish economic exploitation maintains Stoyte in the castle on the California hill, and the suffering of the local poor in the slums is not far removed from the condition of English lower classes found in *Antic Hay*.

Assembled in the castle is an entourage of hangers-on intent on enjoying themselves at the expense of the owner. The first question on Stoyte's mind when he first meets his new employee, Pordage, is his age. When he learns that Pordage is only 54, he remarks that the man should be full of energy at that age. Stoyte's primary measure of life is time — how much time he has left here on earth to enjoy himself. He then unabashedly inquires of Pordage's sex life. Living purely on a superficial and sensual level, Stoyte values only pleasure, power, and wealth. He scorns Pordage's intellectual talents, and he proudly informs his guest that he never had a formal education.

This shrewd, self-made businessman never entertains any ethical concerns in conducting his shady business deals, but his strongest obsession is to remain young and vibrant while indulging with his mistress, Virginia, in all of the pleasures that a wealthy man can buy. His regular injections of testosterone given by his private physician may echo Hearst's own radical attempts at longevity.[38] Meanwhile, his philosophic friend Propter lives a simple but happy life in the valley below. Propter scolds Stoyte for his abusive exploitation of the migrant workers in his orange groves, and Stoyte cannot resist admiring his friend who follows his conscience. He will not, however, contemplate the future in any philosophical sense. At the conclusion of the novel, when he travels to England to discover the ancient, emaciated earl, Stoyte is dismayed but still hopeful. He asks his doctor how long he could be kept from such terrible degeneration.[39] Even if the price for immortality is becoming a living corpse, the gain of a few days, months, or years of life would be worth it, in Stoyte's shallow measure of existence.

Doctor Obispo, Stoyte's private physician, has gladly given up his regular medical practice with its distasteful responsibility of looking after a steady stream of poor or helpless patients. His lucrative post is assured as long as he can convince Stoyte that his laboratory experiments will prevent aging and make Stoyte immortal. The doctor enjoys experimenting with baboons, flirting with attractive young women at Stoyte's dinner parties, and is ever in wait for the opportunity to seduce his employer's mistress, Virginia. She, in turn, is the embodiment of Huxley's concept of the divided self. She is wanton and yet claims to be a devout Roman Catholic. Sexually involved with Stoyte, a man old enough to be her grandfather, she rationalizes the relationship and ultimately betrays Stoyte by succumbing to the sensual demands of Obispo. Virginia finds no contradiction in saying her customary prayers after a sexual encounter with Obispo while Stoyte is conveniently lost in a drug-induced sleep in the next room.

Into this scene of excesses and contradictions comes Jeremy Pordage, the English scholar whom Stoyte hired to catalogue his recent purchase of the historical Hauberk Papers. Pordage is a rational intellectual who relishes order and who shares Huxley's own initial distrust of mysticism. An omnivorous reader, Pordage may be recognized as a caricature scholar that Huxley might have become.[40] On arrival, Pordage is taken on a tour of Hollywood, and this introduction to California's garish materialism is particularly evident in the description of the Beverly Pantheon, a cemetery resembling an amusement park which was modeled after an actual burial ground, Forest Lawn.[41] The irony here is that Stoyte, who is desperately trying to avoid death, owns the cemetery as a commercial enterprise. Huxley graphically described this ludicrous graveyard of splendor and luxury in an earlier travel book, *Jesting Pilate*. It would later provide Evelyn Waugh with the ideal setting for his outrageous 1948 satire on the commercialization of death, *The Loved One*.

The final key character is Peter Boone, a young medical assistant to Obispo, who is also enamored of Virginia Maunciple. An idealist who had tried to volunteer in the 1936 Spanish Civil War, he is naïve and immature, but is searching for a meaningful life. He is consequently attracted to the teachings of William Propter, the wisdom figure who lives a monk-like existence nearby. Propter's advice on spiritual non-attachment helps Boone recognize the foolishness of egotistical obsession with money and power. He accepts that humans must invariably pay for the abuse of their talents. Misplaced seriousness — taking human frivolities seriously — has been mankind's fatal error.[42] Propter preaches a transcendence that is obtainable only in a detachment from the material self, and Boone is ready to respond. William Propter thus becomes the initial spokesman for Huxley's growing conviction that he will articulate repeatedly in his later fiction.

Propter had originally proposed a question and response as an introduction to wisdom: "What is man? ... a nothingness surrounded by God; indigent and capable of God, filled with God if he so desires."[43] Propter recognizes that few people really desire God or are even aware of what they should desire or how they should obtain it. Propter's concern is with eternity and the timeless good to be achieved through enlightenment.[44] He has no interest in extending material life and criticizes Boone for his research into human longevity. The common ideals that society honors, like social justice, patriotism, and romantic love, can be for Propter merely extensions of one's ego. Truth or goodness can only be achieved by a complete transcendence of personality, and with this state comes a full consciousness of the true self, free of desire or aversion that reaches toward a union with God.

Propter's radical message is heard against a cacophony of voices that thwart the silence needed for a meditation of self-discovery. This vocal noise is accurately captured at Stoyte's dinner party. The assembly of diverse personalities thrashing out ideas had become a familiar technique in Huxley's novels. Here once again is the Peacockian style of satiric humor. Thomas Love Peacock was a 19th century English satirist who wrote light, eccentric novels centering around a group of talkative people who usually gathered at a house-party. The crosscurrents of their conversations represented opposing attitudes toward a hodgepodge of subjects.[45]

At this dinner party, Huxley also introduces a satirical criticism of American higher education in the person of Herbert Mulge, the dean of the local Tarzana College. Mulge is basically a professional fundraiser with no intellectual talent or interests. He is lavish in his praise of Stoyte for his generous donation of a new campus auditorium, and Mulge has no scruples in pressing for a new art school and other generous benefactions. During this financial importuning, the dinner guests chatter aimlessly about their trivial concerns. In many ways the mercenary guile displayed at the dinner table is strikingly juxtaposed to the serious economic problems in the city slums below and the far deeper, more transcendent concerns of William Propter at the bottom of the hill.

Propter's spiritual stance reflects concepts advocated by Gerald Heard, an English expatriate and friend of Huxley, who traveled with him to America in 1937. His book *Pain, Sex and Time: A New Outlook on Evolution and the Future of Man*, which was published in the same year as Huxley's novel, advocated the founding of meditation communities separated from material distractions of a soulless, secular society. Heard and Huxley shared a number of lofty interests, and Huxley may have modeled William Propter after his friend.[46] Propter speaks like Heard to Huxley in declaring that contemplation was the true path to a conscious appreciation of a higher life.

Of the main characters, Stoyte, Virginia, and Obispo are extravagant caricatures — one-dimensional personalities that remain unchanged in the course of the narrative. Stoyte is a brutal capitalist dedicated to his own preservation; Virginia is a fatuous simpleton living off her charms; and Obispo is a medical quack exploiting his reputation. Only Peter Boone, the naïve idealist, seeks any spiritual fulfillment. Accepting his mentor's advice, he returns to the mansion with the intent of freeing himself from Virginia to gain total freedom. The jealous Jo Stoyte shoots and kills Boone, mistaking him for Virginia's lover. The innocent youth dies on the verge of discovering the way of life to which he had always aspired.

This killing and its aftermath are reminiscent of Jay Gatsby's murder in Fitzgerald's novel. No one except for the principals on the scene knows what happened, and the crime is covered up. Obispo is bribed by Stoyte to keep silent and to assist in propagating a false report. The 1924 news story of filmmaker Thomas Ince's suspicious death from an alleged illness aboard Hearst's yacht may have been the source of this incident in Huxley's story.[47]

The murder of Boone has profoundly disturbed Stoyte with his own deep fear of death. He and his companions now journey to England to investigate the strange legend of the immortal Fifth Earl of Gonister that is based on information that Pordage discovered in the reading of the Hauberk Papers. The Fifth Earl apparently survived for hundreds of years on a diet of raw fish, and records indicate that the 201-year-old nobleman may still be alive in an ancient English castle. Deep in the crumpling castle they do find the earl alive, but he is only a senile heap of putrid flesh. Stoyte, in his mad obsession for life, however, sees the living corpse as a valid alternative to death. This horrific climax to the novel dramatizes the desire for immortality deep in the human psyche.

Art Imitates Life: A Reflection of Huxley's Progressive Journey in *After Many a Summer Dies the Swan*

During Huxley's initial years in America, with the threat of war in Europe, he judiciously intensified his own moral reflections. He wrote a reasoned argument against war in *Ends and Means* that was published shortly after he reached America in 1937. The concept that people should organize to protest against war was in conflict with the principles of religious detachment or transcendence as advocated by some of Huxley's friends, including Gerald Heard. Both of these themes were found in his novel, *After Many a Summer Dies the Swan*, and the possibility of political reform as advocated in *Ends and Means* was fresh in his mind at the time he wrote the novel. In this popular but controversial collection of essays, Huxley stresses the human predicament inherent in the apparent pointlessness of modern life. The meaninglessness of a simple material existence has left the individual devoid of purpose and significance, a circumstance that Huxley explains is linked to what Gerald Heard had termed the "mechanomorphic cosmology of modern science."[48]

This scientific cosmology regards the universe as a great machine that, through entropy, is moving toward collapse, and humans, as part of that same machine, are advancing toward their own mortal extinction. Physical life is the sole evidence of existence, with personal success and material well being the only valid measure or purpose in life. Huxley's satirical attack on Jo Stoyte's entourage and lifestyle are ample proof of his criticism of this materialistic concept. Having no goal or purpose, individuals try to fill up the internal void with external stimuli — newspapers, games, movies, music, and chatter — anything to compensate for their own emptiness.[49] Whatever will give material significance to life as a temporary goal is embraced. Huxley candidly confesses that he had earlier found specious reasons for believing that life had no ultimate purpose:

> For, like so many of my contemporaries, I took it for granted that there was no meaning [to life]. This was partly due to the fact that I shared the common belief that the scientific picture of an abstraction from reality was a true picture of reality as a whole; partly also for non-intellectual reasons. I had motives for not wanting the world to have a meaning; consequently assumed that it had none, and was able without any difficulty to find satisfying reasons for this assumption.[50]

A world without purpose would mean liberation from common morality, but this sophistry was already the target of Huxley's early satires like *Crome Yellow* and *Antic Hay*. Huxley had come to recognize that true freedom depended on non-attachment — as in the life of William Propter who is calm, lives *in* the world but is free *from* it, is self-directed, and unencumbered by material possessions, much the same as desired by Calamy in *Those Barren Leaves* and Anthony Beavis in *Eyeless in Gaza*. Huxley would particularly express his dismay over the foolish way that mankind has repeatedly alleviated boredom and escaped responsibilities — namely, by the great tragedy of going to war.

In *After Many a Summer Dies the Swan*, Huxley comes to express his new convictions through Propter, the sage who advocates a spiritual basis for living. He discourses at length on the folly of mankind's search for meaning in all the wrong places. He further declares that science may be evil even when it appears to be a benefactor, because it makes warfare more deadly and increases human tragedy.[51] Even the apparently practical applications of science are not guiltless:

> For what do such applications result in? The multiplication of possessable objects; the invention of new instruments of stimulation; the dissemination of new wants through propaganda aimed at equating possessions with well-being and incessant stimulation with happiness. But incessant stimulation from without is a source of bondage; and so the preoccupation with possessions. And now you are threatening to prolong our lives.... I can't quite share your optimism about science.[52]

By 1937, Huxley was acutely conscious of the impending disaster of another world war. He wrote in *Ends and Means*: "Every road towards a better state of society is blocked, sooner or later, by war, by threats of war, by preparations for war."[53] He insisted that war should not be regarded as natural or inevitable simply because man is the only creature conditioned to organize the mass murder of his own species.[54] In order to get rid of war, the psychological causes must be faced and eliminated. Huxley sadly concludes that war exists mainly because people wish it to exist.[55]

Huxley acknowledges, however, that these inclinations towards fighting are complex. The reasons for war are many, including the probability that peacetime occupations are boring and that war fulfills society's insatiable need for success at any cost. While it may be argued that all people desire peace, in reality very few are willing to do what peace demands. These include such measures as unilateral disarmament, a renunciation of arbitrary rule, and a determination to use non–violent measures to resolve disputes.[56] To believe that all of these means are possible without resolving to work for these ends is to deny the truth that Huxley repeated so frequently: one can never have something for nothing.[57] Yet the plight of modern civilization is that of a people unwilling to change their ways. Propter describes this state of stasis:

> For our purposes, the most significant facts are these: the inhabitants of every civilized country are menaced; all desire passionately to be saved from impending disaster; the overwhelming majority refuse to change the habits of thought, feeling and action which are directly responsible for their present plight. In other words, they can't be helped because they are not prepared to collaborate with any helper who proposes a rational and realistic course of action.[58]

In this, his second novel of transformation, Huxley continues to link the malaise of the modern world with economic exploitation. He focuses explicitly on the poor migrant workers who were hired by Stoyte's agent to pick fruit. Their children were forced to work long hours in the hot sun, and their homes were verminous hovels. Their wages were meager and their rent was outrageous, but the agent, described as a decent man, is uncomfortable at Propter's frank criticism of this injustice. He is a man unwilling to examine his ethics for fear he may need to change. This incident is a reference to the 1930s economic depression when California migrant workers were particularly hard hit. John Steinbeck's 1939 classic, *The Grapes of Wrath*, published in the same year as Huxley's novel, offers a full treatment of the tragedy of migrant farmers working in inhuman conditions for a pittance.

Huxley realized from personal experience that soon after the tragedy of war there is a swift return to cynicism and disillusionment in the postwar years. Weak countries will seek even a limited purpose in life by following ideologies like Communism and Fascism that take over like idolatrous religions.[59] In such situations, people cannot act intelligently without secure knowledge, and this knowledge begins with an awareness of self. An appreciation of good on an intellectual plane can heighten this awareness. No one can go beyond the self morally, but by the practice of virtues, detachment, and mystical insight, one becomes fully aware of the purpose of life. This transcendence of self is only possible through total self-knowledge, which nurtures an attitude of complete responsibility.

Propter points out that all disasters must have a cause and that many of these evils are under human control, either directly or indirectly:

> Directly, by the commission of stupid or malicious acts. Indirectly, by the omission to be as intelligent and compassionate as they might be. And if they make this omission, it is generally because they choose to conform unthinkingly to local standards, and the current way of living.[60]

Common evils are often caused by thoughtlessness, and true enlightenment is the only answer. Physical reality and sense experience have been found, even by science, to be merely a small part of the universal world.[61] Huxley concludes that real progress is measured by human charity, and thus can only be achieved when humanity comes once more to embrace religion in the sense of a general belief that all human creatures are sons and daughters of God.[62] The truly happy person, therefore, is one who is free from gross attachments and who works to end suffering by refraining from all malicious acts.[63]

Propter, in his role as a sagacious mentor, is Huxley's first fully developed model of achieved enlightenment, one that is more mystically centered than a Miller in *Eyeless in Gaza*. He stands apart from the lurid plot of the story and, except for his words to the unfortunate Boone, his message has no effect on the other major characters. Huxley recognized that his message was a stark contradiction to the outlook and lifestyles of most Americans. Spiritual transformation was an individual challenge that cannot work without a radical change in attitude, and he had no illusions on this score.

In *Ends and Means*, Huxley's "practical cookery book of reform," he asserts that major social, political, economic, moral, ethical, and educational reform will not work without the conscious, awakened spirit of each individual.[64] Technological inventions that tend to replace warm human contact must be suspect. Along this line, one may speculate, like his widow did in a 1993 interview, that Huxley would be both surprised and appalled at the use of modern computer technology to achieve dehumanizing ends.[65] Social reform, according to Huxley, always needed to be judged by the effect, positive or negative, on the human condition. Ultimately the only sure path toward this enlightenment can be found in religious practices that heighten spiritual consciousness. Like Propter in his novel, Huxley advocates meditation as the traditional means toward this end.[66]

After Many a Summer Dies the Swan: A Critical View of Progress

Technological progress, according to Huxley, is useless unless it is supported or accompanied by a growth in charity and an awareness of humanity's ultimate goal. Indeed, he argues, if technology is used for mundane or selfish purposes, it can only move civilization backwards.[67] This regression was not limited to the wealthy who employ technology to exploit the poor or to expand their power. Anyone can be a victim. For example, his novel describes a migrant farmer from Kansas who is lured by advertisers' enticements to multiply his wants and to base his happiness on possessions and wealth.[68] On his former farm he raised only cash crops, and he fell into debt by overspending. Now homeless and in dire poverty, he moves to California where he must work as a hired hand for very little pay. Huxley describes the sorry state of thousands of migrant workers who had moved West in a vain pursuit of fortune: "All of them had come to California as to a promised land; and California had already reduced them to a condition of wandering peonage and was fast transforming them into Untouchables."[69]

Stoyte's quest for eternal youth is an ancient theme, but his obsession with discovering the technology to serve his misguided purposes resonates with the modern age. Today new and expensive scientific marvels are created for the identical purpose: to promise the older population youth, vitality, and the possibility of a longer life. The latest pills, creams, and chemicals may slow the aging process, improve looks, and increase self-esteem in a youth-oriented society where the old are often neglected or disparaged. The unintended consequences of these technological marvels, however, are frequently dubious and lead to greater misery. Yet so firm is the faith in science, people continue to hope that the next technological breakthrough will be the source of new, if not eternal, youth. In *Ends and Means*, Huxley points out that social changes caused by technological progress have surprised society — not because they suddenly appeared, but because no one in authority foresaw their full effects. What is praised as a scientific miracle frequently has a downside for which people are ill prepared.[70]

The macabre climax of *After Many a Summer Dies the Swan* savagely satirizes the modern American obsession with youth and the fear of death. The horrifying sequence was probably inspired by Swift's *Gulliver's Travels*, whereupon visiting the strange land of Luggnagg, Gulliver meets the immortal *Struldbruggs*. When Gulliver first hears of these people who live forever, he is overjoyed at the chance to learn from these fabulous beings. Gulliver mistakenly confuses perpetuity with youth, fitness, and vitality, but he discovers that the results of great age are horrendous. These human creatures who cannot die have lost all their physical and mental powers. They live in an appalling vegetative state of dissolution, and their last conscious longing is for the pleasure of death. Gulliver concludes:

> The reader will easily believe that from what I have heard and seen, my keen appetite for perpetuity was much abated. I grew heartily ashamed of the pleasing visions I had formed, and thought no tyrant could invent a death into which I would not run with pleasure from such a life. The King heard of all that had passed between me and my friends upon this occasion, and rallied me very pleasantly, wishing I would send a couple of *Struldbruggs* to my own country, to arm our people against the fear of death.[71]

The English earl is Huxley's characterization of a modern *Stuldbrugg*, immortal but devoid of human essence. Huxley describes the evil life of the selfish aristocrat as an 18th century Jo Stoyte. Wealthy, powerful, and cruel by nature, the earl had been wholly absorbed in sensual pleasures. He paid any price to maintain his sybaritic existence — with these horrifying results. Some readers may have been shocked by the grim irony of the climactic scene of the novel. Huxley, who presents himself as a high-minded spiritual guide, does exhibit a cruel streak in his sneering caricature of the American tycoon and his muddled-headed mistress. Like Dante in the *Inferno*, however, he does not flinch from exposing the ugly side of vice and corruption. As Huxley became more aware of the human potential for spiritual growth, he was also resolute in his criticism of the profligates who scorn ennobling grace.

Thematically, the novel demonstrates that the search for immortality by way of technology is as meaningless as looking for final fulfillment through material possessions. Entropy or physical dissolution teaches that these illusions can, at best, lead to an apelike creature, a soulless being. This retrograde image would be developed further by Huxley in his novel, *Ape and Essence*, which describes the apelike degeneration after a nuclear war. This is ironically different from the way the ape-man figured in the defense of evolution by his grandfather, T.H. Huxley, before him.[72]

In *After Many a Summer Dies the Swan*, the young innocent Peter Boone ultimately becomes a symbolic victim of a society obsessed with materialism and blinded by the illusion of a progressive technology achieving human perfection. The death of Boone is deliberately juxtaposed to Stoyte's indifferent attitude toward the crime and his subsequent journey to England to purchase his own immortality — an immortality satirically represented by the obscene Earl of Gonister. This satiric but very serious parable, as Huxley described it, dramatizes the truth that science, or modern technology alone, cannot prevent death or dispel fear, nor can it be accepted as a surrogate religion.

Propter represents the hope that spiritual self-transcendence may be possible — he is the hope sought by Calamy, offered by Rampion, and affectively achieved by Beavis. Following in the footsteps of Miller, this wisdom figure was to become a regular feature of Huxley's fiction. His ultimate purpose was to demonstrate that a way of enlightenment was possible in this world of illusion. His mystical doctrine revealed this possibility, although his approach was more Buddhist than Christian. In Buddhism the way to spiritual insight is central to absolute transcendence.

"I believe that it is essential to appreciate our potential as human beings and recognize the importance of inner transformation ... achieved through what could be called a process of mental development."[73] These words of the Buddhist Monk and Leader of His People, His Holiness the Dalai Lama, resonate throughout the pages of Propter's speech. The goal is to know oneself, to seek what is good, to comprehend and appreciate the duality present in human nature, to see with new eyes, to be *in* the world but not *of* it, to train the mind meditatively toward an inward transformation that will allow one to be ever present in the moment without being a part of the noisy, misplaced pleasure-oriented materialism that consumes the body as well as the soul.

These were the venues that occupied Huxley's mind, body and spirit as he read all of the world's great spiritual texts while seeing his limited vision dwindling. The dogma of *nirvana* consumed his reading, his speaking, and his writing. How could this consummate artist not express what he was experiencing and place these concepts into the mouths of his characters? As Huxley drew on the world about him for his characterizations, the most striking person with whom he was the most inexorably involved was himself. Whether it is the inquiries of a Beavis, the innocent eye of a Pordage, or the wisdom of a Propter, all of these characters are a part of Huxley in his various modes, in his many lifetimes, in his being and his becoming. And so the journey continues.

Time Must Have a Stop

During the troubled years of World War II, Huxley was preoccupied with two serious problems: his own deteriorating eyesight and his search for spiritual reality. His account of his own experience with eye exercises, *The Art of Seeing*, was published in 1942, and *The Perennial Philosophy*, an anthology of spiritual wisdom, appeared in 1945. His 1944 novel, *Time Must Have a Stop*, may be regarded as the fictional interpretation of the other two books. In the first book Huxley demonstrates that physical exercises could improve eyesight, and he was to illustrate how spiritual discipline could improve mystical insight in the second volume.[74] The link between vision and understanding — sight and insight — was to be fictionally dramatized in *Time Must Have a Stop*. This narrative of redemption, along with *The Perennial Philosophy* anthology, may be regarded as the closest that Huxley would come to composing what some critics called religious tracts.

Huxley described himself as unwilling to be listed among the mass of humanity that was content with living at twenty percent of one's potential. He would never cease to explore new ways to realize his full ability.[75] The indomitable urge to employ his talents would characterize his career, and this spirit would be found in the restless pursuits of his fictional characters. Unfortunately for Huxley, serious problems with his eyesight were to plague him throughout his life. In 1951 a bout of influenza led to a painful inflammation in his weaker eye, but Huxley would never surrender to this handicap, and he continued to read and write extensively.

As a boy, Huxley was almost blind for nearly two years, and he remained handicapped with weak vision thereafter. In 1939 he began following W.H. Bates' method for improving sight through eye training, and he claimed that his vision did improve significantly through this practice. Unlike other techniques, the patient relaxes the eye muscles to allow for greater blood circulation. By not straining or staring, he can learn to interpret the visual impression.[76] Huxley explains that after significant experimentation with a large number of patients, Bates, a New York oculist, concluded that many visual defects were the result of faulty habits. The technique he devised aimed at visual re-education.[77] This new methodology, according to Huxley, was bound to succeed since it was based on the same principle as all successful psycho-physical skill instruction: combine relaxation with activity.[78] So improved was his vision that Huxley stopped wearing eyeglasses, and objected to his publisher for continuing to picture him with spectacles on the dust cover of his latest book.[79]

Huxley claimed that his success with the Bates method had broader implications. It demonstrated "the possibility, on the physiological plane, of a complete reconditioning, analogous to that which takes place through the techniques of mysticism on the psychological and spiritual planes."[80] He proposed that similar methodologies in education — both physical and spiritual — would have great possibilities. This educational approach would conform to what he claimed was the best way to learn the nature of reality. This radical education would be based on "the art of seeking first the kingdom of God and thereby having all other things added, from health and virtue to heightened awareness and liberation."[81]

World War II had brought the twin evils of armed aggression and massive destruction, but these calamities were further proof to Huxley that nationalistic brutality and persecution would only lead to further disasters. Peace between the two great 20th century wars had been short lived, and now there was the threat of nuclear annihilation. Only moral reform would bring about effective changes in society. For Huxley, this change began with a transformation of the thought process — humanity could no longer passively or blindly accept conventional assumptions. Huxley would describe this enlightened process more clearly in *Time Must Have a Stop* than he had attempted in earlier books.[82] The ability of humans to transform their lives was to remain a standard conviction for him in all of his subsequent fiction.

Time Must Have a Stop: Theme and Characters

Time Must Have a Stop spans a period of 15 years from an opening scene in 1929 to a wartime conclusion in 1944. An impressionable young Englishman, Sebastian Barnack, is the narrator's innocent eye of the story. Barnack is a self-centered adolescent who aspires to become a poet. His mother had abandoned his family when he was just a child, and his father is a busy social reformer who spends his energies fighting for worthy causes. Sebastian enjoys few luxuries, and is delighted when he is invited to Italy to spend his holidays in Florence with his uncle. Eustace Barnack is Huxley's caricature of the English aesthete, a privileged art connoisseur who, during the inter-war years, reveled in the beauty of Florence and its magnificent treasures. He is also a man of sensual excess with an insatiable appetite for every worldly pleasure. Befriending his young nephew, he parades him about town, gives him a valuable painting from his own art collection, and promises him new clothes.

That evening, however, after a cheap sexual encounter, Uncle Eustace succumbs to a heart attack and suddenly dies in his luxurious home. At this point, the narrative takes an unusual turn as two plots operate simultaneously. While young Sebastian is disappointed at this sudden loss, his uncle is described wandering aimlessly in an after-life limbo. Eustace Barnack cannot release his death-grip on mortal existence and aesthetic pleasures. His obsession with sensual delights renders him unfit to achieve the light of Divine fulfillment. Sebastian, on the other hand, is crushed by selfish inclinations. He is more devastated by the loss of his uncle's hospitality than he is by the man's death. He sells the painting that his uncle had given him to purchase a dinner jacket. When the missing painting is claimed in an audit of the estate, Sebastian allows the blame to fall on others. His cousin Bruno Rontini, a deeply spiritual man, comes to Sebastian's rescue by retrieving the painting from the dealer, but he then is accused of the theft and jailed. Sebastian returns to England with no qualms of conscience over the injustice that he had caused.

Fifteen years later, physically maimed in the war and spiritually bankrupt, Barnack is reunited with Rontini, who is dying of cancer. Rontini, much like Propter and Miller before him, assumes the role of spiritual mentor to his nephew; Sebastian, now broken by loss and pain, cares for the dying man in the last weeks of his life. Barnack is converted to the effortless, detached enlightenment that Propter had advocated in Huxley's earlier novel. No longer identifying himself with a world of materiality, Barnack is finally portrayed as a gentle, spiritually centered, and compassionate man filled with a full awareness of self and his purpose in life.

Time Must Have a Stop: Contrapuntal Plots

In two letters to his publisher, Cass Canfield, the first while he was writing *Time Must Have a Stop* and the second after its completion, Huxley observes that the novel follows a progression from Balzac's realism to Dante's mysticism. Midway through the simple plot, one central character dies, but the reader follows his posthumous experience, which is disquietingly different from his previous hedonistic life. The other principal character is a precocious 17-year-old boy who first appears in 1929 and then in a subsequent epilogue during World War II. Having been wounded in battle, he is now a writer struggling to find the proper relationship between art and religion, between the aesthetic and the spiritual life. Huxley, in this correspondence, recognizes that this was an odd story.[83] In the second letter, he describes the novel as a story treated contrapuntally:

> A theme from the Human Comedy [by Balzac] is in process of development, when suddenly and startlingly a new theme is introduced — a theme from the Divine Comedy [by Dante] of man's eternal destiny. And thenceforward the two themes run parallel, the after-death experience throwing light on what is going on in the material world, the events in time taking on new significance against the background of eternity.[84]

The theme of time is significant here. "Time must have a stop" are the words of the rebel Hotspur in William Shakespeare's *King Henry the Fourth, Part One*, when in facing a critical battle he realizes he may have a short time to live:

> But thoughts, the slaves of life, and life, time's fool,
> And time, that takes survey of all the world
> Must have a stop.[85]

Sebastian reads in the late Bruno Rontini's journal a reflection on this quote from Shakespeare. Rontini explains that time, as a material measurement, not only *must* have a stop, but *does* have a stop on the earth. Only when it is viewed as eternal, however, can time then be prevented from making a mockery of existence.[86] Huxley frequently makes a contrast between mortal time, which is allied with self-identity or disunity, and eternal time, which corresponds to self-transcendence or unity.[87] The life of the spirit is life exclusively in the present, never in the past or the future. Sebastian concludes: "The life of the spirit is life out of time, life in its essence and eternal principle."[88]

The struggle to comprehend time and the purpose of life is described on two levels in the novel: on the present plane for Sebastian, and in the posthumous spirit of his uncle Eustace. Bruno Rontini passes his wisdom onto Sebastian, much in the same manner that William Propter instructed Peter Boone in *After Many a Summer Dies the Swan*. Rontini does not engage, however, in lengthy homilies like Propter. His words are brief and often cryptic, but he succeeds in producing an older and wiser Sebastian.

At 17 years of age, Sebastian is described as a young egoist who prefers his strong attachment to the secular over any sense of enlightenment.[89] His greedy reaction to his uncle's generosity, his selfish disappointment at Eustace's death, and his careless disregard of the suffering he causes are all evidence of his inherent shallowness. After witnessing the servants carrying the dead body of his uncle, Sebastian's first thought was that now he would not get his promised evening clothes. The pang of disappointment and self-pity overwhelm him, and he questions whether anyone ever had such bad luck.[90] Even when Rontini tries to counsel the young man, Sebastian wants to escape any confrontation on such serious matters as life and death. While Rontini generously retrieves the missing painting for him, Sebastian occupies his time completing a poem.

Rontini, in analyzing the character of Sebastian, observes that heredity, environment, and how one reacts to these conditions determine who one is as a person. A possible genius like Sebastian might have the ability to see into ultimate reality and express what is seen. If this same person spends all of his time only in writing about ordinary reality and not in trying to improve his talents, then important knowledge will never be attained. Sebastian is grateful to Rontini, but his words are not persuasive. Rontini's kindness, on the other hand, led to his unjust imprisonment. Under the Italian dictatorship, the angry art dealer was eager to cooperate with the authorities who sought a reason to arrest Rontini as a vocal anti-fascist. Sebastian, dazed and confused, remains silent in order to save himself.

In the epilogue to the novel, Sebastian's subsequent 15 years reveal that, after a university education, he had become a successful playwright. He had married but was unfaithful to his wife, who died of blood poisoning after a miscarriage, cursing Sebastian for his infidelity. Now, invalided from the war, Sebastian finds himself sad and confused. He was once a sensualist with no sense of responsibility, and he denied that God was needed in his life. Now, however, he realizes that ambition and a lust for power drove his career. He recognizes that his greatest offense was living in a spiritual vacuum, reluctant to seek or develop his higher nature. Through Sebastian's new understanding, he represents a basic human attitude. Rontini is a symbol of the mystic; Eustace Barnack, a type of hardened sensualist; and Sebastian Barnack a potential spiritual disciple.[91]

Sebastian comes to realize that he has been a slave to time all of these years while secretly yearning for a deeper understanding of life. He again meets Bruno Rontini who has been released from jail and now, in exile, is dying of throat cancer. Sebastian becomes Rontini's constant companion and nurse through his dying weeks. He finally comes to understand the significance of all that had happened in Florence years earlier. He now looks to the future with a clear vision, and he will no longer be a mindless agent of the world's creed of illusory happiness. Through this final chapter, Huxley once again expresses his personal beliefs through the words of a fictional character. Like Huxley, Sebastian Barnack experiences a form of enlightenment that would lead to a more enriching life.

The evidence of Sebastian's new outlook is seen when his dominating father visits him in the final scene of the novel. Sebastian sees his father as much smaller in stature and more vulnerable. When John Barnack asks his son about Bruno Rontini, the young man speaks of Rontini's simplicity, tenderness, sincerity, and the absence of all pretension. Of the many qualities that Rontini encouraged in his pupil, the most memorable trait was the man's sense of self—he knew what he stood for. This now becomes Sebastian's ultimate aid in his journey toward fulfillment.

In contrast to Sebastian is the sorry plight of his uncle Eustace. A wealthy aesthete, Eustace has enjoyed all of the pleasures of life but has no interest in his destiny. Years earlier he had given up a promising career in politics to marry a wealthy widow with a weak heart. After her death, his days were devoted to sensate pleasures and aesthetic enjoyment among the art treasures of Florence. Cynical of religion and scoffing at ideals, Eustace is the epitome of worldliness. That last evening after a lavish supper, he is reaching for a bicarbonate of soda when he is swiftly struck by a fatal heart attack. Eustace Barnack's after-life experience is that of a soul caught in a dilemma: he cannot rise toward the eternal light, and he is cut off from the life of pleasure that has ended. The account of Eustace's death struggle is graphic:

> There was no pain any longer, no more need to gasp for breath, and the tile floor of the lavatory had ceased to be cold and hard.... Where there had been eternal bliss there was an immensely prolonged uneasiness, an immensely pro-longer duration of pain and, longer and yet longer, as the pain increased, dura-tions of intolerable anguish.... The anguish of being crushed by the pressure of too much light.[92]

Huxley gives a brilliant six-page description of the transformation of this atheistic voluptuary into a lost soul who comes to the chilling conclusion that his whole life was wasted and that he is beyond redemption. The clos-est literary parallel is to Dante in the third canto of the *Inferno* where Vir-gil shows him the opportunists — those souls who were neither good nor evil but lived only for themselves. Both heaven and hell reject them, for they are beneath contempt.

In several subsequent passages of the novel, the lost Eustace is seen as confused by his peculiar state. He even attempts to communicate with his household guests when they hold a séance, but his message comes out dis-torted. Spirit séances were popular in England, and Huxley had previously described one in *The World of Light* in 1931. In his final appearance, Eustace has a terrible vision of a future war on earth. Already observing the horror of World War II, Huxley depicts Eustace as a lost soul outside the dimen-sion of time. Hence, he is able to foresee the atrocity of a world at war a decade after the initial setting of the novel.

Eustace's after-life experiences may have been further derived by Hux-ley from *The Tibetan Book of the Dead,* an ancient Buddhist text on the state of the soul after death and before reincarnation. This *bardo* experience, as it is called, is divided into three parts: the initial passage after death is the time when the supreme vision can be obtained. If this vision is resisted by the spiritually immature, the soul may enter a state of hallucination. Finally, when a weak soul desires a return to the body, reincarnation occurs. The soul must, consequently, reach the highest spiritual level while on earth in order to gain the supreme vision immediately after death. In life, Eustace Barnack ignored his soul and sought no spiritual goals. In death, he clings futilely to earthly memories and pleasures that are meaningless on the immor-tal plane.

The Perennial Philosophy: Huxley's Spiritual Guide in Time Must Have a Stop

Time Must Have a Stop was to take Huxley two and a half years to write.[93] In 1941, he was haunted by the idea that man's conscious mind could function after his body had died. He had abandoned the project, however, because he was experiencing eye strain, a severe case of writer's block, and difficulty in attaining spiritual enlightenment. In a 1942 letter to a friend, Huxley indicates that he had reached an impasse in his personal and professional life:

> I have been meaning to write for a long time, but I have been in one of those states where it seems difficult to get the things done that one wants to do — a state partly due ... to chronic fatigue ... partly to having reached an impasse in my writing, where I don't know if I can achieve what I want to achieve, or how exactly to do it.[94]

In the same period, war had broken out and Huxley was disillusioned by the human inclination to seek only aggressive solutions to problems.[95] He was tired of the social glitter of Hollywood, and he decided to move to an isolated home in the Mojave Desert. Here he would claim that "the desert's emptiness and the desert's silence reveal what we may call their spiritual meanings ... because God seemed nearer there than in the world of men."[96]

While living in the desert, Huxley was to write the three books that were inspired by this experience. In *The Art of Seeing*, Huxley examines vision problems on the physical level. He explains that maladies are frequently the result of an egoism that hinders the natural healing process. Medicine and physicians merely provided the opportunity for nature to heal, and Huxley saw himself as proof of this concept through his success with the Bates' method. The renunciation of self was also essential to attaining true spirituality as rendered fictionally in the second work, *Time Must Have a Stop*. While writing this narrative, a third book, *The Perennial Philosophy*, was ruminating within him, one that would present lucidly his enlightened perception of life that he had dramatized fictionally in his story. With the mind of a scholar who renders the teachings of the world's greatest spiritual leaders and the heart of one committed to a new way of perceiving reality, he embraces his spiritual conversion. All that Rontini teaches and Sebastian learns — and all that Eustace fails to learn — is contained within the pages of this spiritual guide. The thematic connection is strikingly visible in the quotations cited from past spiritual leaders who insist that the human obsession with the self is the greatest obstacle to union with the Divine.

Their basic teaching can be stated thus: "To be a self is, for them, the original sin, and to die to self, in feeling, will and intellect, is the final and all inclusive virtue."[97] Quoting Saint John of the Cross, Huxley confirms that the soul bound by attachments will never be able to achieve true freedom in union with the Divine. This non-attachment advocated by spiritual writers is not mere escapism or indifference. Rather, freedom from greed fosters a spirit of tranquility and humility based on charity:

> The distinguishing marks of charity are disinterestedness, tranquility and humility. But where there is disinterestedness, there is neither greed for personal advantage nor fear for personal loss or punishment; where there is tranquility, there is neither craving nor aversion, but a steady will to conform to the divine.[98]

Only with a full awareness of self and one's motivations can true charity be realized. No longer fearful of a loss of prestige or driven by greed for gain, the egocentric attitude will diminish and the idolatrous worship of things will no longer be an obsession.[99] Even war will end because countries will no longer be selfishly driven to expand their power, and nations will finally consider war as evil — not just because it causes suffering, but mainly because it propagates hatred.[100] The unattached soul will find true freedom, and the empty, solitary heart will experience the fullness of God.[101] All negative pressures will thus be removed and true happiness will finally be achieved. Contemplative prayer is the first means to this end because the nature of man's being determines the nature of his actions; his unique nature is primarily manifest through the mind.[102]

Huxley's fictional version of this concept is reflected in the process of Sebastian Barnack's enlightenment in *Time Must Have a Stop*. The sensual, materialistic lifestyle of Eustace leaves him at death unable to rise to the Divine light in the after-life, and the parallel account of young Sebastian's selfish life is apparently turning him against the Light. In both cases, however, the obsession with the self and possessions thwarts true peace and contentment, both on earth and in the eternal life to follow. It is only in the brief epilogue to the story that takes place 15 years later that Sebastian comes to spiritual insight, a condition never reached by his uncle, who apparently remains a lost soul in limbo. The wisdom of Sebastian's mentor leads his student to the realization that self-denial is the sole path to spiritual enlight-

enment. Through practice, Barnack is now able to attain an effortless serenity that silences the intellect, the will, and all desires.

As Huxley indicates in *The Perennial Philosophy*, a change in the essence
of a person means a corresponding transformation in a vision of reality and
how one responds to it.[103] This is the *Philosophia Perennis*— the wisdom of
the ages that affirms a Divine Reality beyond the physical plane.[104] In his
anthology, Huxley had collected the writings of mystics from the East and
the West, and had chosen quotations both for their deep insights and beauty
of expression. Included among these topics is: God in the World, Charity,
Truth, Self-knowledge, Good and Evil, Time and Eternity, Immortality and
Survival, Silence, Prayer, and Suffering. Among the quoted sages are: Eck-
hart, Chuang Tzu, Pascal, St. Thomas Aquinas, St. Teresa, and St. John of
the Cross. The selections come from such varied works as *The Tibetan Book
of the Dead*, the medieval classic, *The Cloud of Unknowing*, and the Hindu
Bhagavad Gita.

Huxley was reading all of these mystics while on his own spiritual journey, and he was seriously pondering their wisdom while writing *Time Must
Have a Stop*. In a 1942 letter, Huxley reveals that he has come to see mysticism as the ultimate means to an authentic understanding and appreciation
of life. Reflecting on this transformation in thought, he states:

> As a young man, I cared supremely for knowledge for its own sake, for the
> play of ideas, for the arts and literature, painting and music. But for some
> years now I have felt a certain dissatisfaction with these things, have felt that
> even the greatest masterpieces were somehow inadequate. Recently I have come
> to know something about the reality in relation to which such things as art
> and general knowledge can be appraised. Inadequate in and for themselves,
> these activities of the mind can be seen in their true perspective when looked
> at from the vantage point of mysticism. "Those barren leaves of science and of
> art" are barren only when regarded as ultimate ends.[105]

The Perennial Philosophy is Huxley's spiritual goal since it represents
a metaphysic that accepts a Divine Ground of being. It maintains a psychology that the human mind can grasp intuitively the Divine, and it supports
an ethic that leads to an ultimate goal of union with the immanent and the
transcendent.[106] This constant and pervasive wisdom teaches that all religions
of the world become one in seeking this ultimate goal.

In the introduction to his anthology, Huxley provides a series of analo-
gies to support the concept of transformational knowledge. The child is
transformed by physical growth and education into the adult. With this

transformation comes a radical change in a person's manner of knowing as well as the depth of what is known. Likewise, Huxley asks the reader to consider the modern scientist who, with the assistance of highly technical instruments, can approximate the ability of a superhuman creature with superlative vision. For example, the quality and quantity of an astronomer's knowledge of the stars will far exceed those limited to physical eyesight.[107] Thus, every individual can, by conscious effort, attain an enlightened, unitive awareness of the Divine by a growth in insight and understanding. This spiritual vision can come about through a rejection of the material world and its values, through the time spent in silent contemplation, and through reading the transcendent wisdom of those who have journeyed to a nonattached state of consummate awareness. All people have the potential to regain this intuitive power that has been lost in the development of the rational, sensual self.

This new awareness of the primary purpose of human endeavor is fictionally explored in *Time Must Have a Stop*. In the last chapter of the novel, Sebastian Barnack reads of the difference between high utilitarianism and a lower, popular utilitarianism — the basic difference between those who see a world based on the latest in scientific gadgets or greater social reform and those who seek an alternative, spiritual path.[108] These are words similar to *The Perennial Philosophy* indicating that if the kingdom of God is sought before all else, every blessing will be added. In the illusory philosophy of the world, material wants are sought first with the hope that somehow in the future the kingdom of God can be attained. The Biblical words "I shall show you sorrow" reflect the unregenerate, ordinary person, while the words "the end of sorrow" characterize the unitive knowledge of the Divine Ground. In the distorted modern view, sorrow exists in the current world but somehow it will be eliminated in the future through technological progress. This progress, however, has not eliminated tragedy, and humanity continues to experience a grave sense of discontent.[109]

The enlightened Sebastian Barnack reads through a list of principles that are actually the essence of the perennial philosophy: a Divine Ground does exist, and a union with it is the primary goal of life. To achieve this state, the Tao or spiritual way must be followed, the ego must be subordinated, and pride must give way to compassion. It is difficult to subdue an ego that is always obsessed with pleasure, but the inevitable cost of egoism to humanity is heavy:

> They get their good times; but also inevitably they get wars and syphilis and revolution and alcoholism, tyranny and, in default of an adequate religious

hypothesis, the choice between some lunatic idolatry, like nationalism, and a sense of complete futility and despair.[110]

Despite these miseries, humans still go on seeking evil to avoid the difficult full-time job of trying to get to know the Divine Ground of one's being. Huxley portrays his contemporary culture in *The Perennial Philosophy* as a world of external stimuli based on the belief that more noise, gadgets, and possessions will provide greater happiness. Even moral progress is believed to depend on bigger, better machines and a higher standard of living. A materialistic attitude, encouraged by an expanding technological system of mass production, has only led to a desire for more material goods. This universal craving, intensified in modern times by the technology of advertising, has been viewed by saints and religious teachers as a major barrier to self-transcendence:

> The condition of an expanding and technologically progressive system of mass production is universal craving. Advertising is the organized effort to extend and intensify craving—to extend and intensify, that is to say, the workings of that force, which (as all the saints and teachers of all of the higher religions have always taught) is the principal cause of suffering and wrong-doing and the greatest obstacle between the human soul and its divine Ground.[111]

Living in what Huxley terms an "Age of Noise," people disdain or have forgotten the value of contemplation: how to remain apart and gain insight into what is important in their lives. Huxley observes that this mindset has been sustained by technological progress:

> The 20th century, is among other things, the Age of Noise. Physical noise, mental noise and noise of desire—we hold history's record for all of them. And no wonder; for all the resources of our almost miraculous technology have been thrown into the current assault against silence.[112]

While the perennial wisdom sees contemplation or the direct intuitive awareness of God as the ultimate goal of human life, the popular attitude has always held action as the purpose of human existence.[113] Conditioned to believe that aggressive action is a mark of strength, society accepts cruelty, war, and destruction in one's interests as justified. Since they have been less concerned with events in mortal time and more concerned with eternal time, it follows that only in contemplative religions like Hinduism and Buddhism can the principle of non-violence be maintained.[114] Here is the foundation of Huxley's pacifism which he promoted fictionally in *Eyeless in Gaza*. With a modern emphasis on action and change, however, society erroneously equates technological progress that improves physical life with ethical and cultural advancement. In this context, silence and contemplation are not only regarded as antisocial but even as obstacles to human achievement.[115]

Huxley remained optimistic, however, about the spiritual usefulness rather than the destructive application of progressive technology. The humane consideration would require each new discovery to comply with human standards to ensure that it was serving worthy social ends. According to Huxley, humanity has unfortunately allowed some scientific advances to develop like cancerous growths, subordinating all human interests to their development. He concludes that mankind acts erroneously in serving technology rather than the other way around. Since society tends to embrace anything new, it frequently has failed to realize how time-honored cultural traditions must also be adapted to meet the demands of a changing world. In this respect, society is inconsistent: it lacks the foresight to implement those changes necessitated by its technical advances. Huxley insists that what is wrong in a technological world is clearly mankind's fault.[116]

Huxley's repeated message is that scientific progress has already exacted a serious toll. Society has failed to realize that technological *hubris*, or arrogant pride, in dominating nature, must eventually be paid for in the form of *nemesis* or retribution — that gains in one area entail losses in another. The modern world, however, still holds fast to the secular religion of inevitable progress. Huxley cites the 19th-century French poet, Alfred de Vigny, who attacked Victor Hugo for his lavish praise of the technological marvel of the age, the steam engine. Huxley remarks that Vigny was perfectly right in his assessment that the first travelers on the train read their newspapers and falsely believed it was bringing them to a golden age of peace, freedom, and brotherhood. By 1944 this mechanical concept had turned into a gigantic four-motored bomber dropping incendiary high explosive bombs on helpless cities.[117]

Huxley connects an evaluation of technological progress with spiritual goals by insisting that the standards used to evaluate the usefulness of any technology must ultimately take into account man's ultimate purpose in life.[118] Paraphrasing the Gospels, he affirms that to those who first seek the kingdom of God, all things necessary for a good life will be added. Those who become the modern idolaters of progress — who seek only material gain — will eventually lose everything.[119] By refusing to live in harmony with the Tao or the Divine nature of things, Huxley contends, society is paying the price in the anxieties and sicknesses directly related to an over-indulgent, materialistic lifestyle. Well-paid workers are frequently bored or frustrated on mass production lines created to satisfy the artificially stimulated demands of the public for more goods. Huxley notes, however, that free people have the option of changing to more humane ways of life. The process may be difficult, but any suffering endured may, according to Huxley, contribute to spiritual maturation through self-abandonment, love, and a more complete, conscious awareness of God.[120]

In *Time Must Have a Stop*, Huxley deals only indirectly with technology proper, but he offers a searing portrait of the soul of modern man caught in modern, insatiable materialism. Parallel tales of Sebastian Barnack struggling against his selfishness and his sensual uncle finally exiled in a bleak hereafter dramatize the point. Sebastian's final, hard-earned vision at the conclusion of the narrative represents Huxley's hope for the future of mankind, while Eustace's crippled soul epitomizes the human predicament of the self-obsessed materialist. The war-veteran Sebastian finally speaks for Huxley in criticizing the human misuse of military technology that has contributed to the modern mood of disillusionment.

Connecting Threads in Huxley's Journey to Enlightenment

While Anthony Beavis in *Eyeless in Gaza* may find in a pacifistic doctrine the roots of a mystical dimension to life, William Propter in *After Many a Summer Dies the Swan* has made great strides in working toward a negation of self and an abandonment of material pleasures for more lofty ideals. On the threshold of a major conversion in the person of Peter Boone, the young man is killed — literally and figuratively — by the ruthless, carnal covetousness symbolized in the person of Jo Stoyte. Playing out like chapters in a parable running parallel to each other and intersecting with happenings in his own life, Huxley offers a moral tract in *Time Must Have a Stop*, the contrapuntal tale of a sensualist who comes to enlightenment, and a soul in limbo that never is able to ascend to the light.

All that Huxley philosophically had come to embrace is included in this masterful tale of a life in process, and one refusing to accept the eternal aspect of time. Time temporal will have a stop, but time eternal knows no end. *Time Must Have a Stop* is, in essence, the fictional counterpart of Huxley's *The Perennial Philosophy* published just one year later. The two should probably be sold as companion pieces, for the man who read the teachings of all of the world's great religious leaders, had now come to a firm assessment of the purpose of life and the path to self-understanding and ultimate enlightenment. The Huxley of 1921 and the Huxley of 1944 are the same man in the flesh — albeit somewhat tattered — but the vision of the two men is strikingly different. The young Huxley objectively rendered satirical portraits of the outlandish world he observed; the mature Huxley was now compelled to present and promote an enlightened perception of reality in his fiction. Before, during, and after this transformation comes the Huxley of utopian fiction, but clearly in each work, as in each phase of his life, is the voice of the artistic genius speaking through his characterizations.

FOUR

Thesis, Antithesis, Synthesis: Three Futuristic Novels

Utopian literature generally attempts to portray a future society as a model against which one may judge current conditions. This genre may be traced historically to classic versions like Plato's *Republic* and to St. Augustine's *City of God*, books that offered, in turn, a rational and a religious version of an ideal world. Sir Thomas More's 1516 *Utopia* (Greek for *no place*) represents a later example that describes an ideal world in satiric contrast to the faults of his contemporary culture. The complex task of holding up two mirrors — one reflecting contemporary tendencies while the other shows how the world should develop — is so difficult a feat that aesthetic success in the genre is rare.[1] That Huxley wrote an enduring version in *Brave New World* is a tribute to his imaginative power and skill.

The satiric aspect of this fiction was skillfully demonstrated in Jonathan Swift's *Gulliver's Travels*, in which strange civilizations are described with detailed realism, and the fascination with this verisimilitude leads the reader to accept the author's savage criticism of the evils of his time. In modern examples of this fiction, a distinction is sometimes made between utopian novels that portray an ideal world and dystopian stories that predict a more dismal future. George Orwell's *1984*, for example, is clearly dystopian in describing a future slave state. Huxley, on the other hand, is more subtle in his ironic depiction of a new world devoted to pleasures. Many moderns would be inclined to accept this apparently happy future, but this society would represent a hell for sensitive and humane people. In either case, whether utopian or dystopian, these novels describe innovations that are suggested by the social conditions at the time when the work was written.[2]

Aldous Huxley wrote three utopian novels: *Brave New World* (1932), *Ape and Essence* (1948), and *Island* (1962). In all three narratives, he questions the future of humanity if technological progress divorced from humane principles remains the ultimate goal. In *Brave New World*, the reader is dropped into a technologically controlled utopia where all suffering has ended and everyone is apparently perfectly happy. To achieve this end, however, all expression of individuality has been outlawed. This novel is the first full exposition of Huxley's thesis that technology without human wisdom will lead to a seemingly blissful world made up of mindless, human automatons. In an antithetical mode, *Ape and Essence* depicts the ultimate tragedy that may ensue when advancing technology is used for destructive ends. Here nations, blasted by nuclear war, are awaiting extinction in the 21st century. A savage race of deformed and degenerate beings populates Los Angeles. Civilization has regressed thousands of years, and mankind has reverted to an apelike existence.

Huxley's third utopian novel, written a year before his death, is based on a synthesis of themes to produce a perfect culture. On an idyllic island, Western technological ingenuity has blended with Eastern philosophy to produce a genuinely happy civilization that is fully conscious of its purpose and destiny. Although the novel ends tragically, the basic premise is not pessimistic. Huxley realized that people who have been conditioned to behave aggressively and to equate happiness with possessions can create chaos, but they could change with time, and their enlightenment is worth the struggle. Huxley was to explore in these three futuristic novels the unintended consequences of technological progress. Even in the realm of science fiction, he reflects his own personal quest for self-understanding and meaning in an increasingly spiritually bankrupt and materially obsessed universe. He posits within the plot of his futuristic tales both the prospect of a dismal future for those who would continue on a faulty course, and the hope for those who would seek both wisdom and truth. He offers to the reader divergent propositions: one in which humanity's overweening pride and need for self-gratification will lead down the path to extinction; the other in which its quest for spiritual meaning and understanding will lead to peace and personal fulfillment. The three different fictional approaches reflect successively his own thirty-year progression in formulating his basic ideas.

Thesis: *Brave New World*

Through his popular science fiction, the novelist H.G. Wells was a significant propagandist for a technological future for mankind. Born in 1866 to working-class parents, Wells's early years are described in terms of a Dickens' hero as a "Pip Without Great Expectations."[3] He was, however, a bright student, and he won a scholarship to the Norman School of Science to be trained as a teacher. There he studied biology under Thomas Henry Huxley, Aldous's grandfather, who was by then the staunch campaigner for Darwin's evolutionary theory. Deeply impressed by the elder Huxley, Wells was to spend the rest of his life exploring, through his writings, the full impact of a materialistic evolution of society.[4]

As a young writer, Wells's fascination with scientific theories was imaginatively described in such widely read novels as *The Time Machine, The Island of Dr. Moreau, The Invisible Man,* and *The War of the Worlds.* While his science fiction describes some scientific dangers or disasters for dramatic effect, Wells's blind trust in the ultimate evolutionary progress of humankind and his tendency to view the future through rose-colored glasses was the dominant tone of these books.[5] His highly acclaimed *The Outline of History* (1920) explains how mankind finally reached its highest fulfillment in the 20th century. In 1929, Aldous's brother Julian collaborated with Wells on a popular biological study entitled *The Science of Life.*

Another of Wells's prophetically optimistic books, *Men Like Gods* (1923), actually gave impetus to Huxley's writing his most famous novel, *Brave New World.* In a 1962 letter, Huxley explained how the facile optimism of *Men Like Gods* greatly annoyed him. Determined to compose a parody of Wells, in 1931 he began writing a novel satirizing the notion of a scientific utopia, a satire that was published the following year and became his most widely read narrative.[6]

Unlike Huxley, who would later search for positive spiritual answers for modern problems, H.G. Wells' increasing disillusionment over continuing wars and the dangerous misuse of technology was eventually to destroy his faith in science. Wells sadly came to realize that modern technology in World War II and the nuclear destruction of Hiroshima and Nagasaki both gave and took away hope in human progress. His final book, *Mind at the End of Its Tether* (1945), expressed his bleak pessimism over the future of a technological society he once championed.

In his first utopian venture, Huxley exhibits all the imaginative flair of Wells in detailing a scientifically controlled society of the future, but his worldview is vastly different. *Brave New World* depicts a technologically advanced, minutely organized world state whose inhabitants are programmed to eliminate individual differences in order to enforce a stable society. The promise of total happiness is portrayed as a dubious compensation for this repression. The novel opens in the year A.F. (After Ford) 632, an apparent reference to Henry Ford and his factory assembly line. The opening chapters take the reader on a tour of the London Hatchery and Conditioning Center. Here babies are conceived artificially in test tubes in batches of identical twins to create intimate social bonding. At conception, embryos are assigned to levels of a caste system designated by the letters Alpha, Beta, Delta, and Epsilon. The role of natural parents has been completely eliminated, and children are brought up in State Conditioning Centers where electric shock or neo–Pavlovian techniques assure that social lessons are permanently learned. The infants are given electric shocks to make them hate art and beauty, while pleasurable stimuli entice them to embrace their work roles in society.

In this orderly, mechanical, Godless, yet perpetually youthful and pleasure-driven culture, members live for 60 years before they are assigned to the crematorium. At any sign of discontent or rebellion, there are prescribed doses of the pleasant drug *soma*— Greek for "body"— available, a drug that Huxley describes as having all of the advantages of Christianity and alcohol with none of their drawbacks.[7] Observing the smoke rising from one of the crematorium chimneys, a passerby momentarily ponders who they were in life or to what caste they belonged. There is, however, one thing that is certain. Whoever died was happy when alive for "Everybody's happy now."[8] The certitude of an ideal life is never questioned, since inhabitants have heard this conviction repeated 150 times nightly for the first 12 years of their lives.

One troubled character in utopia is Bernard Marx, a specialist in hypnopaedia or sleep-learning. He is a loner whose small physical stature and odd behavior may have resulted from a mishap when he was originally decanted from his test-tube origin. Unlike his companions, Marx is sensitive and self-conscious. He questions his personal worth, and he feels disgust at the crass behavior of his fellow workers. Marx shares his thoughts with Helmholtz Watson, who through another decanting miscalculation has turned out exceptionally intelligent. Watson writes clever conditioning slogans for the masses, but he yearns to express himself in an original way without quite understanding this human urge. Huxley here begins to intimate that all is not happy in paradise. The two men secretly share the angst of individuals who are forced to live in a society that outlaws diversity.

Marx attracts the attention of Lenina Crowne, a vivacious young woman, and she accepts his invitation to visit a reservation in New Mexico, the isolated preserve in the desert for outcasts who could not adapt to the new world order. These exiles maintain customs from the old world, like reading, monogamous marriage, and the enjoyment of art, but they are scorned as crude *savages* by visitors. Marx, however, discovers an exceptional young man named John the Savage, who was born on the reservation. He is the offspring of a woman exile and the powerful Director of Hatcheries, who, as a member of the elite ruling class, is guilty of procreating a child by the forbidden natural means.

A major occurrence in the novel involves John, the innocent eye figure, who is taken from the reservation to the utopian center. At first he is enthralled by the technological novelties of this brave new world. There is a significant difference, however, between John and the new world citizens. He is better educated and has lived with greater freedom. He has read forbidden books like Shakespeare and the Bible, and he has experienced original thoughts and natural feelings. He views the happy, carefree, superficial people who surround him as mindless automatons. Rebelling against the suppression of individuality, he refuses to be programmed, and when his mother dies of an overdose of the drug *soma*, he displays the typical reaction of a savage by staging a violent scene at the hospital.

John the Savage's travels in the utopian center further reveal the problems of this perfect society. In the final section of the novel, the ruling World Controller explains to John that this new world order came about because mankind yearned for total happiness. This happiness had to be paid for, however, at the cost of the outworn ideals of truth, beauty, religion, freedom, and individuality. A perfect world required total control, but John the Savage replies: "But I don't want comfort. I want God. I want poetry. I want real danger. I want freedom. I want goodness, I want sin.... I'm claiming the right to be unhappy.... Not to mention the right to grow old and ugly and impotent."[9] After a series of escapades, John the Savage chooses to endure a self-imposed exile. He lives in an isolated lighthouse separated from the world he detests but unable to return to his refuge on the reservation. He is regarded as a newsworthy curiosity by the public media, and the inquisitive arrive by helicopters to gape at this rare specimen of a free man. John, however, becomes a victim of his own isolation. In a state of despair, he consumes the drug *soma*, and after a night of sensual frenzy, he takes his own life.

Brave New World: Background to the Narrative

An unpublished 1930 letter written by Aldous Huxley to Simon Blumenfeld offers insight on the author's intention in writing *Brave New World*. Huxley reveals that recently he had been impressed by a Russian propaganda film entitled *Earth*. In the movie, Ukrainian peasants had pooled their resources to purchase a tractor for their village. They then run through the streets, dancing before the technological marvel, and treating the machine as though it were a god. Huxley remarks that their ecstatic reaction is comparable to a revivalist meeting or a religious procession. He wonders whether science had the capability of producing new gods for humanity to worship.[10]

In the film, the new technology promises to improve the lives of the peasants but it only creates trouble. A peasant is murdered in retribution after the tractor destroys a fence — a personal tragedy indicative of society's failure to regulate technological progress. The final scene depicts the stolid mass of villagers at the peasant's funeral sadly proclaiming that there is no God. Huxley may have recognized in this scene a prophecy of the long-range failure of technology gone awry.[11] Certainly the symbolic images in the film inspired Huxley and influenced his criticism of scientific progress.

The English philosopher Bertrand Russell, an earlier fellow guest with Huxley at Garsington Manor, published his views on technology in *The Scientific Outlook* (1932) the same year that *Brave New World* appeared. Similar concepts of technology are found in both books, and some scholars have questioned which writer influenced the other.[12] While this critical attitude was common among intellectuals of the time, these writers took different approaches to the danger of a technocratic world-state and their skepticism of technical progress. Robert Baker points out that both writers saw the pursuit of power as an underlying principle driving modern technology.[13] At the time, Huxley was also particularly impressed by the ideas of the social theorist, Max Weber. In his *Protestant Ethic and the Spirit of Capitalism*, Weber expresses deep concern over the menacing alliance between politics and modern technology, a subject clearly emphasized in Huxley's fiction.[14]

In Huxley's *Brave New World*, the threat that technology may take on a life of its own and bypass human volition is horrifyingly illustrated in the dreamlike trance in which the people live. They cannot escape this nightmare state, and they are not even aware that they are living an illusion. Huxley's choice of a title for his anti-utopian work relates to this theme. The words, *Brave New World*, are taken from William Shakespeare's *The Tempest*.

In Shakespeare's play, Duke Prospero has long been exiled to an uncharted Mediterranean island for 12 years with his daughter Miranda. From her youth, Miranda has only known her embittered father and their slave, Caliban. In her ignorance she sees the shipwrecked visitors as glorified human beings. She proclaims: "How beauteous mankind is! O brave new world, /That has such people in 't."[15] By *brave* she means handsome, noble, or courageous, but the irony is that these newcomers will destroy the island paradise. In like manner, the novel appearance of Huxley's future world may be attractive, but beneath the surface the lack of humane principles will ruin the utopian dream.

Brave New World: Huxley Revisits His Narrative

In *Brave New World Revisited*— a collection of essays written a quarter of a century after his novel — Huxley provides a unique re-examination of the narrative's themes, as well as the rationale behind them. In 1931, the world was troubled by a serious economic depression and social unrest, and some countries were threatened by dictatorial governments. Huxley's totalitarian, totally organized state was projected far into the future, but now, in 1958, he thought that the prophecies of *Brave New World* seemed to be coming true much faster than he anticipated. He notes that George Orwell's *1984*, the brutal portrayal of a dictatorial state published in 1949, appeared at that time to reflect the somber mood of postwar Europe. Ten years later, however, the rapid growth of science and technology robbed Orwell's warnings of their shock value and moved *Brave New World* closer to the realm of possibility.[16] Although nuclear war was still a threat in the 1950s, Huxley points out that Orwell's totalitarian control by threat of punishment was waning in the modern world. The non-violent but pervasive manipulation of common citizens through technologically advanced and heavily organized systems of government and industrial control had subtly programmed society in the direction of a *Brave New World*. To paraphrase Winston Churchill's famous words, Huxley concludes that "never have so many been manipulated so much by so few."[17]

Huxley saw a future world as dominated by ominous trends already found in contemporary society. Incessant inducements to greed through advertising, conscious and subconscious mind control through media propaganda, genetic manipulation, the political, economic, and social life dominated by a power elite — all these pressures demonstrate how the public is coerced today. As in *Brave New World*, today's victims of this manipulation are not always aware of this fact. Huxley explains how it is possible for an individual who is not in jail to be a prisoner, or for one who is not physically constrained to be a psychological captive in the sense of being compelled to think, feel, and act according to the agendas of a national state or powerful economic interest groups. As Huxley commented in a 1948 essay about *Brave New World*, the myths of inevitable progress promoted by advertising and political propaganda have infected the attitudes and actions of the general population.[18] Communist countries behind the Iron Curtain were the obvious examples at that time, but capitalist powers had more subtle ways of promoting a false but seemingly glorious future for mankind.

Huxley saw that progress in technology — both in organization and scientific application — had led to a dangerous concentration of economic power in the hands of a few. Since mass production is both complex and expensive, it is generally beyond the capacity of the small entrepreneur. With big companies increasingly taking over small firms, real economic power is exercised by fewer and more powerful elites. Huxley alludes to the common practice of wealthy conglomerates buying local newspapers so that even the news is managed in support of special interests. In a dictatorship, the state has acquired this absolute power, but in a capitalistic democracy like the United States, the culture can be controlled by a power elite in its place.[19]

Huxley argues that a country's power elite are not only employers. They include the bankers who lend the money to the workers so that they may purchase more products, and the stockholders of corporations who demand quarterly profits. They control the media and communication through which they persuade their audience that their happiness and well being depend on owning all the latest technological wonders. Consumerism has replaced capitalism as king, according to Huxley, and even politics is merchandised to appeal to the voter's self-interest. In a highly conditioned mass audience with limited powers of concentration, electronic advertising takes the form of short, snappy appeals, and even important broadcast news stories are delivered in sixty-second segments.[20] So much of Huxley's argument and examples are exponentially present in the modern world of the 21st century that his perception becomes all the more visionary.

One of Huxley's primary theses in *Brave New World Revisited* is that the spread of technology over the past century has been accompanied by advances in organized systems. Complex technologies have required complicated social arrangements to operate effectively. Mass production, the assembly line, management structures, and consumer manipulation all mean more controls over the individual, so that a rich social variety has been reduced to an unnatural, dull conformity. In the process, people have come to act like robots. They are described as dehumanized, anonymous, divorced from human contact, alienated, and lonely. Forced to live in large impersonal cities, the majority of people live meaningless and futile lives.

The characters in Huxley's *Brave New World* are victims of an extreme conditioning process, and they are willingly drugged into a mindless submission. They cannot mourn the loss of what they never enjoyed or even remember. Huxley would later offer his own plan for resisting this inhuman condition of life:

> Therefore, if you wish to avoid the spiritual impoverishment of individuals and whole societies, leave the metropolis and revive the small country community, or alternatively humanize the metropolis by creating within its network of mechanical organization the urban equivalents of small country communities, in which individuals can meet and cooperate as complete persons, not as the mere embodiments of specialized functions.[21]

Freedom, to Huxley, was too sacred a right to be given up lightly. As he saw it, it was the essence of what it meant to be human. Although strong forces may be at work to reduce and destroy individual personhood and freedom, they must be resisted at any cost.

Huxley once again repeats his warning that the nature of reality rules that nobody ever gets anything for nothing. Technological advances are paid for in human terms much like the monthly payments in an installment plan. The problem is that these installment payments keep getting higher as time advances.[22] In an essay entitled "Over-Organization," he points out that historians, sociologists, and psychologists have insistently complained about the outrageous price that Western society has paid and will continue to pay for its technological progress.[23] At the conclusion of *Brave New World*, the resident World Controller for Western Europe, Mustapha Mond, candidly reveals that "Happiness has got to be paid for."[24] The residents of Huxley's fictional world have paid dearly for their happiness through the loss of the authentic values of home, family, culture, and morality. In return for avoiding physical want and suffering, they have lost enabling love, individuality, and freedom — the freedom to think, to criticize, to choose, and to know the difference it would make in their lives.

Mond relates that one of the former world's abandoned features was God, religion, and the concept of immortality. Yet this new world order is rampant with religious allusions. The World Controller is referred to as his Fordship; "Thank Ford" is a common invocation; the sign of the "T," like the sign of the cross, is a regular act of reverence; and the Solidarity service depicted has all of the trappings of a religious, revivalist meeting. Yet books on spirituality are banned, and the only acts of self-transcendence sanctioned are those of service and social cohesion — this meticulously ordered world is programmed to engage continually in mindless, pleasurable activities.

Like modern totalitarian countries, the new world is run on catch phrases: "Community, Identity, Stability" is the motto of this minutely organized society. In the factories, the city streets, the infant nurseries, and the conditioning rooms, loudspeakers constantly praise the wonders of this Brave New World. Having survived a Nine Years' War, death from the anthrax bomb, and an economic collapse, these people are more than willing to submit to a supreme organization that promises perfect happiness. This orderly civilization requires drastic social changes. The primitive system of people falling in love and producing babies, therefore, has been abandoned. Children are now decanted or born from bottles, and they accept this strange parentage as the song extols: "There ain't no bottle in all the world like that dear little bottle of mine."[25] The Director of Hatcheries and Conditioning supervises the bottling plant, and he decides the caste level of each child according to the current need to sustain social order. Conditioning from birth ensures that everyone acquires an irrevocable social destiny which relieves the child of the responsibility of earning one.

In rearing these children, genetic manipulation is followed by sleep-learning, and this process is reinforced by a regular diet of subliminal conditioning. Two central characters in the novel, Bernard Marx and Helmholtz Watson, work in these areas. These men are deeply disturbed by the social enslavement they promote, but they lack the courage to complain or rebel against what they see as inhuman practices. In their throwaway society, old people must be destroyed since science prevents them from aging to the point of death. The conditioning slogans enforce the rules by proclaiming: "Ending is better than mending"; "The more stitches, the less riches."[26] A constantly renewed population sustains consumerism and a healthy economy. The local director asserts that the best method for total control and social stability was not through force but by the slower and more certain formula of ectogenesis (bottle birth), neo–Pavlovian conditioning, and hypnopaedia (sleep learning).[27] In this world of the obedient slave, there is no need for a ruthless dictator. Obedient people are products of technology and their minds are manufactured just like any other commodity.[28]

Huxley describes the novel's heroine, Lenina Crowne, as a model product of this fully ordered system. A beautiful young woman, she enjoys her work, her leisure, and her stable but formulated existence. She has never known or wanted an original thought. As do most women in this new world order, she enjoys a series of sexual encounters with a variety of men. She, therefore, accepts Bernard Marx's invitation to visit the distant reservation in the hopes that the trip may lead to a sexual adventure. The reservation exiles have retained some of the values associated with former cultures such as marriage, traditional belief, and strong family ties. They are also less conformist in that they are superstitious, unclean, and crude by new-world standards. Lenina Crowne is horrified by witnessing the brutality of their rituals, but is equally fascinated by the strong personality of John Savage. When they bring John back with them to the new world, Lenina Crowne cannot understand why he rejects her. He explains the concept of true love and the need to transcend a purely sexual attraction, but she cannot understand what he is talking about.

John Savage in this Brave New World reacts much like Tarzan of the Apes after he has left the familiar jungle. At first he is fascinated with this technologically prosperous society and the attention that he receives, but he soon comes to feel troubled in a world that is devoid of God, philosophy, and literature. Asserting his own precious will, he refuses to take *soma*, the wonder drug that cures anxiety. He flees this false civilization, but he cannot escape notoriety and he ultimately chooses death.

Brave New World: Technology as Liberator, Threat, and Instrument of Power

Huxley's *Brave New World* demonstrates Ian Barbour's model of the three relationships between technology and mankind: those of liberator, threat, and instrument of power.[29] Both as a liberator and a threat, new-world technology has apparently freed these future people from pain, anxiety, want, and all fears associated with the common human condition. The populace is laboratory germinated, nurtured, and conditioned to love their role under a totalitarian caste system. There is no hatred, class envy, or crass desires for what belongs to others. The ambition to improve one's status has been eliminated through conditioning techniques. Since promiscuity is encouraged and marriage is outlawed, there are no standards of morality or basis for guilt. Science prevents aging and bodies remain handsome and healthy until the prescribed age limit when they are cremated and recycled into the living whole. In this sense, everyone belongs to everyone else. Perfect happiness is the routine expectation, and when mental or emotional distress occurs, the drug *soma* is available to restore a state of euphoria.

The assembly line and mass production systems of the era "After Ford" have eliminated tedious manual labor. Streamlined production (as in the Bokanovsky process of human replication) has increased prosperity and created a worry-free society with abundant leisure time. Technological advances have enhanced recreational activities as well. For example, people can fly anywhere by helicopter, join in a game of aerial "Obstacle Golf," and then dance to synthetic music at the Westminster Abbey Cabaret. Huxley describes a visit to the Alhambra Feelie Palace for a sensual, sense experience of virtual reality. Metal bars attached to the theater seats transmit the *feelie* effects of "Three Weeks in a Helicopter," a pornographic experience. The interactive form of amusement depicted here closely resembles the virtual reality entertainment now being developed by computer technology.

Huxley's imaginative novel realistically details the regression in human worth or moral stature through a blind trust in technological achievement. In positing a utopian world of perfect happiness in the future—when the inhabitants are conditioned not to think or relate to one another as human beings—he shows that the ultimate threat of technological dominance divorced from humane concerns can become an ominous reality. Once readers suspend disbelief, they can accept the possibility of this plausible scenario of a culture based on pleasure but devoid of authentic happiness. Huxley's satiric wit is still savagely at work as he mocks the pathetic human condition in this technocratic state. Here is a society where fidelity is scorned, where intelligence and empathy are psychological abnormalities, and where creative literature and art are no longer possible because there is no natural joy, sympathy, or meaningful suffering in life. Solitude, in this new world order, is a threat to peace, and freedom is incompatible with artificial happiness. The future world depicted is more frightening than any horror fiction. Uniform comfort is little compensation for the loss of truth and beauty. Shutting out religion tends to empty life of meaning. The population remains young and energetic, but no one ever matures or achieves wisdom.

Late in the novel, Huxley has the World Controller give his candid rationale behind this technological system of power. The ruling group has long determined through experimentation that the ideal population of the world is analogous to an iceberg—eight-ninths of the common herd is below the water line in importance. The select few above the surface are wise in the way the whole system works, and they make all of the decisions for the benefit of the masses.[30] Social stability is achieved because the vast majority gets what they want, and they have been conditioned never to want what they cannot have. The controllers, as the power elite, are not subject to the general law, and they can even break the laws without accountability. The organized systems based on the laws affect all aspects of common life from birth to death. Decisions on genetic manipulation predetermine an individual's fate, the caste, employment, hours of labor, and leisure activities. Aware of the nature of scientific research, the leaders are wary of any new discoveries that might raise questions on the validity of the present technology.

Yet the new-world rulers revere the science that produced this present technological state. Even Huxley's choice of names for the power elite team in *Brave New World* recall three famous physiologists of the 19th century: Foster, Bernard and Helmhotz. Michael Foster was a former assistant of Huxley's grandfather, T.H. Huxley; Claude Bernard was a noted French physiologist; and Hermann von Helmhotz was a German physiologist best known for his formulation of the theory of the conservation of energy.[31]

In this safe, secure, perfectly ordered world, everyone is blissfully ignorant, and they are free from facing any unpleasant situations. In 1946, Aldous Huxley was to write a foreword to a new edition of the novel where he admits that he limited John the Savage's final fate to either insanity in utopia or a primitive existence in exile. He now saw a further possibility: he would have allowed the Savage the opportunity to settle on the outskirts of his reservation and live in a humane community with a band of exiles and refugees from the Brave New World. In this communal environment, "science and technology would be used as though, like the Sabbath, they had been made for man, not (as at present and still more so in the *Brave New World*) as though man were to be adapted and enslaved to them."[32]

In this same preface, Huxley goes on to explain that in any worthwhile civilization, either religion or a unitive knowledge of the Divine must be the conscious pursuit of the community. A higher or moral utilitarianism should be the prevailing philosophy of life, and the quest for happiness must be only a secondary goal. The condition for establishing this civilization would be to evaluate all of human thought, as well as organizations, to determine how they might either contribute to, or interfere with, humane development in pursuit of this ultimate goal.[33] Again he notes that the standard for the evaluation of all proposed technologies should be the degree to which human values are advanced. Huxley here reveals that the ultimate purpose in writing *Brave New World* was to encourage his readers to question the current human condition, to determine how it developed, and to foresee where it may be headed.

Hence, the probing mind of Huxley is asking the reader of his novel whether pursuing the possibility of a perfect world was the right course for humanity. Perhaps, he suggests, it may be better to settle for a less perfect world that offers the human race greater opportunities to remain free. This is the gist of a statement by the Russian philosopher Nikolai Berdyayev that Huxley quotes in French as the epigraph to his novel. In 1927, the philosopher questions why the Communists abandoned the old order in the establishment of the Soviet State. He wonders whether the new utopian model may not be a more troubling one, and *Brave New World* asks a similar question: Would a technologically advanced perfect world mark the end of human civilization?

Technology's massive power to mold, condition, control, and determine the quality of life is imaginatively portrayed by Huxley with such memorable impact that this one novel would assure his place among the significant writers of the 20th century. His theme continues to be relevant in a modern age that increasingly sees many of his predictions becoming a reality. Huxley's novel anticipated an expanding technology that would force humanity to face the ethical dimensions of human cloning, an irrational obsession with youthful vigor, and a passion for uniformity. His projected image of a technologically controlled, passive, pleasure-bound throwaway society that is detached from traditional values and a moral standard is strikingly close to contemporary culture.

Brave New World:
The Modern Prometheus, Circa 632AF

In Huxley's treatment of the two aspects of life that humanity holds the most sacred — birth and death — he deliberately offends and alienates the reader with an objective, emotionless, and hardened perspective that chillingly strikes home. No longer do people determine that they would like to continue their legacy in the form of a child within a loving partnership, but a sterile laboratory germinates the next caste of species. A technician, rather than a mother, determines the proper dosage of those elements that will allow the offspring to mature into a competent — or not so competent — member of society. Likewise, one reports for death in the manner that one has led his or her life — in complete obedience, submission and acceptance to the rule of the State. No joy or mournfulness marks the coming or the going of any one individual — he or she is just simply a small part of the whole, and it is the whole that dictates the synergistic functioning of its parts.

In Huxley's foreword to the 1946 reissue of *Brave New World*, he notes that humanity is not yet ready to produce babies in test tubes or send new-borns off into Bokonovsky sets, but he does suggest that someday we may.[34] Could Huxley have envisioned a world in which babies may be germinated without the union of the sexes? Could he have anticipated the genetic manipulation in the womb? Was he warning of a day when the birth of a child is a "sterile conception," scientifically rendered for reasons other than love? Since love, marriage, and family are no longer aspects of this Brave New World, Huxley's diminishment of birth to a State function removes from the human species one of its fundamental and instinctual obligations — the reproduction of its own. Far removed from his grandfather's vocal and persistent argument for an understanding and appreciation of the evolutionary chain, Huxley has taken his reader to a realm above and beyond human tolerance. Could science advance to such an extreme that it devolves rather than evolves humanity? Could we — like Dr. Frankenstein's intellectual pursuit to destroy death — create life that has no connection to the living? And, more importantly, could we fail to recognize the unintended consequences of our actions?

Mary Shelley's exploration of what happens when science exceeds its boundaries is reflected in a far more advanced state in Huxley's treatment of birth through the Bokanovsky process. While the monster in Shelley's account is created by a modern Prometheus driven to break through the mystery of life and tear down the barrier of death, so the State in Huxley's vision has instituted a scientific process whereby the correct number of Alphas, Betas, Gammas, Deltas, and Epsilons are born daily in the proper ratio to those who leave earth by way of the Slough Crematorium.[35] Balance is maintained in the world's population and mathematically kept at the proper ratio. Would it not follow that if birth is nothing more than a scientific success, then death would also serve the common good?

The Savage is upset when the nurse at the Park Lane Hospital for the Dying treats him with such disdain. After all, he proclaims, it is his mother who is dying. Disturbed and embarrassed by his use of such a term as "mother," the nurse explains, in a programmed manner, that of course there is no hope — intimating that the very thought of hope within such an institution is a ludicrous concept.[36] Later, the Head Nurse explains that the children present, who are intruding on the special private time John wishes to spend with his mother, are undergoing "death conditioning." She warns the Savage that if he interferes with their conditioning, he will be thrown out of the facility.[37] Death, to this procreation-free society, is no more of an individual event than birth. From cradle to grave, all are manipulated by a power greater than any one entity. The smokestacks that Lenina and Henry fly over are encircled by balconies for phosphorous recovery — more than a kilo per person. Even in death, everyone thereby is socially useful.[38] Lenina may find it "queer" that she even entertains the thought that those on the upper chain of the caste (Alphas and Betas) will not "make more plants grow" than those at the bottom (Gammas and Deltas), but Henry Foster explains that all people are "physico-chemically equal."[39] In our contemporary world, we still take time to honor the legacy of an individual who has died, and his or her family still mourns existence without the presence of a loved one, but in the Utopian Center, there is no love or honor or sense of loss. Everyone works for and belongs to everyone else, thereby creating a classless society within a caste structure. This contradiction in word and form is accepted without question in much the same way that "slavery is freedom" is regarded as a trusted creed in Orwell's *1984*.[40] The conditioning process has allowed humanity to think and accept contradictions without question.

Ignoring for the moment Mustapha Mond's lengthy and detailed explanation of how this Brave New World came into existence, if one removes the emoting factors instinctually present in the polar aspects of life — birth and death — one may foster a species that bears little resemblance to what we consider to be human. The penetrating reality so craftily dramatized by Huxley is that the sterile and genetically manipulated beginnings of life will generate a malleable species whose demise is of no more significance than its conception. Birth and Death become, therefore, simply a fractional embodiment of the whole.

Brave New World: Paradigm Lost

Fritjof Capra, in his intriguing study *The Turning Point*, offers that our contemporary world is in crisis. He presents a laundry list of woes that are all too familiar to any reader: inflation, rising unemployment, the energy crisis, health care costs, pollution, etc. His thesis is that what we are suffering from is a crisis of perception — that we are called to look at the world in a new and different manner. [41] Yet, Huxley — long before Capra's call to perceive reality in a new light — envisioned and described a world that he hoped would never become a reality. Based upon the edict that "science has made us who we are," and that it is "our faith and our age's unique signature," Huxley sought to fictionally create a new species of man who would, while scientifically advanced, branch off in the evolutionary chain to the status of humanoid. [42] While the breed of person created through the Bokanovsky process may look like a human, he or she has been genetically manipulated to assume a specific role within society, and to never think or deviate from the established and respected norm.

To promulgate this norm, Lenina Crowne is advised to obtain her Pregnancy Substitution early, as are all female humanoids of *Brave New World* required to sublimate their biological functions through Mammary Gland Extracts taken three times a day, and Placentin injections administered intravenously every third day. The age of birth control was anticipated by Huxley some 30 years before its arrival, but in the Utopian Center, it is not a matter of choice, but a necessary aspect of the World State's need for "Community, Identity, Stability."[43] What would become of such an advanced society if someone were allowed to give birth to a child through natural conception? The "We" aspect of the world would be destroyed. Individuality would return and the unified, balanced World State would be damaged.

In 1938, some six years after Huxley's publication of *Brave New World*, Ayn Rand, with a specific philosophic agenda in mind, was to create a world where identity has been lost — where all are equal as seen through the eyes of Equality 7-2521. All men and women are alike in Rand's narrative since "there are no men but only the great WE."[44] Perhaps Huxley's depiction of a unified society that has been conditioned through hypnopaedia and neo–Pavlovian measures may have resonated with Rand. Certainly Lenina and Fanny, as well as Bernard Marx, Helmholtz Watson, Henry Forster, and all members of the Utopian Center, have been conditioned to accept their place and purpose within this unified society. Through the constant repetition of clever phrases, they have been brainwashed into accepting their identity, not as individuals, but as a necessary part of the whole — a part of the "WE." No one sees the world in a different light — how could they since there is no way to perceive reality other than the manner in which the State has conditioned them to see it? As Henry Forster puts it, "All conditioning aims at that: making people like their unescapable social destiny."[45] It is in this inability to see reality in a new way — the loss of a paradigm — that the residents of a *Brave New World* cease to be human.

Yet Huxley provides a glimmer of hope, even in this formidable configuration. Is Helmhotz Watson not characterized as one discontent with writing the clever jingles for conditioning? Does he not yearn to write something creative of his own? Is not Bernard Marx — before he is caught up with the attention he gets when he brings the Savage to the Utopian Center — not dissatisfied with the use of *soma* and the world view of sexual promiscuity, especially in his temporary, monogamous relationship with Lenina? Is not Lenina herself confused as to why she prefers to remain with Bernard rather than engage in indiscriminate sex as demanded by the State? Furthermore, is she not bewildered by her feelings toward the Savage that seem to contradict her conditioned need to just engage in sensual sex? Within the framework of this genetically manipulated and conditioned world, Huxley paints a picture of those who "see" things differently than others. Why is this the case? Perhaps their genetic manipulation went awry — as in Bernard and Watson. But maybe — just maybe — the remnants of humanity that differentiate man from beast cannot be programmed out of the species. What are these remnants?

Man's imagination, reasoning ability, and desire to change his environment may be the defining qualities of humanity. Bronowski sees these not as part of a biological evolution but a cultural one in *The Ascent of Man*.[46] Certainly this is the central internal conflict in John the Savage when he arrives at the Utopian Center. Unlike Watson or Marx, he comprehends why he is dissatisfied with the promoted World View. He yearns to witness the human condition in others, but he cannot penetrate through the veneer of conditioning that has sapped humanity out of the residents of this Brave New World. So he retreats to a lighthouse far removed from all "civilization," only to find that he is not alone — that he cannot escape their gaze and hypnotic influence. Ultimately, he sees no way out but to physically leave the world that he cannot accept. Imagining those feet dangling from the crown of the arch, one can only wonder: Is civilization headed in the direction of this Brave New World, or is it doomed to extinction by its own hand, as was the case with John the Savage?

Writers of fiction do not always understand what they have created — sometimes the canvas of the artist embodies much more than what was initially conceived. When Huxley was asked some 25 years after the publication of *Brave New World* if he had any idea that the work would be regarded as philosophically prophetic, he replied that he had only initially intended to pull the leg of H.G. Wells until "he got caught up in the excitement of his own ideas."[47] Was "the excitement of his own ideas" influenced by the world around him? Huxley was writing *Brave New World* during a time of crisis — a time in search of a discerning paradigm.

In a time of crisis, humanity has always turned to its institutional government to solve its issues. Many of these solutions — from government subsidies to statutory regulations — tamper with individuality by collectively banding together all members of society into a unified whole. The concept is that in a time of crisis, what is good for the whole must be accepted by the individual. It is simple to understand Huxley's fears as presented in *Brave New World* since it is written during the initial stages of the Great Depression, a period when government intervention was rampant in all walks of life. Would a World State come into being that would destroy all individuality? Was the world not in need of a paradigm shift? Was Huxley's dystopian view of the future a fearful recognition that the world was headed in the wrong direction? Certainly John the Savage has the advantage — and the distinct disadvantage — of seeing the world in a unique way, a way similar to Mustapha Mond, one of the world's ten Controllers, who knows the history of how this Utopia came into existence. With knowledge of the past, and a steady hand on the controls of the present, Mond concedes that even he sublimated his own quest for truth and individuality to serve the greater good. In his lengthy discourse with John the Savage, he explains that misery, and instability, and passion, and doubt are all far more glamorous than contentment, stability, and happiness. Yet, the underlying truth is "one can't have something for nothing. Happiness has got to be paid for."[48]

As Bernard Marx and Helmhotz Watson are sent off to islands away from the rest of the programmed population, and while John the Savage seeks refuge in an abandoned lighthouse only to ultimately take his own life rather than remain in this sterile world or return to his former primitive existence, it would appear that *Brave New World*— as a work of prophetic fiction — offers no hope for humanity. With this in mind, Huxley was later to toy with the idea of another ending — one that would provide John the Savage with another choice whereby he would seek others like himself and form a new colony of like thinkers.[49] But Huxley resisted changing the ending of his novel. Perhaps he understood that within the ending was a reflection of where humanity stands. How much more relevant are these insights to our contemporary age? Huxley does strongly suggest a solution. He recommends that we decentralize and use our technological prowess not as an end in itself, but as a means of producing free individuals. If we do not, then we may just fall prey to the totalitarian welfare-tyranny of *Brave New World*'s Utopia.[50]

Brave New World:
John's Dilemma — Illusion Versus Reality

One can only imagine what Huxley was experiencing in 1932 with the world in the jaws of a Great Depression and the distant drums of wartime marching feet pervading Europe. Government control at any cost was the social and political battle cry. A totalitarian government had a stronghold on the Soviet Union, and Huxley was aware of its costly loss of freedom. One can only imagine what he may have to say about our modern times when government has grown exponentially as one crisis develops after another. If *Brave New World* is only taken as a satiric swipe at human eccentricities, the power of its political and social argument would be sadly lost. As *Animal Farm* can be appreciated as an imaginative novel and a powerful allegory, so *Brave New World* can be both an entertaining depiction of a world gone mad, as well as an allegorical vision of an appalling future. Running parallel to this issue and intersecting at its core in *Brave New World* is the question of illusion versus reality. This pivotal quandary is astutely characterized by Huxley in the form of the central protagonist's struggle when these two forces — illusion and reality — intertwine.

In a masterful manner, Huxley challenges his reader to question what is real versus what is an illusion — in this case, a craftily created world that appears to be perfect, but under the surface, is anything but. As Mustapha Mond so eloquently indicates to John the Savage, the fundamental aspects of freedom have been sapped out of human existence to protect the individual from harm. In this case, harm is both global and individual. A World State organized and ruled by a team of World Controllers has no need to invade the other's territory since all is part and parcel of one giant domain. To ensure that no one individual desires more than he or she possesses, all motivational drive for a more comfortable existence is both genetically controlled and environmentally monitored. No Alpha, Beta, or Epsilon will ever desire to be anything more than what he or she is. All live harmoniously with neither a jealous nor envious bone in a unified body. So this world has all the appearance of perfection.

Yet this perfection has come with the ultimate sacrifice of one's individuality and freedom. Lenina cannot feel or sense anything more than what she has been genetically, socially, and psychologically meant to feel. When there is any semblance of withdrawal or dissatisfaction with one's state, *soma* comes to the rescue to return one to this illusory world. The most significant horror operating in this Brave New World is that only a non-programmed person like John, or a superiorly created and molded member of an elite class, like Mond, understands what is going on. It is this conflict between the illusion that has been created by this band of World Controllers, and the ability to "see" the world as it really is that torments John the Savage and leads to his ultimate extinction at his own hand. John cannot find happiness in a world of pure illusion. How did this world of illusion come about?

Certainly a period of prolonged bloodshed can cause a nation to bow to a higher authority that will provide peace and security. So it was that after the Nine Years War, Mond elucidates, "People were ready to have even their appetites controlled" for a peaceful existence.[51] It is posited that once individuals willingly give up one freedom, it is very easy to remove other freedoms from them under the guise of social profitability. While no human in the year 1 AF would agree that art and religion and love and family and marriage are hindrances to social order and happiness, if one-by-one they are genetically removed or environmentally conditioned to believe so, there would come a time — like 632 AF — when no one would know any better. It is this lack of knowledge and inability to "see" reality that becomes the foundation for this Brave New World.

One may consider it dangerous that Mond allows John the Savage entrance and interaction with the residents of this Brave New World, but under the tutelage of scientific research, he agrees to have John and Linda visit. He even proceeds further by ordering that John remain in the Utopian Center after his mother's death and Marx's and Watson's exile. Deep within Mond is the arrogance of scientific advancement. What had he to fear when John speaks to his fellow utopians? They would regard him purely as a curiosity item since they would be incapable of truly understanding him. And as for John himself, he either would find this world a breath of fresh air or a sphere of brainless sensory perception. If nothing else is learned from the experiment, a sense of confidence would swell when the "utopians" are repulsed by Linda's appearance and/or bewildered by John's ranting about Shakespeare. Carrying the source of Huxley's novel's title to its ultimate end, John may at first be dazzled by the beauty of this new world so that he may agree with Miranda in stating, "O brave new world that has such people in it," but later would realize that this is a new world uninhabited by thinking, feeling, nurturing, developing, and loving people.[52] The veneer of illusion is peeled away to reveal nothing but a reality devoid of humanity. And since all is programmed, there is no hope for development in the future. It is this deep sense of loss that drives John to seek exclusion.

John the Savage cannot embrace a world without Shakespeare, God, and emotion — a world without art and music and philosophical musings. Huxley deliberately chooses to make John into an unusual half-breed — half the product of utopian parents and the primitive world of a reservation. Not understanding the genetic markers of his superior intelligence — an intelligence that prevented him from engaging in or enjoying the communal activities at Malpais — but appreciating the complexity of human existence, John is the innocent eye who lacks the historical knowledge of a Mond, yet still aspires to seek food for his soul. It may be in the case of the latter characteristic of John's full potential that makes him unlike any member of the Utopian Center: John has a soul — not in the religious sense, but in the anthropological sense. By reading Shakespeare and yearning for true love and understanding, John's development far exceeds Lenina and Bernard and even Mond. For Mond has sold his soul — he has sublimated his humane interest in anything empirical for the common good. He states that he gave up his interest in truth for the happiness of others. John is not willing to make this sacrifice: "But I don't want comfort," he cries out to Mond.[53] In essence, John is claiming the right to see reality and deal with it, rather than living in a world of illusion. Mond's exclamation that "you're claiming the right to be unhappy," is his comprehension that John is claiming the right to continue to develop and nurture his soul.[54] Once John is understood by Mond, there is nothing more than he can do but to retreat from the world of illusion for fear that he will be consumed by it.

For a brief period of time, John is able to find refuge at a lighthouse removed from the physical, mental and emotional constraints of dealing with brainless, detached people. But the utopian curiosity seekers will not leave him alone. Perhaps out of loneliness and a need for human contact — albeit seemingly robotic contact — John falters and succumbs to the wonders of the drug of choice: *soma*. Distraught that he may become one of these automatons, and unwilling, as well as unable, to return to his primitive homeland, he takes his own life. One wonders if Huxley was truly being sincere with his reader when he indicates in the foreword to *Brave New World* that he may have given John a third choice — to seek others like himself and form a new community. While he was to provide this third choice to the protagonist in his other dystopian novel, *Ape and Essence*, the impact of *Brave New World*'s ending would be diminished by any ending other than the one depicted. For with it, reality is left dangling before the reader's eyes.

There is a deafening silence as John's feet are seen "like two unhurried compass needles" moving "north, north-east, east."[55] The ones who uncover John's body hanging from the arch are nameless — their reaction unstated. One could only imagine how divorced from human reaction would be the media and its viewers/readers when the news of John's bizarre behavior in taking his own life is revealed. Yet the reader realizes that when a powerful illusion clashes with a harsh reality, one can only dismiss it as uncivilized and retreat back into the imaginary existence where discomfort is not allowed. And so it is with this Brave New World "that has such people in it."[56]

Brave New World: Insights on Some Major Players

THE DIRECTOR

Huxley cleverly brings us into the world of the future with an explanation of how it functions. The entire Bokanovsky process, the use of hypnopeida and neo–Pavlovian conditioning are explained to the reader by the D.H.C. (the Director of Hatcheries and Conditioning) to a group of students taking a tour of the facility. This is the plot device that Huxley uses to explain to the reader how this society operates — later, its history will be provided in the same manner through Mustapha Mond's lecture to John. The Director is almost beside himself with the ingenious manner that life is created. Purely a narrative hook for the thematic setting of the novel, the Director also serves the function of displaying the symptomatic challenge of this society: how to keep the remnants of humanity at bay. After all, despite the scientific superiority of this new world, it still bears the mark of a primitive past since it is Tomakin (aka The Director) whom Linda adores and with whom she conceived John. The Director even briefly reminisces about his affection for a woman he brought to the reservation some 20 or 25 years earlier when Bernard requests permission to visit the reservation with Lenina.

The Director recognizes in Bernard Marx an aspect of himself that he has tried to obliterate with time — namely, an incomprehensible attraction and compulsion to seek a monogamous relationship with another. In the Director's case, it was Linda — for Bernard it is Lenina. Whether he deliberately or accidentally left Linda pregnant on the reservation is of little consequence. His romantic recollection of the event exposes his vulnerability so candidly to Bernard Marx that he shakes himself out of his reverie, and with a fear of humanistic exposure to another, he lashes back by scolding Bernard over his recent unfavorable reports. He follows with a warning that if Bernard continues to deviate from the directed "standard of infantile decorum," he shall order him to Iceland.[57] Bernard was only later to put the pieces of the puzzle together and use the Director's fall from grace as a defense for his conduct and a means of advancement. The end product of the Director's act of love with Linda has conceived a child by way of an outdated, outmoded, outlawed means that cannot be tolerated. Hence, the Director becomes both the vehicle for an objective explanation of the workings of this Brave New World, and a pivotal means to foreshadow what will become of anyone who violates the creed of "Community, Identity, Stability."

LENINA CROWNE

The reader finds in Huxley's characterization of Lenina Crowne a woman who neither desires nor comprehends anything beneath the physical, unvarnished surface. Lenina is a perfect product of the hatchery and conditioning process as described in glowing terms by the Director — the play on words with her name (Lenin) is purely intentional and speaks, on a sociopolitical level, of what a person may become when a totalitarian state controls all aspects of life.

The reader first meets Lenina as she is injecting typhoid and sleeping sickness into the gelatinous contents of what would later be rhapsodized as "that dear little bottle of mine."[58] Ironically, distracted at a later moment when events and feelings overwhelm her, she forgetfully does not inject a bottle which results some 22 years later in a death from "trypanosomiasis" — the first case in over half a century.[59] Huxley interjects into this perfect woman of the Brave New World some of the conflicting elements of the primitive humanity of the past that cause Marx and Watson — and even the Director — some unsettling moments. But unlike them, she is true to her conditioned self and resorts to *soma* to excise the tentacles of the aesthetic and the humane. Her attraction to Bernard — despite the fact that his behavior is "queer" — as well as her bewilderment about John, whom she lustily desires but who rejects her, are disturbing and distracting to her robotic sensibilities. She is overwhelmed, at times, by sensations that she can only equate to what she feels at the beginning of the Violent Passion Surrogate treatment.

Once again, only that which is programmed into her can come out of her. She does not understand why Bernard is dissatisfied with life and refuses to take his *soma*, nor why John the Savage, who is attracted to her, curtails their love-making and calls her a whore. When these things happen that are not part and parcel of her genetic makeup or packaged self, she resorts to her *soma* to make it and the annoyance of thought go away. Even the sights and smells of the reservation are so revolting to her sensibilities that she once again embarks on a chemical holiday.

Whether taking advice from Fanny about her anti-social monogamous relationship with Henry Foster, listening with fascination to John — yet failing to comprehend what he is dramatizing in the words of Shakespeare's *Romeo and Juliet*—or arriving at the lighthouse in the final scene of orgiastic pleasure and pain, the reader knows that Lenina will survive because she is a textbook creation of the ideal utopian woman. Happy in her own body, lusting for the pleasures of life, mindless to the feelings of others, and obedient to the creed of the World State, Lenina is the ultimate utopian survivor.

Long after Bernard Marx has been sent to Iceland and eradicated from Mond's annals, Lenina will be engaging in a daily stream of vivaporpus sexual relationships; long after the synthetic music of the cabaret has faded, Lenina will be happily dancing home escorted, perhaps, by the new Director or even Mond himself; and long after John's body has been sent to the crematorium, Lenina will choose *soma* to avoid recalling his presence in her life. Lenina accepts and believes in her role to inject antibodies into the assembly line bottles of ova in the London Hatchery and Conditioning Centre. If she momentarily falters and begins to feel any semblance of discontent, she will dismiss the thoughts and feelings as odd, and remedy them in the dictated chemical escape. Yet the reader cannot help but superimpose over her cold, solitary characterization a sense of isolation and aloneness that will never be satiated by the varied pleasures of this Brave New World. Lenina truly is a "Crowning" achievement of this utopian society — forever young, forever beautiful, forever sensual, and forever mindless.

MUSTAPHA MOND

As one of the ten World Controllers, Mond is only momentarily present during the tour of the London Hatchery and Conditioning Centre in the opening of the novel, then again when he provides his approval to Marx to allow Linda and John to visit the Utopian Center, and, finally, at the demotion of the D.H.C. and the promotion of Bernard when Linda exposes Thomas as the father of her child. But his place in the novel is pivotal to an understanding of how the World State came to be. His voice dominates two central chapters of the novel. Structured as a meeting with John the Savage when Marx and Watson are excluded from the Utopian World, he acts as the *Larger Bottle* decanted for the purpose of keeping order.

As he explains it to John, for the benefits of health, happiness and peace, the world controllers recognized that force was not the answer, but rather the surer methods of ectogenesis, hypnopaedia and neo–Pavlovian conditioning. Freedom, art, religion — all of these had to be sacrificed for the greater good of world peace and happiness. Each person, the Controller explains, is in a bottle throughout his or her life — similar to the bottle within which they were decanted. Some bottles — like those of the Alpha Plus — are larger. These are the bottles that comprise one-ninth of the world's population while the masses of humanity are submerged below the surface — submerged in conditioned ignorance. Understanding the historical construct of this Brave New World, and certain of what is necessary to keep peace and stability, Mond represents both the arrogance and impunity of a supreme dictator. As such, he does not need to be seen as the embodiment of a substantial person.

Mond is, therefore, merely an allegorical figure who argues against John's unwavering stance for human rights. Except for an occasional, small, personal revelation that he had to give up his own desire for truth for the greater happiness of all humankind, Mond is pure abstraction to John's concrete assertions. The Controller proselytizes to John in a manner that no one else can understand, with the exception of another Alpha Plus Controller, since John is a "savage" and knows both the old and the new worlds. Failing to convince John that the Utopian way of life is the ideal — an argument that the Controller knows from the start will not render John a subservient citizen — he proceeds to punish the Savage by insisting that he remain in the Utopian World as an object of derision and study. In essence, John may have won the battle but lost the war. The Savage may represent the person that the Controller was at one time. His desire to keep John close may be regarded as a paradoxical act. He may look on John as the embodiment of who he was, while subjecting him to the unyielding power that he now employs — a power only realized by the sublimation of his former self.

Huxley uses Mond as a centerpiece of ideas — concepts that may become a reality if taken to their extreme. Mond is the alarum bell calling humanity to a futuristic hell if it pursues a utopian ideal divorced from humane principles. Huxley does not attempt to make Mond into a flesh and blood individual, but rather a one-dimensional representation of the elite. If knowledge is limited to a chosen few, then power ensues. With power at the helm, ignorance can be scientifically germinated to the masses. And with this ignorance comes dependence on the renowned rulers who orchestrate a symphony that has no individual parts.

Mustapha Mond is only one of ten Controllers — so there is still a check and balance system even for those in command. Mond originated from a long line of Controllers dating back to at least the Nine Years War, a period in which a psychologically tortured humanity abandoned all of its freedoms for the greater glory of peace and happiness. Mond may be seen as the antithesis of John. The reader is not only enlightened by his theoretical and scientific explanation of the origins of this Brave New World, but Mustapha Mond does foster a fear in the heart of the reader — a fear for what an abstract concept may be capable of accomplishing in an ectogentically generated world of Epsilons.

BERNARD MARX

Bernard Marx is another inconsistent character who may epitomize the fickleness in human nature that has not been conditioned out of the residents of this Brave New World. At first, Bernard is the antithesis of the proper social being and a misfit in terms of the typical Alpha Plus. But when he becomes the center of attention and brilliance by introducing the Savage and his mother to a gawking populace, he enjoys the notoriety so much that he completely abandons his "true" self by taking *soma*, and publicly destroying the Director who violated the very creed that he so unabashedly previously denounced. From refusing to take a *soma* holiday, and being upset because Lenina is regarded solely as a piece of flesh, he falls prey to the attentive adoration and willingly accedes to the power that comes with a celebrated and rewarded action. No longer literally looked down upon by those of an inferior caste, his desire to search for something more in this superficial utopian world is sublimated by the warmth of the spotlight.

In the opening chapters of the novel up to the time that he and Lenina visit the reservation, the reader may think of Bernard Marx — once again a play on the name Karl Marx — as the central protagonist. He is an outcast and an individual thinker in a world that promotes sameness. It may be credibly anticipated that his trials and tribulations in this sterile world may be the agent for revolt. When he meets John and Linda, however, all of this changes. He listens to their story and makes the connection to the previous meeting with the Director when Thomas (Tomakin) reveled in remembering a time when he brought a girl to the reservation. Bernard seizes this opportunity to expose the Director and thereby save himself from the ignominy of expulsion to Iceland. Once he sets this action into motion and becomes a favorite of Mustapha Mond, there is no turning back or remembrance of the Marx that once was. Rather than being a leader of the proletariat, he joins the mindless game of life that he so vocally abhorred. It is at this point in the novel that Bernard hands the baton of the central protagonist to John, the innocent eye, with whom and through whom we observe, react, and interact with the passionless social order.

Even Bernard's interest in Lenina wavers, and he gloats at the bevy of women who now wish to be with him. His discontent was to return when the Savage refuses to attend a party that Marx arranged with the elite echelon of society. He can only comprehend that he has suffered embarrassment at the hand of John, failing to comprehend the damage that he has wrought upon the person he now regarded as merely a successful scientific experiment. Despite the fact that Bernard had the capacity to comprehend what the Savage said about preferring unhappiness to the false, deceptive façade of pleasure, Bernard now regards him as an accessible enemy upon whom he would try to wreak revenge.

Finding in Helmholtz Watson a commiserate companion who also was in trouble with authority for the rhymes that he created that were deemed anti-social in nature, he pours his heart out to Watson and is uncomfortable with the other man's magnanimity — a magnanimity that Marx had lost along the way. In the falling action of the novel, Bernard, fearing recrimination, hesitates when asked if he is a friend of the Savage after the latter's breakdown following his mother's death. Mond clearly informs Marx that he is not above the law and must accept its just sentence. Bernard, however, does not go quietly but falls on his knees and begs Mond not to send him to Iceland; he states he will do anything than face that punishment. Ultimately he points to Helmholtz and the Savage, and in a final act of self-denial and a fall from grace states, "I swear it was the others."[60]

In a humiliated and cowardly manner, Marx is led out of the room by four security guards. Perhaps he will find his true self again in the isolated land of misfits, but it may be more accurately speculated that he will suffer the fate of a Linda who could never adapt to an "uncivilized" environment. Rather than graciously accept his fate, as does Watson, Bernard is taken away kicking and screaming and begging to remain in the very land that he so vehemently once detested. While the Savage ate the utopian civilization and declared that it poisoned him, Bernard found the fruit of the tree of knowledge was pleasing. Submissive and apologetic for his spineless acts to the Savage and thankful for the selfless guardianship that Watson had bestowed on him, Bernard departs the Utopian Center at the same time that the Savage seeks refuge and meaningful isolation.

JOHN, THE SAVAGE

Like John the Baptist in the wilderness, the noble Savage John is lifted from the primitive uncivilized world of the reservation and dropped onto the land of plenty; unlike John the Baptist who heard the voice of God, John was to hear the cacophonous, barren voices of the robots created by the likes of Mustapha Mond. John the Savage is the innocent eye who observes, tastes, and questions the utopian world that everyone else so admires. His is the voice of reason in a world of irrational beings; he calls to Lenina and Bernard and all whom he meets to be baptized in the waters of understanding, but these conditioned and genetically manipulated beings do not have the capacity to value his wisdom.

Disillusioned, he tried to communicate the concept of love to the young children for whom he recites *Romeo and Juliet*, but they laugh at the preposterous idea that these two young lovers would take their lives rather than exist without each other. He reaches out to Bernard, but although he may comprehend what John states, Marx discards it because he has been willingly cloned into a hypocritical, utopian model. John is so strongly attracted to Lenina at their first meeting that he blushes and turns away. When she willingly begins to undress so they may unite in a moment of sexual passion, he rejects her because she fails to understand that he does not want to regard her as merely a sex partner but as a love partner. Playing with role reversals, Huxley has the promiscuous female aggressively pursuing a sexual relationship with a hesitant male.

Only Helmholtz Watson seems to understand John; Watson shares his original poetry with John who fully comprehends its intent. John even asks Mond for permission to accompany Watson to the islands — this would have been a reasonable alternative for John, for with Watson and other misfits he may have lived his life with passion and meaning. But his request is denied. Alone in a world of noise and superficial pleasure, John cannot find a companion with whom he can share a like-mindedness. He feels that he is left with only one option: to seek refuge from this world that he so patently detests.

But he soon finds that there is no escape from this overpowering, all-consuming entity — it is a World Power. He lacks the desire and means of returning to the reservation, and cannot bear the thought of remaining in this sterile atmosphere. Since an outward and an inward escape were not possible, only a bodily escape through death will fit the bill. But this decision comes not as an ultimate theoretical conclusion, but rather after he succumbs to a *soma*-driven orgy — an orgy precipitated by the frustration of one unable to overcome a naturalistically determined fate.

In John — the most developed character in the novel — the reader comes close to finding the catastrophic hero of an Aristotelian tragedy. John's error in judgment cannot be regarded as his willingness to accompany Lenina and Bernard to the Utopian Center, for although he did not know what he was in for, he was not finding meaning on the reservation. To have not accompanied them would have been to deny his mother her roots, and his lack of action could never have been determined as tragic. Once he was to comprehend what this Brave New World was all about, his error cannot be seen as his inability to adapt to the utopian world, because the reader would have been outraged by such an act — the very outrage that Aristotle indicates cannot be the substance of a tragic hero. While the rashness of his action to seek a retreat in the lighthouse may seem somewhat naïve, it was the only course of action immediately available to him, and the least repugnant. Did he honestly believe, however, that he would be left alone there, and that this all-powerful world of self-gratifying beings would not search for him and seek to satisfy their unremitting curiosity? Had he not experienced their need for the *Feelies*?

Nor is it in John's submission to the orgy that he errs. Although the orgy represents all that is repulsive and contradictory to his true self, it is not in the action but in the reaction that John falters. He considers himself so far above the fray that he cannot bear to recall what he has done. In essence, this noble savage — perhaps the last remnant of humanity — cannot bear to accept Alexander Pope's adage that "to err is human; to forgive, divine." He is unable to forgive himself and accept a momentary lapse in judgment — a momentary weakness. Perhaps John also fears that he may eventually enjoy the way of the flesh and become one of these utopian robots. In either case, the reader feels true pity for John, a thinking, feeling human being unable to find human companionship in a world populated by programmed machines.

As part and parcel of a dystopian tragedy, the ending clearly does fit. The one remaining human in a world of superficial creatures cannot live — his death is analogous to martyrdom. As his mother consumes too much of a "good" thing in her addiction to *soma*, so John states that he ate civilization and it poisoned him.[61] Although Huxley in his preface remarks that he may have given John a third alternative — to form a community of his own of like-minded thinkers — it would appear that Mond's denial of John's request that he move to an island with Watson, his failure to find others like himself, as well as his inability to find a safe haven at the lighthouse, may seem to have exhausted his options. Huxley could have craftily created a fictional scenario much as he was to do in *Ape and Essence*, where it might work, but the tragic end of John in *Brave New World* appears far more suitable to the intent of his initial utopian thesis.

Antithesis: *Ape and Essence*

Brave New World depicts a passive society conditioned and controlled by technology to assure stability. After World War II, Huxley was to write a novel describing the tragedy of a degenerative, chaotic future caused by nuclear devastation. From 1942 through 1945, Aldous and Maria Huxley lived in the Mojave Desert of California. The desert would serve as the opening and closing scenes in *Ape and Essence*, a bleak futuristic novel that describes a descent into barbarism following a nuclear war. The United States had recently engaged in World War II, and Huxley, a fervent pacifist, was appalled by the massive power of military technology in that conflict. As indicated earlier, during these years Huxley was to deepen his own search for spiritual answers to the human predicament. Huxley had felt somewhat isolated in the wartime Hollywood scene, but film work was a necessary part of his income. In a letter, he describes script writing as "tiresome work, but unavoidable, since books at the moment do not keep wolves very far from doors" — the latter a statement very similar to what he wrote when he felt pressured to quickly publish *Eyeless in Gaza*.[62]

Huxley's son, Matthew, served in the wartime Army Medical Corps, and on August 10, 1945, Huxley was to write to Victoria Ocampo: "Thank God we are to have peace very soon. But I confess that I find a peace with atomic bombs hanging overhead a rather disquieting prospect."[63] Huxley was particularly worried about nuclear power. Attempts to control it reminded him of the scene in Swift's *Gulliver's Travels* in which the tiny Gulliver is manhandled by a gigantic Brobdingnagian monkey. He concludes that "reason, human decency and spirituality, which are strictly individual matters, find themselves in the clutches of the collective will, which has the mentality of a delinquent boy of fourteen in conjunction with the physical power of a god."[64]

One critic concludes that Huxley's writings in the years following World War II contain a mix of optimism and pessimism. The optimism reflected the triumph of the free world over the forces of Nazism and Fascism, while the pessimism grew from a fear of mankind's indifference to further militarism and dangerous technology.[65] In 1946, Huxley was to focus on the problem of how scientists could utilize their gifts to ensure a safer technological world through a commitment to humanity's interests. He addressed this issue in a tract, *Science, Liberty and Peace*, and he donated the royalties to a pacifist organization, the Fellowship of Reconciliation.[66] His positive efforts for peace were, however, to find negative (dystopian) expression in *Ape and Essence*, which shows a world obsessed with destructive power.

Ape and Essence: The Frame of the Novel

Huxley's new novel is written appropriately in the form of a film script. Two motion picture executives accidentally discover a rejected movie screenplay, and they find it an engrossing tale written by one William Tallis. They visit Tallis's residence in the desert, but they find he has recently died. The manuscript's story, set in the year 2108, then becomes the main plot contained within the frame of the novel.

The frame, entitled "Tallis," stands in sharp contrast to the serious tone of "The Script" that follows it. Within this section, the bitingly satiric ink of Huxley's pen floods the page in his depiction of the frivolous pursuits of one Bob Briggs, a studio executive who fancies himself as one of the Romantic poets but, according to the first-person narrator, lacks both the talent and certainly the sexual potency of his models. Mr. Briggs relishes the messiness of his life. "To be, or not to be" is the line satirically illustrating his vainly trivial inability to decide, over a span of two years, whether he should make Elaine his mistress or even ask Miriam for a divorce. A trip with Elaine to Acapulco becomes the symbolic dividing line that makes Elaine act "strangely," and irrevocably turns him into an adulterer, a commitment compared, according to the narrator, to Gandhi's dedication to nonviolence and prison and even assassination, but with greater misgivings. Briggs's accumulating debt, as well as his inability to get a raise from the frugal film studio that uses the economic conditions as an excuse to deny increased compensation, aggravates his plight. Bob Briggs admits that he wants too much, and all of this is mockingly played out against the backdrop of the day that Gandhi is assassinated, a contrast that cuts deeply into Huxley's thematic intent.

The script of William Tallis affords the executives some promise of financial reward, but the author has, unfortunately, died. The final request of the dramatist to be buried in the desert is even thwarted by the legal process which prevents it from occurring. All of this information is related to the film officials by the Coultons, landlords of the deceased. Mr. Coulton is described as a leprechaun, and his granddaughter Rosie is referred to as Lady Hamilton, principally because Bob Briggs pursues her amorously; the naïve and impressionable young lady is swept away by the executive's promise of a screen test, to which the narrator remarks that he sees another trip to Acapulco on the horizon. William Tallis's verbal biography allows the narrator to engage in a romanticized form of reality.

Nevertheless, the facts are actually that Tallis had married and divorced, and his former wife and child remained in Germany. He remarried someone on the stage, but she ran off with someone else. His desire to bring his granddaughter to the States is forbidden by the government; alternatively, he had hoped to send her money from the successful sale of his script if only to provide her with food and a proper education in a war-torn region of the world. Unfortunately, he died suddenly at the age of 66, unable to fulfill his dream. When Coulton is asked what became of the rest of the family, he replies that they all died, surmising that they were Jewish or something. Then, he paused, and Huxley provides in one line the ugly head of anti–Semitism prevalent in his time when Coulton adds that he had nothing against Jews, but perhaps Hitler was not so dumb.

The juxtaposition of this vicious comment with the resident infant crying due to chronic diarrhea, as well as Briggs's promise to provide naïve Rosie with a screen test, forces the narrator to try to make a swift exit from the Coulton domicile. But it is to no avail: paraphrasing scripture that they have ears but do not hear, he tells the reader that he will now relate "The Script" of *Ape and Essence* without change or comment. And so the narrative begins.

Ape and Essence: Plot, Theme, and Characterization

The opening scene is Los Angeles decades after the atomic bomb has devastated the region. An exploratory team from New Zealand, a region safe from nuclear damage, arrives in California to study the destruction, but they are unprepared to witness the barbarism that followed World War III. One scientist, Alfred Poole, is separated from his colleagues and is taken captive by the local savages. The few thousand survivors in the region have resorted to beastly methods for continued existence. They burn books to bake bread, and they despoil the graves of the Hollywood notables. Their beliefs have degenerated into devil worship of Belial, the personification of evil, according to the teachings of their supreme ruler, the Arch-Vicar. Sex is allowed only once a year during an orgiastic festival to Belial. Continued nuclear-bomb radioactivity has caused many deformities, but when these are detected at birth, the infants are sacrificed to the Lord of the Flies. The Arch-Vicar attempts to recruit the captive scientist to the power elite that rules the savages. His words express Huxley's own fear for humanity's future if it continues to misuse technology toward destructive ends. Much like Mustapha Mond's explanation in *Brave New World*, the Arch-Vicar's rationale reveals how a power-hungry and manipulative government can destroy civilization.

The Arch-Vicar points out that, historically, humanity has always fought to control nature. After thousands of years of indecisive battle, the tide has changed in the last few hundred years. Beginning with modern machines, people began to make headway in dominating their environment. The unfortunate price paid by mankind was, however, to become a slave to the machine. Ultimately, the perfect machine would be foolproof, but it also would be independent of human skill, purpose, and inspiration. Technology thus advances inexorably and one problem leads to another, as overpopulation leads to war.

Overcrowding the planet had inevitably led to the exploitation and loss of natural resources. Great nations with large appetites for riches lead to a hungrier race of mortals. In this mad materialistic pursuit, the evil god Belial stood back and waited. If the atomic bomb had not been invented, the forces of evil would eventually be victorious because foolish humans would finally find a way to destroy the world in one way or another. The Arch-Vicar explains Belial's view:

> He foresaw that men would be made so overweeningly bumptious by the miracles of their technology that they would lose all sense of reality. And that's precisely what happened. These wretched slaves to wheels and ledgers began to congratulate themselves on being the Conquerors of Nature and were about to suffer the consequences.[67]

Modern material progress was for the Arch-Vicar too rare a possibility to have been solely the product of human intelligence — it required satanic guidance. He argues that new technologies have continued to provide people with the tools for ongoing and indiscriminate destruction.[68] A blind belief in scientific progress and substituting the national state for God has led the human race, ever more docile and gullible, to believe in the false hope of a future utopia. People gave up freedom to support an Unholy Spirit, and they destroyed civilization in one war after another. Between World War II and World War III, countries had both time and the abilities to change their ways. Instead, they amused themselves and allowed the nuclear tragedy to take place. Once these conditions were set, the bomb was a swift and inescapable conclusion.

The Arch-Vicar elucidates the very essence of the apelike, primitive nature of humankind that Huxley progressively came to recognize as the root of destructiveness — both physically and morally. A staunch pacifist, Huxley advocated a peaceful solution to all human conflicts only to witness the death and devastation resulting from two world wars. Hence, the Arch-Vicar's words are Huxley's written in the silence of the desert as he pursued a calling to discover a peaceful path to self-knowledge and spiritual awakening. Huxley's fears that the forces of evil, both within and without humanity, would ultimately lead to its extinction are vociferously expressed in the pompous pronouncements of the Arch-Vicar. His words prophetically forecast an ultimately devastating reality that will culminate if mankind continues to pursue its destructive ways.

In earlier novels, Huxley introduces a wise character to elucidate the way to spiritual enlightenment. Here, in this somber scene of human depravity, the wicked Arch-Vicar assumes a learned role and explains the horrifying consequences of bad choices. By purely natural means, using humans and technology as his instruments, Belial has produced a deformed race of beings who are stupid, inept, surrounded by squalor, and without hope, for ultimate extinction is inescapable. "Yes, it is a terrible thing to fall into the hands of the Living Evil," concludes the Arch-Vicar, misquoting scripture.[69] Poole, as an innocent observer, questions the Arch-Vicar as to why the people, knowing their fate, continue to worship Belial. The Arch-Vicar compares their conduct to those who would throw food to a growling tiger — to gain some breathing space, some time to put off the inevitable.

Poole falls deeply in love with Loola, a local woman, and together they rebel against the bestial ruler. The couple successfully escapes to the desert, which gives this novel the exception of a happy ending in Huxley's utopian narratives. They find their way to an isolated community, an ideal repeatedly advocated by Huxley. In this monogamous land, they join with other refugees who seek a common path to harmony and authentic happiness. Meanwhile, the dominant savage culture continues unabated. Huxley calls this future world inevitable if nations continue the present course of choosing destructive technologies over human values.

Ape and Essence: Background to the Novel

Before leaving for the United States in 1937, Huxley had been highly impressed by H.G. Wells's 1933 novel *The Shape of Things to Come*, a grim depiction of a future world war that was also adapted as a popular film. In Wells's story, a bombing is followed by a biological attack that destroys both mind and body through a "Wandering Sickness." General chaos results and a dictator takes control and shoots all dissidents. In the end, however, citizens try to revolt against the government and the technological weapons that produced the terror. Wells provides a fortuitous solution when a "Gas of Peace" subdues the government. In the film version, which Huxley saw in 1936, the scientist hero lands his aircraft in the war-torn nation and is bullied by the dictator into supplying the technical knowledge to save the country from a fatal sickness. The scientist in *Ape and Essence* is likewise held captive to force him to supply the Arch-Vicar with new farming techniques.

The title of Huxley's futuristic novel, *Ape and Essence*, comes from William Shakespeare's *Measure for Measure*:

> But Man, proud man,
> Dress'd in a little brief authority,
> Most ignorant of what he is most assur'd,
> His glassy essence, like an angry ape,
> Plays such fantastic tricks before high heaven,
> As makes the angels weep.[70]

These words, spoken by the heroine Isabella, expresses her contempt for the pride and ignorance of those in power. "Only in knowledge of his own Essence has any man ceased to be many monkeys," explains the omniscient narrator of the film scenario that contains the central plot of *Ape and Essence*.[71] For Huxley, the angry ape represents human nature without its essential qualities. Ignorance of the true self includes an unwillingness to face up to the problems of society. The sorry state of humanity after a nuclear strike indicates that humankind is slow to question its actions, or to change its ways, until it is ultimately too late to stop its spiraling fall to extinction.

Science, Liberty and Peace: Huxley's Companion Piece to *Ape and Essence*

As *The Perennial Philosophy* was ruminating within the mind of Huxley during his writing of *Time Must Have a Stop*—and much of its intent can be found within the pages of his fictional narrative — so Huxley was to scribe *Science, Liberty and Peace* two short years before the publication of *Ape and Essence*. Much as one was a reflection of his moral tract, *Ape and Essence* is the fictional equivalent of his previous discourse. *Science, Liberty and Peace* may be both the *ape* and the *essence* of his novel, and can certainly be regarded as a companion piece to it. Within the pages of his treatise may be found the thematic intent of his novel; the dystopian tale was created to promote the principles that had become the very spirit of an enlightened soul.

It was shortly after the completion of *The Perennial Philosophy* that the United States dropped bombs of nuclear destruction on Nagasaki and Hiroshima. Huxley felt compelled to offer his view of the human condition and the effects of scientific progress and prowess in his treatise *Science, Liberty and Peace*. His preface quotes the words of Leo Tolstoy who, 50 years earlier, declared as intrinsically evil any society that allowed the few to have enormous power and control over the many. Huxley proceeds to explain that, with every new conquest of nature, more power falls to the select few, so that every advance in technology has led to a greater centralization of control.[72] As he had declared earlier in his *The Perennial Philosophy*, scientific progress can be beneficial if it is accompanied by an intelligent evaluation of humane principles. Disinterested scientific research geared toward mass production and mass distribution, that is divorced from human norms, is not acceptable. Improving human welfare must be the goal for future scientific research and its industrial application.

Huxley analyzes how scientific progress has historically led to economic and social insecurity. New technologies often result in mass unemployment and, in times of financial chaos, the public has often permitted a strong authority or dictator to take control. Although a strong dictatorial authority generally means security, this central power endangers individual freedom. Today, highly specialized, complex technologies are designed for mass production and mass distribution — a pattern that leads to ever-greater financial gain or political control by the elite few. Huxley idealistically concludes that scientists should make economic self-sufficiency and political independence of humanity the goal of all of their technologies. Such resolve would help guarantee that social freedom would not be sacrificed to national security.

In the same treatise, Huxley also raises the modern concern for a healthy environment. He maintains that the psychological and spiritual needs of a people cannot be realized if individuals are alienated from their natural surroundings and creative work. Routine labor offers little satisfaction, and factory workers on fixed wages resign themselves to having no voice in their destiny. Unfortunately, he concludes, all technologies and their systems have ultimately demonstrated so far that the belief in real human progress is a wishful dream.[73] Huxley once more contends that all technological power involves *hubris*, or an overweening pride, that has no regard for consequences. Mankind must ultimately pay the price for material progress and the cost, more often than not, means a regression in a humane civilization.

Huxley looks further into the cause of technological *hubris*, and he claims that the dominant reductionist philosophy popular in modern thinking has contributed to a growing indifference to human values. This materialistic philosophy reduces the total human person to a mere biological entity, as Huxley explains:

> Human beings, it is more or less tacitly assumed, are nothing but bodies, animals, even machines; the only really real elements of reality are matter and energy in their measurable aspects; values are nothing but illusions that have somehow got themselves mixed up with our experience of the world; mental happenings are nothing but epiphenomena, produced by and entirely dependent on physiology; spirituality is nothing but wish fulfillment and misdirected sex; and so on.[74]

In modern war, this crass attitude has led to general massacres and wholesale destruction, and in peacetime it has encouraged brutish beliefs and ruthless conduct. Human attitudes must be changed to see that the final aim of life is not in the distant utopian future, but human fulfillment is outside of time in the "timeless eternity of the Inner Light." A reductionist outlook as promoted by modern technology is the source of false and fatal modern values.[75]

Huxley proposes that non-violence should become the natural condition of human nature. He sees the quiescent attitude as a product of Eastern thought, while aggression has been implanted in the Western psyche. Reform can only come from a change of heart that can happen when people recognize non-violence as a practical aid to political action. The Hindu leader Gandhi is cited by Huxley as a prime example of this view. Gandhi was not only an idealist and a man of principle, but he was also a practical and shrewd politician. He organized a successful form of non-violent opposition that he termed *satyagrapha*. Against overwhelming odds, his non-violent followers won their struggle in India.

As he forecasts the future of science and technology in *Science, Liberty and Peace*, Huxley makes a number of remarkable predictions: wars fought over the control of oil; the expansion of solar and wind power; the rapid increase in global commerce; Asia's eventual technological superiority; and nuclear proliferation with its attendant threat to human survival. He also predicts that the responsibilities of scientists will be profound in light of the ubiquitous influence of technology in future years. This is why Huxley recommends that all scientists take a pledge not only to share their knowledge, but to insist that the development and application of all technologies be directed solely toward the good of humankind and not for any harmful or destructive ends.[76]

The elements of all of the concepts presented in *Science, Liberty and Peace* may be found in the pages of *Ape and Essence*. It is, therefore, fitting that Huxley opens the story on the day of Gandhi's assassination. Like Gandhi, Huxley believed that revenge is foolish because the injuries people inflict on others will only come back to harm them. The film-script narrator of the novel thinks about the death of Gandhi and concludes that the holy man really did believe that he could change evil into good. He is afraid, however, that if people are simply extensions of their machines, they will be used by the system and eventually be destroyed by it.

Ape and Essence: A Dystopian View

David King Dunaway suggests that *Ape and Essence* is an unacknowledged forerunner of science fiction films like *Planet of the Apes*, a series based on a 1963 novel by Pierre Boulle. In the latter work, intelligent apes rule a future civilization, whereas Huxley proposes that clever scoundrels will one day govern a degenerate people. In either case, society has been foolishly responsible for massive destruction and devolution, or a reversal in evolution, has resulted.[77]

After America entered the atomic age, Huxley's call for a return to a simple lifestyle in small communities appears more frequently in his novels and other writings. In a 1945 letter that alluded to the recent political election, he notes the following historical fact:

> No person or class or institution can possess undisputed power for any length of time without being corrupted by it. Personally I come more and more to believe in decentralization and small-scale ownership of land and means of production.[78]

Huxley came to realize, however, that this utopian solution was not always feasible. When mass production and mass regimentation are dictated by economics, any sudden decentralization tends to weaken morale and national defense. Nations were not ready to give up military might as a safe course, and Huxley concluded that a strong decentralization policy required to maintain a small community culture may be a long way off.[79]

Ape and Essence is a dystopian narrative that focuses directly on the threat of unrestricted technology. In a 1949 letter, Huxley indicates that he had struggled with the appropriate form for his novel. He tried to write a straightforward narrative first, but the theme would not lend itself to simple realism. To achieve imaginative but persuasive narration, he chose the film scenario. Huxley further notes that he again had the problem of balancing the exposition of ideas with the narration. He explains that only two ways would resolve this problem: either write a lengthy work like *The Brothers Karamazov*, or a fantasy in the compact style of the satirist Thomas Peacock. He finds himself caught between the two approaches, and ultimately he tries a compromise that he knew was not wholly satisfying.[80] Huxley, his own best critic, admitted to the weakness that critics did find in the novel. It has been critiqued as a contrived story with a negative view of the future and aesthetically inferior to his earlier futuristic narrative.

The novel's opening scene that described a truckload of rejected film scripts bound for the incinerator could easily have been based on Huxley's own experience in Hollywood in 1948.[81] Satirically, the rejected script that becomes the novel was never returned to the foiled writer because it did not include a self-addressed, stamped envelope. His one final wish — to be buried in the desert—was thwarted by state regulations. At the end of the narrative, the surviving hero and heroine crack a hard-boiled egg on the film writer's tombstone, which is dated *1882–1948*.

Between the opening and the closing of this frame story, the futuristic film scenario proceeds with few digressions. Background exposition is limited to the Arch-Vicar's discourse of how the nuclear destruction occurred. Technology had been blindly promoted for decades, and the resultant civilization pictured in *Ape and Essence* offered no redeeming qualities. The scenario opens with the voice of the narrator, who reflects on the material excess that characterized Los Angeles in the 1940s:

> And in the midst of them the City of the Angels.
> Half a million houses,
> Five thousand miles of streets,
> Fifteen hundred thousand motor vehicles,
> And more rubber goods than Akron,
> More celluloid than the Soviets,
> More Nylons than New Rochelle,
> More brassieres than Buffalo,
> More deodorants than Denver,
> More oranges than anywhere,
> With bigger and better girls—
> The great Metropolis of the West.[82]

But the camera focuses closely on the metropolis, and it is now seen as a ghost town. All of the city machinery stands idle and the inhabitants are a mass of primitive savages who live by plundering graves. For three generations the few survivors of nuclear annihilation have lived in this wilderness. The radioactivity following the nuclear attack has left a race of deformed, stunted people, humans who have regressed to the primitive state of existence before the year 900 B.C.[83] Their sexual habits are based largely on pure instinct: "Thanks to the supreme Triumph of Modern Science, sex has become seasonal, romance has been swallowed up by the oestrus and the female's chemical compulsion to mate has abolished courtship, chivalry, tenderness, love itself."[84] The polluted environment has contaminated all sources of food and left a ravenous, savage population.

Mankind has thus made the worst of both worlds by combining Eastern despotism, passivity, and superstition with Western nationalism and aggression to ruin any chance of social recovery.[85] Love, joy, and peace—the qualities essential to human culture—no longer exist, having been replaced by the characteristics of the brute mind: antagonism, hate, restlessness, and chronic misery.[86] So extreme is the degradation of humanity in Huxley's future world that critics like Sanford Marovitz question whether he intended to write a dystopian warning or a hideous tragicomedy.[87] The horror of the nuclear bomb in 1945 had intensified Huxley's fear of unrestrained technology. This fear led to a more dire warning of a possible holocaust — a shift in attitude that is clearly evident if one compares his depiction of a future society in the pre-war *Brave New World* with the projected horrors of the postwar novel.

While the surviving community at the end of *Ape and Essence* strikes a hopeful note, the novel does reflect both the contemporary threat of nuclear war and the other long-range forecasts by which science and technology threaten to increase human suffering. As he had in earlier works, Huxley sounds an ecological warning in *Ape and Essence*. The hero reflects on the long parasitic relationship between people and the environment that despoiled natural resources. The human exploitation of nature represented an attack on the essential order of things — the Tao or the Logos — an evil that Huxley termed a form of lovelessness.[88] The Arch-Vicar's criticism of the human reckless disregard for nature parallels Huxley's censure in *The Perennial Philosophy*, where mankind is accused of trying "to dominate and exploit ... waste the earth's mineral resources, ruin its soil, ravage its forests, pour filth into its rivers and poisonous fumes into its air."[89] This warning was well ahead of Rachel Carson's *Silent Spring* (1962) and the environmentalists who publicized the modern depredation of nature.

Huxley saw the massive human attempt to dominate nature as a reflection of mankind's spiritual bankruptcy. Human spiritual progress is frequently thwarted by materialism, which is manifest in an obsession with advancing technology. Pride in cleverness and aggressive impulses have ultimately doomed mankind in *Ape and Essence*. Those not killed or mutilated by the nuclear devastation have no check against pillaging the land or destroying one another. Even in this chaotic world, however, there is still hope for the few who have the brains and the will to retain their principles and to live simply, in accordance with human values. A harmonious synthesis between technology and human needs is Huxley's answer.

Ape and Essence: Huxley's Allegorical Dystopia

While remnants of the earlier novelist may be found in the repeated form of an innocent eye like Poole, who in this narrative is the lens through which the reader is introduced to a barbaric world, the protagonist is not as well characterized as was the case in the development of a character like John the Savage in *Brave New World*. In earlier Huxleyan novels, someone is often cast in the role of a learned one who articulates an omniscient World View. Rontini or Propter in Huxley's novels of transformation are spiritual guides, and Boone and Barnack benefit from their instruction; Mustapha Mond speaks with full candor to John the Savage about how the utopian configuration of the world came about. In the depiction of the Arch-Vicar in *Ape and Essence*, however, an unabashed agent of evil has membership in the power elite and rules this bestial community. He holds the "wisdom" on how the world came to this dismal state, and he attempts to recruit the cultured Poole and his expertise to the ranks of those who control an inhumane populace. Poole rejects the invitation and takes flight from this morally destitute community. In essence, Huxley now provides a companion for Poole, unlike the aloneness he projected in John the Savage; likewise, as was the case with John, Poole is an outsider who saw life contrary to the conditioned populace. But even though he provides an alternative for Poole that he did not provide for John, the force and power of *Brave New World* is missing. Did this genius, who was so artistically talented, actually misfire and create an unrealistic dystopia?

The list of bizarre aspects of *Ape and Essence* include: a film script containing the censorious voice of an omniscient narrator; the semi-chorus contributions of a fanatical worship session hinting at the voice of the Greek chorus intoning pronouncements of the degenerative people; and an ending to the script that has the two lovers cracking hard-boiled eggs on the tombstone of the implicit writer of the narrative. All of this seems too peculiar to be a part of the Huxley arsenal. And yet it is. So why did he write it? Is it meant to be a tragicomedy? Had Huxley lost his hold on what makes for an interesting story? Is *Ape and Essence* a failure? Or is his novel simply misunderstood?

Huxley struggled with the form of the novel. What was the best means of conveying his ideas? In this case it was not just his views on pacifism and humanity's erroneous road to happiness, but it was the very real consequence of destructive tendencies that could annihilate the world. In *Brave New World*, he projected a mindless society some 600 years in the future; the world of *Ape and Essence* is set less than two centuries from the present. The world of *Ape and Essence* is, therefore, a world of the here and now as evidenced in the devastation of Hiroshima and Nagasaki. To picture such a world would pose great difficulty in resorting to the satiric genre. Hence, Huxley's dystopian novel is very serious.

In the desert, he reflected on the hedonistic, careless world of Hollywood of which he was part as an earnest and conscious observer. As such, he is able to blend the satiric aspects of a lost script that flies off a truck bound for the incinerator. The agents believe that it has potential, but how much of this potential would be lost because the writer failed to provide a self-addressed envelope for its return? In this scene, Huxley gets in his digs at the absurd actions of the motion picture industry with which he was at this time well acquainted. He sardonically places the discovery of the soon-to-be-burnt script on the very day that Mahatma Gandhi is assassinated. The man who devotedly advocated non-violence — a position championed by Huxley in essays, speeches and fiction — is brought down by the hatred and destructiveness of mankind symbolically reflected in the desolation pictured in his novel following World War III. Humanity, lost in its ways, was on the road to annihilation, and Huxley wanted to fictionally forewarn it.

There are two distinct features of Huxley's dystopian novel that beg critical evaluation: the form Huxley chose (a film script) and the evil incarnate personages and happenings. Huxley states that he had tried to write the story "straight," but the topic would not lend itself to proper expression. He resorted, therefore, to what he terms the "fantastic" — both in form (the film script) and content. He was to write to Philip Wiley of the "possibility that the thing may actually be turned into a film in France. If well done, it might be rather astonishing."[90] Perhaps this is one of the challenges that Huxley and the reader faces — we are asked to read the contents of a script rather than see it. The cinematic directions are sometimes awkwardly rendered, and the reader finds it difficult to make a visual transition to the printed page. The bestial incantations of the people and the Arch-Vicar's Popish description border on the strange and render passages not in keeping with the "verisimilitudinous terms" for which Huxley's was striving.[91] Yet one must pause to ask if Huxley was misunderstood.

What if Huxley decided to create a "short and fantastic" work whose form and content were deliberately rendered as bizarre, in the same manner that humanity's desire for power leads to its own self-destruction?[92] What if the Last Will and Testament of a William Tallis is the clever creation of a talented seer wherein art becomes merely an imitation of life — where fiction and reality meet? What if the voice of irrationality (the Arch-Vicar) is purely a symbolic foil for William Propter and Bruno Rontini? What if Huxley was creating a modernistic allegory with all of the trappings of a Greek tragedy? If all of these "what ifs" receive an affirmative reply, then Huxley's dystopian novel is a success and the author is fully understood.

It is posited that *Ape and Essence* is an allegory filled with symbolic intent, abstract substance, and a confirmatory vision. As an allegory, the bizarre nature of the setting, the people, and the events becomes a nightmarish vision of the future if humanity continues along its same path. Throwing more meat to the tiger to buy time before the inevitable happens is where it stands. But it has the means to change its way — of becoming more enlightened. The humanly and spiritually corrupt world of the future can be avoided if humanity takes the time to seek the virtuous path to discernment. Both Mond in *Brave New World* and the Arch-Vicar in *Ape and Essence* are foils for the very doctrines Huxley advocated in his transformative novels. As an allegorical abstraction, the world of *Ape and Essence* is not all that pleasant to observe. It is within the very heart of the bizarre that Huxley has brought his reader, for the very actions of humanity had far too frequently epitomized the bizarre. Perhaps humanity may take a respite from its ways by visiting the island of Pala, the setting of his final novel. His last venture into utopian literature is a reflection of the synthesis of ideas that he believed was within the grasp of his fellow man.

Synthesis: *Island*

Between 1949 and 1961 Huxley wrote only one short novel, *The Genius and the Goddess* (1955), a relevant study of a brilliant scientist who fails as a human being, a work that stands alone in this genre study. During these years he devoted his energies to preparing anthologies, collections of essays, and delivering a series of university lectures at campus conferences around the United States. In 1962 the last of his novels, *Island,* was published, and in 1963, just months before his death, he produced his final book, *Literature and Science,* a study of the two cultures that were important in his life. The final novel would reiterate themes that were significant to Huxley and his experiences at the time. He would now explicitly advocate the basic life principle that solely through non-attachment — the conscious transcendence of self from material concerns — could one secure inner peace and union with spiritual reality. This principle had been explored through history in

The Perennial Philosophy. It had been suggested in *After Many a Summer Dies the Swan*, and it had been vividly dramatized in *Time Must Have a Stop*.

While writing his last novel, *Island*, Huxley was diagnosed with malignant cancer of the mouth, but he refused the radical procedure that called for the removal of one-third of his tongue. As a boy Huxley had seen his mother die from the same disease, and now, in his sixties, he feared that he may become another cancer victim. His first wife, Maria Huxley, had been his constant companion and assistant through 36 years of marriage until her death in 1955. In an attempt to come to terms with her final illness, Huxley had first studied *The Tibetan Book of the Dead*. He had become more Buddhist in attitude, but he now sought a more practical means of experiencing ultimate reality.

Believing that hypnosis and mind-enhancing drugs aided this mystical endeavor, Huxley found in the dying Maria a willing subject. He tirelessly remained by her side, and he gently eased her entrance into an afterlife that both he and she had come to accept: "I told her to let go, to forget the body, to leave it here like a bundle of old clothes, and to allow herself to be carried, as a child is carried, into the heart of the rosy light of love," related Huxley of her death bed experience.[93] After her peaceful death, he openly defended the use of psychedelic drugs like LSD as a means of enhancing conscious awareness, and he experimented with mind-altering drugs himself. Huxley wrote *The Doors of Perception* and *Heaven and Hell* during this time, shockingly controversial studies supporting the beneficial effects of these drugs.

Huxley never recommended that psychedelic drugs be taken solely for their hallucinatory effects, but only as an aid to initiating mystical enlightenment. He insisted that they be taken under controlled conditions, and the information available suggests that he may have tried the drugs only on a dozen occasions.[94] Given his celebrity status, however, it is possible that Huxley's reputation may have suffered at the time by his willingness to speak openly on this controversial subject, especially since he had earlier satirized the drug-happy culture of a *Brave New World*. Later, he was to keep his own terminal illness a tightly guarded secret from the public.[95] The fictionalized accounts of mystical experiences as found in his postwar novels, however, may have been based on his own drug experiences.

In 1956, one year after Maria's death, Huxley happily married Laura Archera, a concert violinist and a psychotherapist whom he had known since 1948. Otherwise, the last decade of Aldous Huxley's life was mostly filled with sorrow. There was the death of his first wife, his son's divorce, the loss of his home and library in a fire, and his own diagnosis of cancer. Despite these difficulties, Huxley still published close to one book per year, including *Brave New World Revisited*, *Literature and Science*, and *Island*—works that were unique reflections of a man coming to terms with his mortality. Huxley died on November 22, 1963, the day of President John F. Kennedy's assassination. In a *New York Times* article published after his death, Huxley is reported to have taken up painting ten years earlier. He was pleased that one of his works was displayed at a local festival in Lancaster, and he remarked that at a gallery a short distance from this site hung a drawing for which the artist, Goya, had received no such recognition. The painting represents an old man walking with the aid of two sticks, and below the drawing Goya had written the words, *Aun aprendo*, which translates to "still learning." Huxley concludes that if heraldry were still popular, these words and the accompanying image would be his crest and his motto.[96] There is, therefore, no reason to assume that Aldous Huxley would not have continued to pursue his theme of a spiritual versus material culture had he lived beyond his 69 years.

Island: Plot, Theme and Characters

The novel *Island* indicates that Huxley never lost his fascination with a story that introduces a curious visitor to a strange locale. Will Farnaby is a young journalist who is shipwrecked on a Pacific island called Pala. All his life he has been a typical product of a materialistic, power-driven culture. He works for a man who not only owns the newspaper where Farnaby is employed, but his boss also has a vested interest in a petroleum company in search of new oil reserves. Farnaby had actually been assigned to infiltrate this remote island as a friendly explorer when his small boat capsizes in rough seas. Recuperating from injuries sustained in landing, he becomes fascinated by the hospitable natives who possess an inner peace and joy. Neglecting the original purpose of his visit, he eventually accepts their ways.

In the process of gaining an appreciation of the spiritual culture of the Palanese, Farnaby suffers guilt over his past failings. Huxley uses two techniques to convey this enlightenment on the basic spiritual tenets that he had long advocated. In a series of question-and-answer dialogues, Farnaby receives wise instruction that is shared with the reader. Farnaby also reads a book by the Old Raja, who was a repository of spiritual wisdom. The title of this work suggests a pragmatic approach to ultimate reality: *Notes on What's What, and on What It Might Be Reasonable to Do About What's What.*

Through his spiritual training, Farnaby learns not to dwell on the past or the future but to concentrate on enjoying the present. He is strongly attracted to a young woman whose hardy ancestors had originally sailed to the East Indies as merchants. Their descendants combined the best of Western culture with the Eastern meditative philosophy of the ruling Raja. The Palanese have lived for many years in peaceful harmony, and they are endowed with the wisdom to evaluate Western progress insofar as it benefits their enlightened culture. Life in Pala is well organized and planned on a material basis. Free love is practiced, all children are members of an extended family, and drugs are used religiously to attain mystical experiences.

The idyllic paradise, however, is not free from evil. Three greedy plotters assault this utopia: the Rani or queen mother of the realm, her son the young Raja, and the military dictator of a nearby island. The opportunity of oil exploitation, greed, and power ignites the passion of their followers, and in the climactic scene, the island is overtaken by a military invasion. The dictator unites Pala with his own island and declares himself supreme. The peaceful utopia has fallen, but Farnaby, a changed man, has hopes that the paradise may be restored again.

As Huxley's last fictional work, *Island* is again an adventure of discovery, this time through the quest of the central character Will Farnaby. A comparison can be made between Farnaby's adventure on Pala and Lemuel Gulliver's in Jonathan Swift's *Gulliver's Travels.* A further connection may be seen between Huxley's novel and the English novelist James Hilton's *Lost Horizon* (1933) that is set in the idyllic Shangri-La. Cast upon an island, Farnaby finds a superior civilization of wise people. They explain to him that hunger, war, crime, cruelty, and squalor are all caused by the foolish actions of people. The inhabitants of Pala have realized the perfection of their species by seeking only what is beneficial to human culture.

Huxley once again suggests through the depiction of this consummate model that people have the power to change themselves and to change the world. Even Huxley's tone in his final novel is more compassionate and less caustic than in his other futuristic narratives, especially when compared to *Ape and Essence.* The theme supports Huxley's view that a materially obsessed Western civilization based on power and wealth thwarts any chance of human fulfillment, which can only come through meditative self-understanding. Only when Will Farnaby is cut off from modern society on an island where he can be guided by spiritual insight can his enlightenment and happiness be attained. Along with the journey toward self-discovery, the process involves a cultural synthesis, a union of Eastern philosophy with Western technology.

This ecological and holistic way of life is possible, according to Huxley, if people are open to change. The island Pala is not utopian in an impractical sense, but it is described as a plausibly conceivable society created by a people with lofty ideals. Farnaby's search for enlightenment embodies Huxley's hope for all of humankind. Although the Palanese civilization may be destroyed at the end of the novel, the message gained by Farnaby and the readers of his narrative will continue to be taught: To know oneself. For example, Farnaby reads in the little green book of wisdom written years earlier by the Raja:

> Nobody needs to go anywhere else. We are all, if we only knew it, already there.... If I only knew who in fact I am, I should cease to behave as what I think I am; and if I stopped behaving as what I think I am, I should know who I am.[97]

In a 1962 letter to an Indian potentate, His Highness the Maharaja of Jammu and Kashmir, Huxley explains that "*Island* is a kind of pragmatic dream — a fantasy with detailed and (conceivably) practical instructions for making the imagined and desirable harmonization of European and Indian insights become a fact."[98] Huxley admits that this story cannot be reality — a point he emphasizes at the conclusion of the novel. He believed, however, that if people were not so preoccupied with the business of existence, they might create a culture fit for enlightened beings.[99] Huxley saw *Island* as one of his most provocative works, and he was delighted that it had attracted the interest of many readers.[100] The novel reflected the mood of the rebellious American youth of the 1960s, particularly in their search for a communal life that promoted ecological principles. In this regard, the critic Gerd Rohman states that, since its publication in 1962, Huxley's *Island* "has become a seminal influence on modern ecological thought."[101] Many of the concepts contained within Huxley's narrative were also to find their place in such contemporary science fiction novels as Kurt Vonnegut's *Cat's Cradle*.[102]

Huxley's description of the island civilization mirrors his own social philosophy. The Palanese, in their industrialization policies, were prudent, and they weighed the introduction of any new technology against its contribution to the quality of life. They measured the quality of life from the viewpoint of eternity, inner peace, and enlightened consciousness. Ultimate union with the Divine was the purpose of their existence. Although the pro-grammed restrictions of *Brave New World*, like birth control, education through conditioning, and a ban on the nuclear family are found on Pala, they are more reasonably applied. The basic difference on Pala is that the inhabitants are truly free and consciously aware of their ability to develop the social systems that promote human welfare.

The Tantrik doctrine that is the basis of the island's beliefs is derived from Hindu scripture on mysticism. One does not renounce or escape from the world, but rather one makes use of all the good that the world has to offer to reach the goal of ultimate liberation. All sense awareness or experi-ence is used toward this higher purpose. The revered book of the old Raja proclaims:

> But Good Being is in the knowledge of who in fact one is in relation to *all* experiences. So be aware — aware in every context, at all times and whatever, creditable or discreditable, pleasant or unpleasant, you may be doing or suffer-ing. This is the only genuine yoga, the only spiritual exercise worth practic-ing.[103]

Hence, when the original European explorer arrived on the island, he brought with him his earlier painful experience of famine and starvation in India. Vowing that he would never again accept human devastation, he devel-oped an agricultural technology and raised better crops and farm animals. When the inhabitants began to overpopulate the island by living more health-fully and longer, technologies were developed to promote birth control rather than face the alternatives of famine, pestilence, and war.

While the Palanese acquired skill in technology, they consciously avoided exploiting it for selfish gains. As a pacifist society, they rejected all military enterprises. They refused to establish an army and banned all weapons. By not building port facilities, they remained isolated and free from all traders and missionaries that they looked on as invaders. Alternative forms of medicine promoted the health and well-being of the people, and a simple lifestyle sup-ported this goal. Aggression and crime were non-existent in this stress-free cul-ture that was unselfish, meditative, and community oriented.

The government on Pala was reduced to a minimum, and Farnaby is told that leadership roles are avoided since they might produce an abuse of power. The sound wisdom of the old Raja on this subject reads: "The beings who are merely good, are not Good beings; they are just pillars of society.... Most pillars are their own Samsons. They hold up, but sooner or later they pull down."[104]

With no army, there are no commanders, and with limited personal wealth, governing units are established to run the island. Formal religions based on hierarchies are forbidden, and the only sanctioned beliefs promote individual spiritual experience. Transcendental meditation is a common practice, as well as a healthy skepticism toward all dogmatic beliefs.[105] Despite this attitude, however, the natives of Pala are intrinsically trustworthy, as well as naïve in dealing with the deceptive ways of the outside world. The destruction of their culture results from the treason of Murugan, their young Raja, who was educated in Western duplicity.

The Palanese were taught from an early age to concentrate on the present moment and allow no regret for past experiences or anxious anticipation of the future. "Attention" was the byword repeated in school and the term "karuna" (or compassion) was associated with it. Disciplined through concentration, rational thinking, and spiritual exercises, the islanders sought the self-knowledge that leads to the good life. Seeing God in all reality, they recognize that human sorrow comes from false ideas and that this sorrow was an unnecessary emotion. Compassion for others and the acceptance of destiny as a personal responsibility were the basic moral precepts.

The fortunate fusion of the Eastern and the Western thought originated in the 19th century when the first European sailed for the South Seas. This narrative incident may have been derived from a similar voyage by Huxley's grandfather at about the same time.[106] On a visit to the "forbidden" island, the first doctor cures the sick Raja by surgically removing a growth while the patient is under a hypnotic trance. He remains with the island colony, and his medical skills introduce Western technological ingenuity into the traditions of the cultivated Eastern philosophical way of life.

As in all cultures, the children of Pala are vital to the future of the community, and they are indoctrinated into Palanese traditions during their formative years. Their parents are not, however, possessive, and the children are always free to leave their biological family for the more extended family of their neighbors. A "MAC" or Mutual Adoption Club consists of between 15 to 25 couples that range from the newly married to the widowed and the elderly. All these families are thus interconnected, and their children can absorb loving relationships and respect within the entire extended community.

One controversial aspect of the community is the promotion of drugs as a religious rite. Huxley had learned of such rites with mescal or peyote among Indian tribes in the United States Southwest. In the novel, the deepest truths of revelation are revealed through the practice of taking 400 milligrams of the moksha-medicine, a mind-enhancing drug that produces heightened awareness and a state of transcendence. As an aid in achieving a mystical state, Huxley was not reflecting in his novel the practices of his young contemporary readers who were advocating the use of recreational drugs in the early 1960s. These "flower children," as they were called, used drugs to either escape reality or to achieve a blissful state, an objective far removed from the spiritual enlightenment for which Huxley advocated their usage. Farnaby does participate in a drug-enriched out-of-body experience — one that allows him to perceive a spiritual dimension that he had been prevented from attaining in a world of distractions. He also witnesses a serene submission to physical death as a stage in the natural cycle of life. This experience occurred in the profoundly peaceful passing of the doctor's wife with the loving acceptance and assistance of her family.

A transcendent communal philosophy of life contrasts with the selfish greed of the young Raja, who wants a return to a traditional government on his eighteenth birthday, the occasion he believes for his assumption of power. He openly reveals to Farnaby his plans to use Western technology to develop biological and chemical weapons, to industrialize the island, and to exploit the natural resources for profit. In league with the dictator of a neighboring regime, the young rogue schemes to use future oil royalties to finance a plan for World Reconstruction — a brain-washing program that will corrupt the will, the mind, and the spirit of the Palanese and force them to accept the crass values of the outside world. Through the Raja's evil plot, Huxley thematically describes the inevitable tragedy when greedy desires contaminate right thinking — when the mechanized powers of the West are divorced from human values. This tragedy now happens in the form of a military invasion of the island. After a volley of gunfire, loudspeakers on the invading military vehicles proclaim that modern progress is now the standard of this New World.

The novel's narrator cynically describes how society has repeatedly wrecked all efforts to improve itself. The work of a century is destroyed in a single night, but the struggle upward remains. An ultimate note of optimism permeates the final scene of the novel when the omniscient narrator remarks: "Disregarded in the darkness, the fact of enlightenment remained."[107] On the island, the trained mynah bird calls on the demoralized natives for compassion and "attention" to the present moment. Recognizing that a civilization based on a synthesis of thought, will, and perception

176

would not come easily or soon, Huxley in *Island* wrote his final fictional testament to the human cost of technological progress.

The transcendence of self, an awareness of the battling duality of the human psyche toward good and toward what *feels* good, the peaceful co-existence of a people, and the mystical goal of life, are all part and parcel of the island of Pala. Since the island is exploited for selfish means, Huxley realistically intones the creed that even a Utopia can be lost to a world that fails to see reality in a new way. Huxley repeatedly intones that mankind's aggressive response to its problems has only led to destruction and devolution of the race. Hence it is fitting that the reader be forewarned of human tendencies and perceive the destructive force at work, even in the realm of a Utopia. *Island* is Huxley's most enduring and lasting testimony to who the man was and who he had become. Awaiting death and accepting the inevitability of it all, he offers his own Utopia, his own *Lost Horizon*, and prays at the closing of the novel that it may not only fictionally return, but it may someday become a realistic possibility.

What better place than to use the literary artist's perfect setting for a microcosmic view of the macrocosm — an island untainted, far removed from "civilization" and intelligently selective about what is included and, most especially, what is excluded from its domain. Huxley was witness to a mass of humanity sandwiched within domiciles towering over the metropolis separated from any natural environment. Far too frequently he knew the sorry state of those whose wealth and power diminished their souls and made them servants of the very machines they created. And he — for a time — counted himself among their numbers. But far more in his readings, his conversations, and his isolation had he come to appreciate the meditative quality of life and see within it his realized destiny. This spiritually principled, open-minded intellectual now yearned for the very *Island* that he fashioned.

Huxley posits in his *Island* that humanity will always be subject to its egocentric ways; unfortunately, it has often had to learn the hard way that carnal pleasures are fleeting and that time must have a stop. While *Brave New World* may be his seminal work, *Island* is the synthesis of his beliefs. He must have known that it may take its place as his final fictional achievement, and as such, it does leave a lasting imprint. Within its pages may be found selections from the Old Raja's *Notes on What's What* that are lucidly the voice of the author speaking through the pages of a wisdom figure. For this is what Huxley had become in the later years of his life — a man of wisdom who had lived much, read much, and written even more. The Raja writes that the sorrow that humanity experiences is home grown — both without and within. Huxley advocated that people take the time, meditatively, to know themselves, and then to live in the moment of life by doing good. This is the creed underpinning *Island*— it is the essence of Huxley's soul in his final years.

FIVE

Standing Alone:
The Genius and the Goddess

He always returned to the single theme that dominated his later years:
the condition of men in the twentieth century. — Sir Isaiah Berlin[1]

Background and Plot Review

In 1955, Huxley published a unique novella entitled *The Genius and the Goddess*. He wrote it before, during, and after the Huxleys' trip to the Near East. As was the case with several of his novels of transformation (particularly *Ape and Essence* among the futuristic tales), this was a difficult task requiring many revisions. In the end, Huxley felt that it came "off pretty well."[2] The novella demands significant inquiry since it does not conveniently fall into any of the three genres posited in this writing. It is not a utopian tale, since it is a story told in the present looking back reflectively; nor is it a satiric novel, albeit it does dig into the foolish and inadequate thoughts, words and deeds of a misguided humanity. It certainly is not a transformative novel, although one could argue that the narrator is in a different time and place due to the happenings described in the tale. After reading the novella one is struck with the realization that this singular work stands alone as both an amalgam of parts and a unique piece in the Huxley collection.

This tightly woven short narrative is a first-person account of a John Rivers to an unnamed writer. It is a dramatic monologue of sorts because, through the telling of the tale, we learn so much about the narrator. Infrequently does the unknown listener interrupt and/or intrude on the narration. Coleridge's "Rime of the Ancient Mariner" comparatively comes to mind; within the poet's narrative, the old navigator tells a tale to a transfixed wedding guest as a liberating means to redemption, thereby temporarily, at least, converting the listener's perception of the world. Likewise, the frame of Huxley's story provides the means for the telling of the tale, but the reader knows from the start that this is reminiscence, a story set in the present about a past experience.

In the narrative, Rivers, Dr. Henry Maartens' former pupil and lab assistant, objects to the latest biography of the man since he knew him very well. He calls the edition "biographical fiction" because it cannot possibly render the true essence of the person. The interesting aspect of the narrative is that the chronicler knowingly relates the story to a writer who may use the storyline in his next novel. The anonymous listener promises that he will keep it a secret, but Rivers neither believes him nor requests that he do so. No matter, he states, as long as a footnote indicates that the main character bears no resemblance to anyone, living or dead.

One cannot help but look into Huxley's life and locate what was happening at the time of the writing. Huxley met and corresponded with a variety of individuals dealing with the issues of health, psychosomatics, psychopharmacology, hypnosis, and experimentation with mind-altering drugs for the purpose of a more heightened visionary awareness. Dr. Humphry Osmond, Carl Jung, and Dr. Roger Godel were among these learned individuals. In the case of Dr. Godel, Huxley — posing as a physician — accompanied him on his rounds while in Egypt. He writes that Godel epitomized what he always wanted to be, which was "a physician who is also a philosopher and psychologist."[3]

About the same time, Maria, Huxley's first wife, had been diagnosed with a terminal illness. She met with Dr. Mondor, a French specialist, to confirm the prognosis. She adamantly told him and her friends that she did not want Aldous to know of her illness: "He has a book to finish and must have peace of mind," she asserted. In addition, she maintained that she would not give in to the disease, because it would be wrong to die before Aldous: "How could he manage without me?"[4] The coincidence of a man of intelligence like the fictional Dr. Maartens desperately needing his wife Katy to survive, and Maria (the goddess) willing herself to live in order to care for her needy husband Aldous (the genius), is a biographical correlation that cannot be overlooked.

In 1954, the Huxleys found that their finances were low, and the prolific writer had no book in sight. They were to embark on an extensive journey to the Middle East — Egypt, Jerusalem, Lebanon, Cyprus, Greece — all paid for by Eileen Garrett's foundation. With lectures and visits with eminent persons along the way, Maria was to try her best to not let her illness hamper their plans. Ironically, when it was first brought to his attention that Maria might not be healthy enough to travel, Huxley himself fell ill for a couple of weeks,[5] another undeniable parallel to the novella's storyline. At any rate, Huxley was inspired during the journey to work on a fictional narrative that he originally entitled *Through the Wrong End of the Telescope*: he also suggested *The Past Is Prelude*, but it was later changed in December, 1955, to *The Genius and the Goddess*.[6]

Maria was dealing directly with mortality, a subject that Huxley had pondered and struggled with from his youth — brought about by his mother's untimely death and his brother Trevenan's tragic suicide. He had a constant fear of the insidious disease of cancer, and now he was subjected to — even though it was not directly discussed — the imminent death of his beloved wife from the ghastly illness that haunted him. He took mescalin and was hypnotized, along with Maria, to achieve the "Other Worldly" quality that they both sought even before the illness arrived.[7] He lectured in Washington at the Institute of Modern Art and read a paper he had written on visionary experiences to the students at Duke University and U.N.C.[8] A few days after his return, Maria was delighted to hear that *The Genius and the Goddess* was finally completed. As she wrote to her son, Matthew: "Aldous has just finished his best ever (I believe) long short story ... [and] there is Trev in it. I read it in M.S. ... it seems much stronger than anything else."[9] Hence, the life experience of Huxley filters into his fiction. Maria was to lose her battle a few months later after the novella's publication. The whole of the novel is not Huxley and Maria — be she Katy or Helen — nor Trevenan and his tragic lost love, but a reflection of a man who speaks of the past and the present as a "physician who is also a philosopher and a psychologist."[10]

Huxley was a sponge soaking in all of life's experiences. As he traveled through the squalor of Greece and on rounds with Dr. Godel, he looked also to the frail woman who he loved at his side and the images flowed into ideas, and those ideas became words that generated his novella. *The Genius and the Goddess* can be considered pure allegory — the figures of the past representative of abstract concepts that occupy the human mind, sometimes becoming tangible realities. The reader only knows Katy as "Goddess" and Maartens as "Genius" through the innocent eyes of Rivers; they become for him symbols of ideologies that he transmits to us as he speaks to the unknown listener. Four vital aspects of the novella are apparent from the beginning to the very end. First, there is the concept of time: the person we become is very much the essence of the person and experiences that we were — that is, if true growth has been achieved. Huxley was to write earlier that "the truth that perception and vision are largely dependent upon past experiences, as recorded by the memory, has been recognized for centuries."[11] Second, the ongoing struggle of what it means to be human — within and without — in our private soul and in relationships with others. Third, the yearning for that "Other Worldliness," which may be witnessed in authentic love, both physically and idealistically. Last, but not least, the finality of life in Death whose inevitability cannot be ignored.

The story takes place on Christmas Eve — a time of secular and religious anticipation filled with hope. While the present moment should be lived to its fullest, it requires the death of all past moments. Rivers explains that "Time regained is Paradise Lost." He continues, defining God as "the son of Immediate Experience."[12] Hence, one cannot dwell in the past but must dismiss it and live in the present moment (a lesson he learned from his wife, Helen). If one is to seriously heed Rivers' words, the past he is about to express is significant only to the degree that it makes the present moment meaningful. Hence, the analogy to Coleridge's tale of the mariner appears to fit. And so Rivers begins.

As the son of a Lutheran minister and later the possession of a widowed mother, the "shy, stupid, and hopelessly provincial" Rivers is astonished when, after receiving his Ph.D., Henry Maartens, a renowned physicist, invites him to be his lab assistant.[13] Maintaining his virginity until his wedding night — a promise he kept to his mother — Rivers leaves the "prison" his mother has provided for him and arrives at the Maartens's home feeling quite inadequate. Rapidly, however, he experiences authentic freedom that comes from living with genuine people; his life becomes pure poetry. So thrilling is his experience that he has to "debellish" — Rivers states, if there is such a word — his weekly letters to his mother so that she will not perceive his utter joy while in another place away from her. The Maartens insist he live with them rather than take lodging elsewhere. Soon he is running errands for Mrs. Maartens; reading Ruth's lifeless poetry (both in subject matter and form); tutoring young Timmy; becoming Beulah's Prodigal Son; driving Mr. Maartens to his laboratory; and falling madly in love with the most beautiful woman on earth.

Henry Maartens is described as a self-centered, detached individual who lives off of Katy Maartens — he is incapable of doing anything without her devoted attention which she gives freely. The resemblance to the head and heart counterparts of Philip and Eleanor Quarles in *Point Counter Point*, or even the impractical Rampion and socially graceful Mary (in the same work) is striking.[14] Henry's manifest feature is his total disregard for all humanity, mainly because he is not aware of his own. His life is centered on quantum theory and epistemology, with sex between the two. His wife is his material counterpart in body, in social graces, and in soul. The genius cannot live or function without his goddess. It would be difficult to call the interdependence "love" since the relationship is one-sided — Katy gives and Henry takes. The man finds not only children but most adults boring and incompetent for they had nothing to offer his superior intellect

Rivers spends many an evening with Mrs. Maartens. They read, and she speaks of the three men who courted her, and her broken engagement to a wealthy gentleman because of Henry Maartens — a man old enough to be her father. How different her life would be today if she had married the person who had her parents' approval rather than Henry. Rivers listens to her with rapture — he has fallen deeply in love with her — "metaphysically, almost theologically."[15] Nevertheless, she was Henry's wife and it is beyond moral and ethical reason to suppose anything will come of it. Fifteen months of this bliss transpires — with the exception of a ten-week period when the family spends the summer in Maine and he is forced to return to his metaphorical prison with his mother.

Much of this narrative of Rivers is tongue-in-cheek, the ramblings of an older gentleman looking back at the inexperience of one's youth. And yet there is a graceful, kind, and empathetic tone in the recall. Rivers explains that he was to spend a great deal of his spare time with Ruth — the fourteen-year-old daughter of the Maartens — taking nature walks, gathering caterpillars, and talking about her obsession with Death. They take a walk one night while at the Maartens's farmhouse in the country. A stray horse appears in the dark, but Ruth is scared and insists it is a ghost. Rivers enjoys participating in the ritual of fear. Ruth tries to relate Poe's "The Fall of the House of Usher"; Rivers marvels at how she is so absorbed with death and corruption in the evening, yet the following morning she is vibrant and sings, "If You Were the Only Girl in the World." He then ruminates on the fact that the song was written during World War I, revived during World War II and revived yet again while the slaughter was going on in Korea. He wonders if, while looking back at all three massacres, one should not feel despair about the human race. (Certainly Huxley's pacifistic doctrine is underpinning these remarks.)

The attentiveness given to Ruth is mistaken by the impressionable young lady. Rejected by the star football player at school, Rivers becomes her main infatuation. Rivers rejects her proclamations of love by insulting her poetry and ignoring her. Jealousy sets in as the young lady intuitively feels that Rivers prefers her mother — which he does — and he marvels at how she could possibly have known such a thing. Katy Maartens is called to her mother's deathbed in Chicago, and almost immediately upon her departure, Henry becomes irritable and has paroxysms of his asthma. Believing she is to return, he comes alive again and even plays with the children. But this is short lived as her absence continues. He goes out one night and becomes very drunk, walks home and loses his briefcase containing chapters of his latest book that had to be redone. When Katy's stay at her mother's home is prolonged because her mother may actually recover, he imagines that his wife is having an affair with the doctor.

One night in a stupor of self-indulgent anguish and rage — after learning that Katy's absence would be extended — Maartens grabs hold of the defenseless Rivers and provides graphic details of the couple's past and Katy's insatiable sexual appetite. The account at first blemishes Rivers's perception of the goddess, yet it also intrigues him. Suddenly, Henry Maartens becomes very ill and is confined to his bed. Beulah relates the story of how this had happened before when Mrs. Maartens took a European vacation that had to be cut short. Henry Maartens cannot live without the care of his wife; Rivers speculates on the power of psychosomatic illness. (Once again, Huxley's association with Godel and Osmond and others in this field of research can be seen as influencing the fictional account.)

It appears that Mrs. Maartens's mother may recover, but this is transitory since once again there is a relapse. Torn between the prospects of death at both ends of her being — mother and husband — Mrs. Maartens at last gives in to her husband's demands and returns home. Rivers describes her as pale and without "virtue," the quality that Beulah prays will return so that Mr. Maartens may recover. (It is here that Huxley uses Rivers as a mouthpiece in a soliloquy about death and those who minister to the dying.)

The prospect of death affects both the dying and those who minister to them, Rivers relates. The dying may eventually welcome death to end their misery; ironically, in this case, life and death are identical as in the maxim "Give me liberty or give me death."[16] But the nurse or caregiver must always continue to maintain a cheerful exterior, ever fighting the battle even when the patient has given up all hope. This wears on the caregiver — mentally, emotionally, and physically. And so, Rivers looks at Katy Maartens and declares that she is "bankrupt." He, at 28, did not have any experience with death. Yet, that evening, Katy Maartens turns to him for solace and understanding.

Rivers remembers the date — April 23, 1922 — as his "spiritual birthday," for that night, in trying to console the anguished goddess who had just learned of her mother's death, the two made love.[17] She had awakened him from his sleep — she was crying because she was "all alone" — death was all around her: first her mother and now the possibility of her husband. Reaching for her cold hands, Rivers moved her under the covers and then he followed suit. The four elements of the novella come together in this one scene. Here is the horrendous face of death beaming powerfully in their path; here are the two trying to leave this world of torture and enter into the wonders of the "Other World" of love; and as this humanity struggles for consolation in each other's arms — the metaphorical act of at least one divided soul — the clock strikes, "a symbol of time's incessant passage."[18]

And so the struggle of a humanity that knows what it should do, yet does just the opposite, begins. Rivers explains that Katy Maartens was a goddess — she had faced the abyss and sought consolation in an act of love. It was natural for her and, therefore, good — there was no guilt or self-incrimination. But for Rivers — the son of a Lutheran minister, a widow's consolation, and a virgin in mind as well as body — it was difficult to cope with his remorse. He was a divided soul whose sin was even worse because he enjoyed it so much.

Rivers explains the dilemma by drawing three lines in the air: one representing Katy Rivers, the other the John Rivers of 30 years ago, and the third the John Rivers of today. While Katy was beyond goodness and he mired with the imprint of sin, the John Rivers of today can see both as half right and yet wholly wrong. With the lies beginning the following day — Katy would ask Beulah if Rivers had been told of her mother's death and he would need to call the woman he made love to the night before Mrs. Maartens — John Rivers feels like a criminal. For like Macbeth in Shakespeare's tragedy, his host had been kind to him; he should not have betrayed that trust. And yet he continues to betray it.

Renewed in body and spirit, both of which are nurtured by her nights of pleasure with John, Katy Maartens's "virtue" returns, and her husband begins to recover, a sign that Beulah ironically terms the "Grace of God."[19] Rivers rationalizes: Had he not been the reason why the woman beamed with grace and vitality once more? Indirectly, was he not the reason why Henry Maartens did not die? Did this not render the act of love as good and not evil? No matter, he feels like a sham as he goes about his daily activities; his guilt is destroying him, yet Katy Maartens refuses to speak to him about it. And each evening with the children still away, she comes to him and they continue their liaison of pleasure.

Rivers digresses about spiritual grace, animal grace, and human grace.[20] He indicates that all three are part of the same mystery. Humans, however, either close themselves off completely from all three, or only allow one of them to enter, which is never enough. The morning of April 24, Katy Maartens's animal grace has been restored, and although Rivers has resolved that he will leave, he changes his mind when he sees Katy in all of her transcendent beauty.

Rivers tries to tell Katy that he loves her and that he is tormented by his lustful and traitorous actions, but she stops him from speaking, or pats him on the hand and dismisses it. Rivers once more soliloquizes about a subject, in this case, "Words, words, words."[21] With an analogy to Hamlet's words to Polonius, Rivers explains that, in silence, an act is just what it is; but when spoken or discussed, it becomes an ethical issue. Therefore, he has learned to remain silent, but the dialogical struggle within his mind torments him.

One evening he fears that his betrayal has become known when Henry Maartens, on the road to recovery, asks to speak with him. John did not need to worry — it was merely an apology for his ranting about Katy on an earlier evening when he was distraught; none of it was true and Rivers is asked to blot it from his memory. Maartens admits that, without her, he would have gone mad or died. Rivers continues to think of himself and Katy as "a pair of cheats, conspiring against a simpleton."[22] Finally, one evening, Rivers is able to relate to Katy all that he is feeling. She laughs at him — not a laugh of derision — but one of amusement. She asks if he ever thought of anyone other than himself? What of her? What of a woman constantly fighting against the crazy intellect of a genius? She dismisses his "Sunday School Twaddle" and turns away from him so that he is gazing only at the exquisite back of "Aphrodite."[23] Rivers wonders if she thought that their consummation was inevitable — wonders if there were others at another time, in another place. He, however, never receives an answer to his contemplation.

Rivers finds himself loving Katy Maartens insatiably — beyond all limits. She fears that his very gaze on her will reveal their secret — they had to be "sensible," since Henry is recovering and the children are returning.[24] Perhaps reflective of her concern, she is a changed woman on the day the family is reunited; Rivers describes her as "too all seeing."[25] She inspects Timmy's ears and goes into a tirade about Ruth's cosmetics, throwing the make-up kit into the garbage and pouring the perfume down the toilet. As a result, Ruth does not speak to anyone for days. The hatred is brewing within her.

Ruth is a young woman being treated as an "irresponsible child."[26] The complexity is that she hates her mother, because she is jealous of her mother's relationship with the man that she "loves" and who had rejected her. All of this is conflicted within her. With Henry's full recovery, the doctor recommends a stay in the country. John and Katy are to travel there with a picnic lunch to ready the place for occupancy. Ruth fumes at the fact that she will not be included because she has to go to school. Rivers and her mother will be alone — her suspicions are confirmed in her mind. She sets about solidifying these suspicions in the form of a poem she will craft.

Rivers comes into the living room the day before the trip to the farmhouse and asks if he may read Ruth's poem. She indicates that it is not finished, but she will gladly provide him with a copy when it is. The following morning he finds on the table a mauve envelope addressed to him; it contains the poem which he inattentively places in his jacket pocket and takes with him. At the farmhouse — in full view of "Big Brother" (namely a massive portrait of Henry and a mirror reflecting the lovers), he and Katy make love. These are symbols of his guilt. A short time later, as he is putting on his jacket, he feels Ruth's envelope and reads her poem.

The poem is a narrative of a faithless wife and her lover before the Last Judgment. All of their garments are removed and they stand naked and transparent. There is a detailed description of their internal organs, and the verse concludes with a crowd denouncing their actions and calling for vengeance. Rivers understands that jealousy and rejection, mixed with injured pride, has produced anger and now the ultimate: righteous indignation. He hands the poem to Katy, who at first accepts it with the usual amusement she shows all of Ruth's poetry, but soon she is quietly pondering its intent.

Katy articulates her dilemma: if she does nothing, Ruth will continue in her assertive righteous anger; if she openly confronts Ruth, there will be no telling what the young juvenile might do. Of course, she needs to maintain her home, her family, and her relationship with Henry, who needs her so completely. On the way back to the Maartens's home, John and Katy discuss what is to be done. Rivers insists that the only legitimate choice is his departure; Katy reluctantly agrees. Upon their return, Ruth baits John by asking him what he thinks of her poem. He answers that it is the best she has written. Prepared for the question about its subject matter, Rivers laughs and says that it resembles one of his father's sermons during Lent. With a chuckle, he immediately leaves the room, evading any further discussion.

Rivers's letter from his mother — a Friday ritual — offers the opportunity for the pretense of deteriorating health. Consequently, Henry gives him a two-weeks leave. In the interim, on Saturday morning, they pack up two cars — Katy driving the first with Ruth and Timmy in tow; Henry Maartens, Beulah and the luggage in the second, which Rivers is to drive. They are to have one last picnic together before he leaves. The first car is far ahead of Rivers's because, as usual, Henry has forgotten some book at home, forcing them to return. When, however, they are just two miles from the farmhouse, they encounter the treacherous turn where visibility is hampered by overgrown trees and the woods. One had to always honk one's horn before turning. When Rivers and his passengers make the turn, the scene around the corner is one of devastation: Katy's car is upside-down in a ditch and, near it, a big truck with its radiator smashed. There is a man in blue denims, a young child screaming, and two bundles nearby with blood stains on them. Katy dies a few minutes later; Ruth in the ambulance; and Timmy is saved for a more horrible death at Okinawa some time later.

The young boy explains that Ruth and Katy were in the front seat and he was in the rear; he did not understand what their argument was about because he was thinking of something else, and besides, he mostly ignored them when they were engaged in an altercation. He could only recall that Katy stated that Ruth did not know what she was talking about and that she forbade her to say such things. They were talking and not paying attention to the road. Katy did not honk the horn; she took the turn too fast and hit the truck broadside. Rivers speaks of Predestination, applying it to events and to the temperaments of two people — Katy and Ruth. He theorizes that Katy — the goddess — had lost her divinity for a moment and lapsed into the destructive mode of vulnerable humanity, making a deadly error in judgment.

The gruesome memory of Katy's mangled body haunts him and causes him to contemplate suicide. That is, until Helen comes along. Predestination is at work again because she saves him, ironically at the same cocktail party that the listener within the frame story attended — a party at which the listener is vanquished by Rivers in his bid to woo Helen. The silent presence knows that Rivers cannot help but be successful — he is so handsome, intelligent and unhappy — a trio of qualities that destroyed the competition.

As a postscript, Rivers is asked what became of Henry. He explains that the old man lived to the age of 87 — still full of what his biographer called "the undiminished blaze of intellectual power."[27] But, to John, Henry's real presence was long gone the last time he saw him — just the tapes running, but inside there was still that miserable being who required flattery and sex and a "womb substitute."[28] Henry became ill for a while after Katy's death, but to no avail since he could not get anything in return for his illness. He found consolation in Katy's fat widowed sister whom he married just four months later. Her obesity did her in, but Henry quickly found a replacement in a young, physically and intellectually gifted redhead named Alicia; she was to remain with him until the end.

Rivers concludes his tale and bids his quest goodnight as well as a Merry Christmas. He warns him, however, that since it is Christmas Eve in a Christian country, he needs to be careful, since everyone will be drunk.

The Genius and the Goddess: Looking Beneath the Surface

There is no fictional work by Huxley designed in the manner of *The Genius and the Goddess*; it is short, concise, direct, and if at any time Huxley allows his protagonist to philosophize, it is very brief and intrinsically clear. Occasionally in the course of the story, the frame comes into play with some aspects of Rivers's current life interrupting the recollected narrative. For example, his young grandson Bimbo awakens and Rivers, the grandfather, tenderly holds him; much to his grandson's delight, he imitates a variety of dog barks, and then takes the youngster on a tour of various rooms. Ultimately, as he holds the child in his arms, the two view their forms in a full-length mirror. Rivers calls his guest over to survey the scene.

While gazing into the mirror, he ruminates that it is amazing how we all start off as a "lump of protoplasm" and grow through so many stages, degenerating eventually into one or more of a variety of gorillas.[29] The Wordsworthian concept of the child being father of the man is engaged here. Rivers goes on to remark that it is a shame that the little one, who gazes so peacefully back at them in his crib, must go through so much anguish and agony in the seventy years or so of life. But the guest adds that there is also much fun to experience. Oh, yes, "fun," Rivers agrees. There are many traps waiting for Bimbo, but there is solace in the fact that he will be ignorant before he falls into each one of them, and he will have the treasured human luxury of forgetfulness afterward.

A second interruption is the arrival home of his daughter Molly and his son-in-law Fred. The latter never even utters a word of acknowledgment; Molly states that she has a splitting headache and that the party was "stinking."[30] The two quickly retreat to bed. Rivers once again ponders the concept of Predestination. After all, he had three daughters. They were all brought up by a loving, non-possessive mother, and a father who tried to follow his wife's example. Yet, two of them were married and happy, and then there was Molly — dismal and lost. Bimbo was destined to either be the child of a divorced mother subjected to a series of lovers, or the son of two people who torture each other. Either way he will go through hell, and nothing can be done about it. Maybe he will come out of it stronger; maybe he will be damaged. Perhaps this is the inner Predestination of Temperament versus the Predestination of Events that transpired between Katy and Ruth. Who knows?

Rivers does contemplate his deceased wife Helen; he had been in pleasant competition with his guest for her ardent attention. Helen, he recalls, really knew how to live each moment and taught others by example without ever preaching. He reflects that there is an art to dying, one we should learn. Helen studied it to perfection because she knew exactly how to live; in living each day she was dying by degrees. When the final stage came, there was little left to give. (Once again there is the connection biographically to Huxley when Rivers remarks that the previous year he had been at death's door with pneumonia. Maria's illness, his own recent poor health, the view of disease and death on rounds in Greece, and contemplation of the mystical quality in both living and dying were ruminating within Huxley as he crafted his fictional tale.)

Reflecting on the story he has related to his guest, Rivers ruminates about his guilty conscience after the blissful occasion of his apocalyptic moment with Katy. He recalls that, shortly thereafter, he heard the words "Vile, Base, Foul," like woodpeckers intruding on his psyche. Rivers acknowledges that our language is often inadequate — that words get in the way of emotions — that at 60 years of age, one forgets what words even mean. Unfortunately, all the language of morality consists of bad words. But Vile, Base, and Foul are words that exist in this world, but never exist in the Other

World. The "Other World" is beyond language — good or bad — and time-less before, during, and after a union of love. Lust and adultery debase the dignity of the "Other World," but if one remains within it, all is good. He speaks of the "Otherer," and "Otherness," and the quality of sacredness that comes about in the suspension of time and place when he lies next to Katy in the indefinable "Other World." (This is the "Other Worldliness" that Huxley and his bride were trying to experience through hypnosis or mind-altering drugs. Is it possible to reach that state of *nirvana* even temporarily through sexual consummation? Huxley posits this question within the narrative.)

Rivers continues: "How can one seriously believe in his own identity?"[31] He looks back at the John Rivers who felt that way about Katy Maartens and it is very much like looking through the wrong end of the opera glasses. All of life changed at that moment — everything was spectacular and beautiful. Everything had significance. He asks the question: Why does one love a woman? The answer is "because she is."[32] Tantamount to the Biblical statement of God, "I Am Who I Am," in his union with Katy Maartens, Rivers came to live in this "other world" even while present in an earthly cosmos. Within the awareness of self and the world around one, Rivers finds an essence that did not exist previously.

Often characters within Huxley's novels find that they should not pursue a lustful pleasure for its own sake when the person with whom they are coupling is not an object of their love (Calamy and Chelifer, for example). In this short novel, however, Rivers, the idealist, finds that the alluring object of his love becomes even more divine when he reaches out and satisfies what was once regarded as a base instinct. John Rivers loves Katy Maartens even more after their sexual union than he did before. Time and circumstances — the mores of society — demand that he end the affair and leave his love; her death along with Ruth's predestines an immediate termination of an otherwise irreconcilable situation. The John Rivers of 1954 (the time of the writing and the telling) can make no judgment — the words (in the modern age) have even changed from lust and adultery to "drives, urges, [and] extra-marital intimacies."[33] The desolation of emotions following the deadly incident predestines the arrival of Helen in his life, she who believed in living each moment and letting the "dead bury their dead" in the wasteland of memory.[34] It would appear that several pronouncements result from the cumulative effect of predestined moments as presented in the novel.

First, love has an element of transcendence for both the one loved and the lover himself. While Rivers speaks of love, Katy never needs to; while he loves her before the union, she seeks him in a moment of desperation. Their lovemaking is enjoyable to both, and Katy even wants him to remain, but he convinces her that he must leave. The apocalyptic quality of their union remains with Rivers — and probably would have remained with Katy Maartens also, if given the opportunity — and that will never be destroyed by the ravages of time.

Secondly, human beings are subjects of nature and nurture, yet even with this understanding, there are mysteries of grace and predestined dispositions and events over which one has little or no control. The union of Katy and John may have been inevitable; the end of their affair also a certainty. The arrival of Helen into John's life at a time of suffering is pure grace; the deaths of Katy and Ruth pure mystery.

Finally, the inevitability of death is with us every moment of each day. Better yet, one's mortality is tested in the very act of living. We are all "moving towards the same consummation."[35] Yet despite the pain and anguish and suffering that is inevitable, there is always joy — "fun" as Rivers and his guest call it. It is the fun of life that brings us closer to the Other World for which we yearn.

The Genius and the Goddess is a simple story. Within its simplicity the depth of philosophical understanding of its creator may be missed or misunderstood. Huxley wrote an uncomplicated story wherein he casts a light on people trying to come to terms with life in the present moment that is inescapably intertwined with the past. In essence, each moment fully lived becomes the fabric of a past that cyclically determines who we are. The 61-year-old Huxley writing the narrative, in many ways, is the John Rivers telling the story; the thematic intent inescapably reflects the man creating it. The Huxley who wrote three transformative novels, and whose last lengthy fictional venture reflected his ongoing quest for spiritual enlightenment, is the older and wiser John Rivers, philosophically at peace in the moment, and fully comprehending the meaningful import of the past. In many ways, *The Genius and the Goddess* depicts an enlightened Huxley yearning for a unity of body, mind and spirit — a union he would come to achieve and espouse in his final utopian venture, *Island*. The concept of time ever consummately explored in his novels is underscored by the realization that time must have a stop; in the meantime, as is clearly evident in Rivers's case and profoundly expressed by one of Huxley's compatriots, "We beat on, boats against the current, borne back ceaselessly into the past."[36]

SIX

Integration and Conclusion

> Man has no Body distinct from his Soul for that call'd
> Body is a portion of the Soul discern'd by the five senses,
> the chief inlets of Soul in this age. — William Blake[1]

Huxley's Call for the Union of Two Cultures

Laura Archera Huxley, the widow of Aldous Huxley, quotes these words from William Blake's *The Marriage of Heaven and Hell* in her essay which introduces a later-discovered and never-before-published screenplay, *Jacob's Hands*, which her husband wrote in 1944 in collaboration with Christopher Isherwood. The subject of her essay and the screenplay itself focuses on the theme of healing. She remarks that her husband and she had spent a considerable amount of time discussing and researching healing in all of its forms, orthodox and unorthodox. Although Aldous Huxley was hopeful that in union with Isherwood their combined talents would produce a saleable script that would "solve a lot of economic problems and will make it unnecessary to go into slavery at one of the studios," the script was universally rejected.[2]

Huxley and Isherwood at first did not understand why this was the case, but in July of 1944 it had become clear to Huxley that the medical profession had created such a fuss over its storyline that no studio would touch it. There was a misunderstanding of its thematic intent since doctors were interpreting the screenplay as an endorsement of spiritual healing over mainstream medical treatment. Huxley explains that the doctors were mistaken since the central character's "biggest medical success is a moral failure, [and] his biggest moral success is a medical failure, he retires from all but veterinary business because he feels he can't use his gift rightly."[3]

Huxley once again found his intent misunderstood. The plot of the screenplay involves a simple rancher living a quiet life in California's Mojave Desert in the 1920s. Jacob Ericson inadvertently discovers that his hands hold the special power of healing. A deeply spiritual man, he gives his gift freely, at first, for purely compassionate reasons. Soon the materialistic world latches onto him, and compromised by his own selfish interest in Sharon — a woman he adores — he is coerced into using his gift for worldly, mundane, and temporal pleasures, which ultimately leads to tragedy. Finally Jacob must take himself and his gift far away from the secular world, living simply in the desert, using his ability rarely and purely for humane purposes.

An analogy could be drawn between Jacob's gift of healing and the many tangible gifts granted to mankind. Used for the enhancement of one's humanity — a concept closely allied in Huxley's thinking with one's essence or one's soul — all technologies can improve humanity's well-being; used arrogantly for material gain, control, and senseless delights, it will exact its toll, eroding the very essence of what it means to be human, creating a race of mindless, senseless, and hopeless creatures.

In his final novel, *Island*, Huxley reflects on the harmonious union of Western technological enterprise with an Eastern mystical view of human purpose and destiny. The life led by the noble people on this island represents Huxley's hope for the future of mankind. While baptized in the Anglican faith, Huxley grew up in an agnostic generation. By the 1930s his writings began to show a definite interest in finding a spiritual dimension to life, although there are traces of this search in his earlier novels *Antic Hay* and *Those Barren Leaves*, and certainly in *Point Counter Point*. He never accepted a formal religion, however, and he was finally content to advocate his own holistic vision of spirituality based on Eastern and Western mysticism. Throughout his literary career as a social satirist, he indiscriminately attacked the orthodox restrictions of Christianity. While he was attracted to the mystical teachings of Catholic saints, Huxley was also fascinated by religious scandals. Two historical studies, *Grey Eminence* (1941) and *The Devils of Loudun* (1952) are particularly critical of French religious practices.

Huxley came to accept self-transcendent meditation as the means to enlightenment. The practice of withdrawing in silence from the material world in order to reach a heightened state of edification is a principle in keeping with the religious doctrines of the East and the West. Within an action-oriented, materialistically driven Western world, it may be harder to attain and maintain, but it is a practical approach to life advocated by many devout religious practitioners. Buddhist principles such as non-violence, silent meditation, and the union of God with the whole of life — principles that were not always in keeping with the Christian view of God as a separate entity and the historically violent inclinations of the West — were to move Huxley more in the direction of Eastern religious thought. He was to read selections from *The Tibetan Book of the Dead* to Maria as she lay dying, repeating the mantra as he placed his hands upon her, "Let go, let go ... go forward into the light."[4]

One of Huxley's basic religious principles is that the earthly ego or greedy self is the enemy of the spirit. This core belief is found in Buddhist teachings, in Hindu scripture, and in the Christian gospels. In 1925, Huxley could unselfconsciously write to a friend and fellow novelist this spiritual advice found in his readings:

> It gives the reasons why it is necessary to lose one's life in order to gain it: because it is impossible to have a real and absolute self, so long as the superficial self is allowed to control things. It is the sacrifice of one's egoism for the sake of realizing another and much profounder egoism.[5]

The progression to self-transcendence was illustrated fictionally in Huxley's description of characters struggling against the burden of egoism — beginning with *Eyeless in Gaza*, continuing in *After Many a Summer Dies the Swan* and *Time Must Have a Stop*, and culminating with his extensive commentary in *Island*. In fact, Huxley's editors demanded extensive cuts in his last novel because of the lengthy philosophical expositions.[6]

If there was one repeated criticism of Huxley's novels, it was his use of fiction to not just tell a story but to convey ideas. Huxley unabashedly reveals in an early interview that his main reason for writing was to illuminate an outlook on life that he had at that particular point in time. He does not write for his readers, he states, but rather to clarify a particular outlook for himself: "My books represent different stages towards such an outlook." Each book is a stage and it is a provisional one since he believed that humanity is ever working towards a "comprehensive outlook on the world."[7] In his own words captured in this 1931 interview, we have the essence of the man's intent through each work of fiction examined in this study. Is it any wonder that in the genre of the commercial theater — whether in an adaptation of a novel or an original work — Huxley was to find little success? In a visual medium it is very difficult to convey so many complex and, at times, contrary thoughts. In his essays, however, Huxley was unrestricted in articulation, and here he found the balance between expression and ideas.

Accordingly, he clearly expounds on the age-old debate between the two disciplines of art and science in *Literature and Science*, a collection of essays published in 1963, the year of his death. "Snow or Leavis?" he asks at the opening of the treatise which highlights the famous public argument between the literary critic F.R. Leavis and the science proponent C.P. Snow in the early 1960s. Huxley proposes that the answer lies in the synthesis of the two, not in the continued isolation of one from the other. While both the scientist and the artist inhabit the same world, the scientist, through observation, produces abstract principles that explain material phenomena. Since knowledge is power, these principles invariably control, or at least modify, the environment presumably for beneficial purposes, but sometimes with disastrous results. On the other hand, Huxley explains, the literary artist gives imaginative expression to the whole of human aspirations. The writer is not concerned with changing the physical world but in transforming our vision of the human condition and its possibilities. Hence, Huxley's explanation underscores his intent in writing fictional works, a clarification that could serve as a response to those critical of his narrative techniques.

Huxley recognized that the responsibility of a writer was not always easy to fulfill. Yet he was to successfully satirize the artist's struggle between the aesthetic and the profane in his early novels; stimulate the mind of the reader to wonder what might transpire if human foibles exponentially proliferate in his futuristic tales; and ultimately render a series of transformative beings who have finally attained a new paradigm — a new and intriguing perception of the world. Upon close examination, one may find within Huxley's canon an artist ever pursuing a fusion of two cultures — of philosophy with fictional narrative, of literature with science.

On recalling his own family background, Huxley could see how the scientific bias of his grandfather T.H. Huxley was contrasted with the humanistic writings of his granduncle Matthew Arnold. He asserts, however, that "one can be a practicing scientist without sacrificing one's love or one's understanding of literature."[8] Huxley instances his grandfather, the scientist and champion of Darwinism, who proclaimed that he had found all fields of human knowledge attractive or worthy of his interest. He shows how a Romantic poet, William Wordsworth, could praise the beauty of rainbows and yet admire the science of Isaac Newton, who demonstrated that the phenomenon was merely refracted light.

Literature allows for the free play of thought and imaginative speculation, and Huxley argues that his own favorite genres, the novel and the essay, are the categories that allow for the most digression. If the writing is skillful, any ideas can be examined in an essay and almost any theme, whether public or private, can find expression in a novel. In a scientific age, the socially conscious writer needs to focus not only on the present but also the future. Accordingly, the author has three responsibilities: to convey skillfully shaped human experiences through words; to relate these experiences in an imaginative way that is compatible with reality; and to support the principle that people are responsible for those decisions that will make a better world.[9]

Huxley insists that "literature gives a form to life, helps us to know who we are, how we feel and what the point of the whole unutterably rummy business is."[10] The means of understanding the whole point of existence is a knowledge that involves both literature and science. Literary writers, for example, may not have the deep knowledge of a specialist, but they must acquire at least a broad understanding of how science influences their society.[11] Likewise, intelligent scientists cannot divorce their discoveries or their applied technologies from human experience. It is obvious today that powerful technologies can prove more deadly than any innovations of the past. Therefore, one responsibility of thoughtful writers — according to Huxley — is to draw attention to this danger and to demonstrate that the quality of life should be the goal of all human endeavors, including all technological achievements.[12]

Huxley successfully posits in *Literature and Science* a fusion of the two cultures in a lucid manner. The fusion he advocates is one in which "the traffic of learning and understanding must flow in both directions — from science to literature, as well as from literature to science."[13] In this treatise calling for a new holistic attitude toward natural reality, Huxley claims that Eastern thought or animistic tradition demonstrates that the soundest criticism of modern science is more Buddhist than Christian and more Totemistic than Greek.[14] This is Huxley's credo at the conclusion of his life. *Literature and Science* invites the scientist and the literary artist to travel together in exploring the endless unknown.

The themes set forth in this last collection of essays were explored imaginatively in the novel *Island*. Huxley's ultimate message is that only a basic shift in human attitudes would foster a spirit of universal harmony and mitigate incessant suffering. Huxley's prophecy was that if countries continued to apply technologies toward destructive ends, the world would not have a future. This threat can be avoided, however, if the mind and heart of humanity is changed. If not, either humanity will annihilate itself in a nuclear holocaust, or participate in the "revolutionary revolution," much as he describes in his foreword to *Brave New World*:

> The people who govern the Brave New World may not be sane (in what may be called the absolute sense of the word); but they are not madmen, and their aim is not anarchy but social stability. It is in order to achieve stability that they carry out, by scientific means, the ultimate, personal, really revolutionary revolution.[15]

The contemporary reader of Huxley's futuristic novels, therefore, will not find the verisimilitude that one detects, for example, in Michael Crichton's *Jurassic Park*. Huxley's purpose was not to describe precisely which machines or hardware would be developed in the future. He is more interested in what will happen to future generations as a result of these possible technologies. Huxley's main scientific interests lay in the fields of biology, physiology, and psychology, areas in which he can be remarkably prophetic. In this sense, Huxley's final novel *Island* is both a hopeful blueprint and a dire warning of future possibilities.

Island: A Possible Ideal?

In framing an ideal we may assume what we wish,
but should avoid impossibilities.—Aristotle[16]

Nobody needs to go anywhere else. We are all,
if we only knew it, already there.— Huxley[17]

After her husband's death, Laura Archera Huxley reflected on the significance of his last novel. She reveals that her husband was unhappy over the critical reception of *Island*, especially by readers who did not take the novel seriously. The modes of living described in *Island* were not fantasy, she insists, but practices that had been observed in various cultures. She further maintains that the ideals envisioned by Huxley in *Island* were not hopelessly utopian but could be attained in the here and now.[18] And yet, in contrast, was Huxley not consciously aware that the ideals he envisioned may not be achievable as evidenced in his citing Aristotle in the epigraph to his final novel?

What are the ideals to which she alludes? In the final act of his life the "ideal" for Aldous Huxley was a total awareness of self in each moment — to be aware unremittingly to each moment and one's presence in it. Hence, it is appropriate that the mynah bird shouts "Attention" in the first word of his final novel *Island*—"attention" to the moment of existence and to all that it imparts lest we are lost in remembrance or anxious about the future. The art of knowing who we are fosters a "Good Being," and a "good being" results in "good doing." To achieve this end, Huxley recommends within his narrative that there be a constant need to concentrate, to engage in abstract thinking, and to practice the spiritual exercises that are part and parcel of the authentic yoga.[19]

In 1998, some 35 years after Huxley's death, Dr. Howard C. Cutler assembled the teachings of His Holiness, the Dalia Lama, in a published work entitled *The Art of Happiness: A Handbook for Living*. Upon close examination it becomes evident that the words of His Holiness are the essence of where Huxley had arrived at the conclusion of his life. His Holiness writes that the mind — better yet the psyche, the spirit, the heart combined with the mind — needs to be disciplined in order to transform its perception of the world.[20] The resultant inner contentment will lead one "not to have what we want but rather to want and appreciate what we have."[21] Freedom — true Liberation — will come about when one reaches the stage of highest happiness, a stage where there is no longer any suffering.[22] Perhaps the Dalai Lama may not have approved of the chemically enhanced means that Huxley sought at the end of his life to improve his passageway to enlightenment, but the two do share an identical vision of the path to authentic personal happiness.

Although *Brave New World* remains today as a seminal work in exposing the dangerous tendencies in the modern world's view of progress, *Island*, Huxley's synthesis on the subject of scientific advancement founded on humane principles, may hold an equally strong claim to the interests of the contemporary reader. The island of Pala had achieved a humanly centered relationship to its technology, thereby serving as a consummate model for the modern world. In an interview, Huxley's widow labeled the novel her late husband's legacy — within it may be found glimpses of the whole panorama of Aldous Huxley's life.[23]

Huxley's Legacy

When he was dying of cancer, Huxley asked his wife to give him an injection of LSD. Since he had not taken the drug for over two years, Laura regarded this request as similar to the custom described in *Island*, in which a mind-enhancing drug (the moksha-medicine) is given in extreme circumstances. She recognized this as evidence of Huxley's complete awareness and his acceptance of imminent death. She later described his death as a peaceful transition when "the breathing became slower — and slower — and slower — the ceasing of life was not a drama at all, but a piece of music just finishing."[24]

Aldous Huxley died on the same day that John F. Kennedy was assassinated. The passing of a writer of less magnitude may have been missed by a media that covered every aspect of the tragic murder of a president. Aldous Huxley's death, however, received front-page coverage in the *New York Times* alongside news of the preparations for Kennedy's funeral. Characterized in this obituary as occupying a seat at the literary pinnacle, Huxley's *Brave New World* is said to have set a model for writers of his generation. Huxley's mind is compared in its curiosity to that of his grandfather Thomas Henry Huxley as it probed both the commonplace and the esoteric.[25] He was also eulogized as a distinguished author, scholar, essayist, and moralist by *Time* and *Newsweek* magazines in the weeks following his death. [26]

Orville Prescott indicates in a companion piece to Huxley's obituary in the *New York Times* that "the death of Aldous Huxley removes from the world one of the most brilliant, learned and versatile of 20th century writers."[27] Prescott asserts that Huxley, outraged by the horrors of war and the cruelty of man, had journeyed on his own road to Damascus, and there he was to find refuge in mystical experiences. Ironically, as a result, he ended up alienating two camps of readers: those who enjoyed his early satires did not take kindly to his mystical pursuits, and those who admired his mysticism were upset by his urbane prose. As a result, Huxley was deemed far more popular and critically praised in the 1920s and 1930s than he was in the last decades of his life.[28]

Aldous Huxley was a 20th century writer whose acute intelligence, literary skill, and social conscience have illuminated some of the most pressing problems of modern society. Living through the first two-thirds of the 20th century, he saw how technological progression had come to support the dubious assumption that, since the standard of living has improved, a happier, healthier, and saner world has resulted. The common masses who were absorbed in this material world had little inclination to question whether modern methods and machines were improving or harming human welfare. Social critics and writers have, however, observed the human condition and pondered on the possible future of civilization.

Modern technology has obviously bred a machine culture that depends on labor-saving devices and mass-produced possessions. Sensing the futility of this obsessive materialism, perceptive thinkers from philosophers to psychotherapists have urged moderation and detachment as the authentic way to human fulfillment. Among these proponents, Aldous Huxley can be viewed as a gifted writer who successfully combined narrative mastery with the moral intent to challenge the reader to question the purpose and meaning of existence. In his early novels, Huxley satirized the aimless and pleasure-mad social world in the aftermath of World War I, but he later came to take a more positive stance in demonstrating how human values could be changed. Through this transformation, a more enlightened, compassionate, and humanly oriented society could result.

A convinced pacifist from youth, Huxley continued to question the tragedy of war and why nationalism through powerful technologies remains a threat. As a novelist, however, Huxley concentrated on describing how individuals suffered from the aggrandizement of scientific power that leads to war. He had good reason to decry the evils he observed—the gas chamber, the atomic bomb, and the loss of freedom in great areas of the world. The frivolous application of technology and the gross materialistic attitude it engendered led to further disparagement of the age of science. Huxley followed the only course of action for a responsible and conscientious writer by describing truthfully the false attitudes and the foolish actions of his generation. Through his books he essentially offers a moral evaluation of human errors over four decades, and the ethical state of society from 1921 to 1962 is reflected in eleven successive novels. Whether they stand alone or are classified under the headings of social criticism, novels of transformation, or futuristic fiction, the same critical temperament infuses each narrative.

The worlds depicted in Huxley's novels, with the possible exception of the doomed Palanese enterprise in *Island*, are not always happy places. The inhabitants of the dominant or repressive cultures have manipulated nature for material gain and self-centered pleasure, and they have lost contact with what is humanly important in the process. One central figure in each story is dissatisfied with his world, and his search for a better way is the primary theme of the narrative. The mindless masses, meanwhile, continue to be misled by false purposes, and their plight contrasts with those who seek enlightenment. To aid this process, wisdom figures or spiritual gurus are sometimes introduced, and they comment on the action like a Greek chorus. Huxley expresses his own critical ideas through the advice of these seers, through searching dialogues, or through key excerpts from a book or diary within the frame of the story.

Underpinning these fictional works thematically is Huxley's belief that human hubris, or arrogant pride that corrupts the natural scheme of things, will inevitably lead to avenging nemesis, or retribution. He would further claim that, in all that we term as progress, people pay some price, whether in the long or short term. In all of his novels the societies involved suffer through their innovations, whether self-inflicted or imposed. Yet Huxley never advocated that nations abandon vital technologies. In *Island*, for example, he describes those who follow the Buddhist tantric teachings toward self-transcendence as balanced individuals who do not try to escape from the world, but rather make use of all valuable discoveries in order to achieve a higher level of self-understanding.

Huxley argues that if technology is pursued and promoted solely for self-aggrandizement detached from the human dimension, then greater trouble will ensue. In this early insight Huxley anticipated many of the contemporary world's problems, including nuclear proliferation, overpopulation, depletion of natural resources, and genetic manipulation. Although readers may criticize his spiritual solution to the world's technological ills, Huxley's call for an alternative approach is comprehensible. His concern for human betterment, and his in-depth understanding of people as complex creatures of body, mind, and spirit, further validates many of his conclusions.

Although Huxley could be savagely satirical in criticizing human folly, he was optimistic by nature and sanguine about the future. He had good reason to think otherwise: his near blindness, tragic life experiences, and the pessimistic temper of his age. Despite two world wars, a traumatic economic depression, and the threat of nuclear annihilation, he did not succumb to the cynicism and disillusionment that affected others. On the contrary, if his narratives are reflections of the man, they demonstrate a progression in hope. The aimless societies depicted in the novels of the 1920s (*Crome Yellow, Antic Hay, Those Barren Leaves,* and *Point Counter Point*), the conditioned masses in *Brave New World,* and the illusory pursuits in *After Many a Summer Dies the Swan,* were to give way to the transformed central characters at the end of *Eyeless in Gaza, Time Must Have a Stop* and even *Ape and Essence,* respectively, as well as the enlightened optimism concluding *The Genius and the Goddess* and *Island.*

Huxley's novels demonstrate the maturation of his ideology. All of his novels are engrossing narratives exposing the hazards of human progress. As is the case in all substantial or significant works of literature, Huxley's novels raise many more questions than they answer. Providing solutions to problems, however, is not the province of the novelist — although Huxley's works have been utilized to raise interest in reform.

In Huxley's final published essay, "Shakespeare and Religion," he examines the spiritual legacy of the great dramatist. He finds in the plays the message that mankind must live thoughtfully, and they must develop a spiritual consciousness so that by living in the world, they can improve it. Through his fictional narratives, Aldous Huxley also portrays a world in which his characters suffer even when surrounded by material abundance. He challenges his readers to recognize that the ends and means of scientific production must ever serve and not harm society. This theme resonates even more powerfully in the modern world of increasing technological ascendancy, where the current threat now far exceeds even the author's prescient vision.

It remains difficult to assess the future fame of 20th-century writers who were once highly reputed. Among Huxley's contemporaries earlier in the century, the once-popular Somerset Maugham, Arnold Bennet, and John Galsworthy appear to have lost lasting eminence. H.G. Wells, as the powerful advocate of technical progress, is now remembered as a minor science fiction novelist. The major talents of the pre-war years, novelists of the caliber of Virginia Woolf, E.M. Forster, and D.H. Lawrence, rest their reputations on probing studies of social mores rather than the great public issues of the day. George Orwell is perhaps closest to Huxley in examining the basic threats to modern civilization, but he lacks the range and depth of Huxley's social, critical, and spiritual exploration. Among the post-war English novelists, it is rare to find a writer who consistently tackles the broad themes of mankind's basic purpose and ultimate future.

The legacy of Aldous Huxley is that of a gifted writer who sought not only to entertain through his imaginative narratives, but also to involve the reader by posing the moral dilemmas faced by all people in the real world. Huxley was a skilled teacher whose ideas embody the classical sense of a seer who warns society of impending evils. It has been posited in this study that Huxley's novels successively embody his progressive development not only as an artist, but as a person. In the varied conversations, eccentricities, and internal monologues of his characters, as well as the actions or learned inactions of his personae, we find the creative artist delving into the human psyche for meaning in a materially oriented world. The answers are not always forthcoming, but occasionally the central protagonist learns the hard way that life is more than seductive gratifications. Huxley was to read and meditate deeply, and the spiritually based unitive force of his thinking became for him the answer to a personal quest, as well as possibly a worthwhile remedy to most of the world's ills. The many watershed moments — both sorrowful and joyful — from his youth through the maturation of his body, mind and spirit are inexorably inculcated in the thematic intensity of his fiction. The analysis of each novel, therefore, has been interfaced with Huxley's own words in letters and essays that he wrote before, during, and subsequent to the penning of each work. In essence, the study becomes, for that reason, a literary biography of an artistic genius.

His movement away from satiric observer to proactive ideologue has been analytically substantiated through his essays and other non-fictional writings which are far more explicit in their intent; his novels, however, vividly dramatize the 20th-century social dilemmas in concrete terms that are both cogent and compelling. It is evident that Huxley was ever the open-minded one willing to explore all that the world had to offer. Whether rubbing elbows with fellow pacifists and the gifted array of artists at Garsington Manor, dining with shallow celluloid celebrities at a Hollywood party, or reading the writings of prophets and hallowed philosophers of old, his mind and spirit soaked in all that he saw, heard, and sensed, and he fused it into his fictional creations. His was not a static personality, but a dynamic spirit whose craft became, for him, the means to articulate all that he was thinking about at any given moment in time. It is possible to conclude that of all the major commentators on the modern threat of technocratic arrogance, Huxley remains perhaps the most widely read and influential. While his *Brave New World* remains a standard college text, it would behoove those seeking meaning in an age buffeted by the winds of selfish aggression to re-examine the wisdom of such a scholar. Huxley's thematically allied novels will continue to be read by coming generations of students and all those who seek to understand the moral and cultural underpinnings of not only the past century, but also the transcendent concerns confronting a contemporary age.

Appendix: Selected Books and Articles by Aldous Huxley

After Many a Summer Dies the Swan. New York: Harper and Row, 1939; Elephant Paperbacks, 1993.

Aldous Huxley, Between the Wars: Essays and Letters. Edited by David Bradshaw. Chicago: Ivan R. Dee, 1994.

Antic Hay. New York: George H. Doran, 1923; Dalkey Archive Press, 1997.

Ape and Essence. Chicago: Ivan R. Dee, Inc., 1992.

The Art of Seeing. London: Chatto and Windus, 1942; Harper & Brothers, Publishers, 1942; Seattle: Montana Books, 1975.

"Brave New World." *Life* XXV (September 20, 1948), 63–70.

Brave New World. New York: Harper and Row, 1932; Perennial, 1989.

Brave New World Revisited. New York: Harper and Row, 1958; Harper Perennial, 1989.

Brief Candles: Four Stories. London: Chatto and Windus, 1930; Penguin, 1973.

"Chawdron." In *Brief Candles: Four Stories.* London: Chatto and Windus, 1930; Penguin, 1973.

Christmas Sketch: An Unpublished Playlet by Aldous Huxley. Boston: David Godine in collaboration with the Dartmouth College Library, 1972.

Collected Essays. New York: Harper and Row, 1923; Harper Colophon, 1971.

Collected Short Stories. New York: Harper and Row, 1958; Bantam, 1973.

Crome Yellow. London: Chatto and Windus, 1921; New York: Bantam, 1955.

"A Defense of the Intellect." *UNESCO Courier* 46, no. 12 (December 1993), 42. Printed excerpts selected by Edgardo Canton from Huxley's Address to the International Institute of Intellectual Co-operation in Paris, France: October 16–18, 1933.

The Devils of Loudun. New York: Harper and Row, 1952; Carroll and Graf, 1989.

The Doors of Perception. New York: Harper and Row, 1954; Perennial, 1990.

Ends and Means: An Enquiry into the Nature of Ideals and into the Methods Employed for Their Realization. London: Chatto and Windus, 1937; 1946.

Essays New and Old. New York: The Forum Publishing Company, 1925; George H. Doran, 1927.

Eyeless in Gaza. New York: Carroll & Graf Publishers, Inc., 1995.

"Further Reflections on Progress." *Vedanta for Modern Man* (1947). Reprinted in *Huxley and God.* Edited by Jacqueline Hazard Bridgeman, 111–115. San Francisco: Harper, 1992.

The Genius and the Goddess. London: Chatto and Windus, 1955.

Grey Eminence: A Study in Religion and Politics. New York: Harper, 1941.

"Has Man's Conquest of Space Increased or Diminished His Stature?" In *The Great Ideas Today, 1963,* "Part One, A Symposium on Space," 21–33. Chicago: Encyclopædia Britannica, 1963.

Heaven and Hell. New York: Harper, 1956.

"How to Improve the World." *Nash's Pall Mall Magazine,* xcviii (December 1936), 84–88. In *Aldous Huxley: Between the Wars.* Edited by David Bradshaw, 220–229. Chicago: Ivan R. Dee, 1994.

The Human Situation: Lectures at Santa Barbara, ed. Piero Ferrucci. New York: Harper and Row, 1977.

"If We Survive." *The Star* (16 March 1936): 4. In *Aldous Huxley: Between the Wars.* Edited by David Bradshaw, 215–217. Chicago: Ivan R. Dee, 1994.

"The Individual Life of Man." A Lectured Delivered at the University of California, Santa Barbara, September 21, 1959. In *The Human Situation,* ed. Piero Ferrucci. New York: Harper and Row, 1977.

Island. New York: Harper and Row, 1962; Perennial Classic, 1989.

Jesting Pilate. New York: G. H. Doran, 1926; Paragon House, 1991.

Leda. London: Chatto and Windus, 1920; 1922.

Letters of Aldous Huxley. Edited by Grover Smith. New York: Harper and Row, 1969.

Literature and Science. New York: Harper and Row, 1963; Ox Bow Press, 1991.

Now More Than Ever. Austin: The University of Texas Press, 2000.

The Olive Tree and Other Essays. London: Chatto and Windus, 1947.

On Art and Artists. New York: Harper and Brothers, 1960.

"On Deviating into Sense." In *On the Margin: Notes and Essays.* London: Chatto and Windus, 1923; Phoenix Library, 1928.

On the Margin: Notes and Essays. London: Chatto and Windus, 1923; Phoenix Library, 1928.

The Perennial Philosophy. New York: Harper and Row, 1944; Perennial Library, 1970.

Point Counter Point. New York: Doubleday Doran & Company, 1928.

"Progress: How the Achievements of Civilization Will Eventually Bankrupt the Entire World." *Vanity Fair,* January 29, 1928.

"Reflections on Progress." *Vedanta for Modern Man* (1947). Reprinted in *Huxley and God.* Edited by Jacqueline Hazard Bridgeman, 94–109. San Francisco: Harper, 1992.

Science, Liberty and Peace. New York: Harper and Brothers, 1946.

"Shakespeare and Religion." In *Aldous Huxley, 1894–1963: A Memorial Volume.* Edited by Julian Huxley, 165–175. New York: Harper and Row, 1965.

"Sincerity in Art." In *Essays: New and Old.* The Forum Publishing Company, 1925; George H. Doran, 1927.

Themes and Variations. New York: Harper, 1950.

Those Barren Leaves. London: Chatto and Windus, 1925; 1928

Time Must Have a Stop. New York: Harper and Row, 1944; Perennial, 1965.

Tomorrow and Tomorrow and Tomorrow and Other Essays. New York: Harper and Row, 1952; 1956.

An Unpublished Letter. In Suzanne R. Begnoche, "Aldous Huxley's Soviet Source Material: An Unpublished Letter." *English Language Notes* 34, no. 3 (March 1997): 51–56.

Huxley, Aldous, and Christopher Isherwood. *Jacob's Hands.* New York: St. Martin's Press, 1998.

Chapter Notes

Preface

1. Aldous Huxley, *Brave New World* (New York: Harper Perennial, 1989), 235.
2. "Progress Is Overrated." *Parade* (June 14, 2009), 17.
3. William Shakespeare, *Hamlet, Prince of Denmark*, 3.1, lines 80–81.
4. Aldous Huxley, *Literature and Science* (Woodbridge, CT: Ox Bow Press, 1991), 82.
5. Boethius, quoted in Aldous Huxley, *The Perennial Philosophy* (New York: Harper and Row Perennial, 1970), 161.
6. Aldous Huxley, *The Genius and the Goddess* (London: Chatto & Lindus), 87.

Introduction

1. Clifton Fadiman, *The Lifetime Reading Plan* (Cleveland: The World Publishing Company, 1960), 237.

Chapter One

1. David King Dunaway, *Huxley in Hollywood* (New York: Harper and Row, 1989), 4.
2. Adrian Desmond, *From Devil's Advocate to Evolution's High Priest* (Reading, MA: Addison-Wesley, 1997), 617.
3. *Ibid.*, xiii.
4. Sybille Bedford, *Aldous Huxley: A Biography* (New York: Alfred A. Knopf/Harper and Row, 1974) 197.
5. *Ibid.*
6. Bedford, 33–36.
7. Juliette Huxley, *Leaves of the Tulip Tree* (London: John Murray, 1986), 226.

8. Bedford, 32–33.
9. *Ibid.*, 34.
10. Julian Huxley, ed., *Aldous Huxley: A Memorial Volume* (New York: Harper and Row, 1965), 22.
11. Bedford, 39–43.
12. Harold H. Watts, *Aldous Huxley* (Boston: Twayne, 1969), 20.
13. Bedford, 39.
14. Aldous Huxley, *Letters of Aldous Huxley*, ed. Grover Smith (New York: Harper and Row, 1969), 63.
15. Bedford, 69.
16. T.S. Eliot, "A Memorial Essay" in *Aldous Huxley: A Memorial Volume*, ed. Julian Huxley (New York: Harper and Row, 1965), 30.
17. Aldous Huxley, *Letters of Aldous Huxley*, 673.
18. Jonathan Swift, *The Writings of Jonathan Swift*, eds. Robert A. Greenberg and William Bowman Piper (New York: W.W. Norton, 1973), 375.
19. Jonathan Swift, *Gulliver's Travels* (New York: Bantam, 1981), 134.
20. Aldous Huxley, *The Genius and the Goddess* (London: Chatto and Windus, 1955), 7.
21. Aldous Huxley, "Sincerity in Art," in *Essays: New and Old* (New York: George H. Doran, 1927), 300.
22. *Ibid.*, 303–304.

Chapter Two

1. Aldous Huxley, *Letters of Aldous Huxley*, ed. Grover Smith (New York: Harper and Row, 1969), 198.
2. *Ibid.*, 198–199.

3. Sybille Bedford, *Aldous Huxley: A Biography.* New York: Alfred A. Knopf/Harper and Row, 118.

4. Aldous Huxley, *Letters of Aldous Huxley,* 203; 202.

5. *Ibid.,* 202.

6. Bedford, 121.

7. Aldous Huxley, *Crome Yellow* (London: Chatto and Windus, 1921; New York: Bantam, 1955), 41.

8. *Ibid.,* 109.

9. *Ibid.,* 18.

10. *Ibid.,* 110.

11. *Ibid.,* 119.

12. *Ibid.,* 113.

13. *Ibid.,* 116.

14. *Ibid.,* 166–177.

15. *Ibid.,* 120; 121.

16. *Ibid.,* 152.

17. *Ibid.,* 31.

18. *Ibid.,* 45.

19. *Ibid.,* 75.

20. *Ibid.,* 21.

21. *Ibid.,* 22.

22. *Ibid.,* 24–26.

23. Bedford, 122.

24. *Aldous Huxley: Between the Wars, Essays and Letters,* edited by David Bradshaw (Chicago: Ivan R. Dee, 1994), 13.

25. F. Scott Fitzgerald quoted in Bradshaw, *ibid.,* 17.

26. Aldous Huxley, *On the Margin: Notes and Essays* (London: Chatto and Windus, 1928), 25.

27. *Ibid.,* 25.

28. *Ibid.,* 24.

29. *Ibid.,* 25.

30. Christopher Marlowe, *Edward the Second,* in *The Complete Plays of Christopher Marlowe,* ed. Irving Ribner (New York: The Odyssey Press, 1963), 285.

31. Aldous Huxley, *Antic Hay* (New York: Dalkey Archive Press, 1997), 39.

32. *Ibid.,* 40.

33. Bedford, 137.

34. Aldous Huxley, *Antic Hay,* 212.

35. Guinevera A. Nance, *Aldous Huxley* (New York: Continuum, 1988), 23–24.

36. Aldous Huxley, *Antic Hay,* 189.

37. *Ibid.,* 115.

38. Aldous Huxley, *Letters of Aldous Huxley,* ed. Grover Smith (New York: Harper and Row, 1969), 224.

39. *Ibid.*

40. Jerome Meckier, *Aldous Huxley: Satire and Structure* (London: Chatto and Windus, 1969), 68.

41. T.S. Eliot, "A Memorial Essay" in *Aldous Huxley: A Memorial Volume,* ed. Julian Huxley (New York: Harper and Row, 1965), 32.

42. Huxley, *On the Margin,* 45–52.

43. Huxley, *Antic Hay,* 139.

44. Harold H. Watts, *Aldous Huxley* (Boston: Twayne, 1969), 52.

45. Huxley, *On the Margin,* 127.

46. *Ibid.,* 128.

47. *Ibid.,* 129–130.

48. Milton Birnbaum, *Aldous Huxley's Quest for Values* (Knoxville: University of Tennessee Press, 1971), 144.

49. Aldous Huxley, *Themes and Variations* (New York: Harper, 1950), 207.

50. Evelyn Waugh, "Youth at the Helm and Pleasure at the Prow," A Critical Symposium on Huxley, *London Magazine* (August 1955): 51–64. Review reprinted in *Aldous Huxley: The Critical Heritage,* ed. Donald Watt (Boston: Routledge and Kegan Paul, 1975), 398.

51. *Ibid.,* 397.

52. *Ibid.,* 399.

53. Alexander Henderson, *Aldous Huxley* (New York: Russell & Russell, 1964), 135–136.

54. Aldous Huxley, *Antic Hay,* 59.

55. *Ibid.,* 48.

56. *Ibid.,* 141.

57. *Ibid.,* 142.

58. *Ibid.,* 152.

59. Aldous Huxley, "On Deviating into Sense, in *On the Margin: Notes and Essays* (London: Chatto and Windus, 1928), 81–82.

60. Aldous Huxley, *Antic Hay,* 212

61. *Ibid.,* 208.

62. *Ibid.,* 48.

63. George Woodcock, *Dawn and the Darkest Hour: A Study of Aldous Huxley* (New York: The Viking Press, 1972), 96.

64. *Ibid.,* 98.

65. *Ibid.,* 99.

66. *Ibid.*

67. *Ibid.*

68. Keith May, *Aldous Huxley* (London: Paul Elek Books, 1972), 41.

69. Aldous Huxley, "Reflections on Progress," *Vedanta for Modern Man* (1947).

Reprinted in *Huxley and God*, ed. Jacqueline Hazard Bridgeman (San Francisco: Harper, 1992), 107.

70. Aldous Huxley, *Letters of Aldous Huxley*, 228.

71. *Ibid.*

72. *Ibid.*, 235; Bedford, 152.

73. Bedford, 152.

74. Aldous Huxley, *Those Barren Leaves* (London: Chatto and Windus, 1928), 72.

75. *Ibid.*

76. *Ibid.*, 195.

77. *Ibid.*, 60.

78. *Ibid.*, 72.

79. *Ibid.*, 379.

80. Aldous Huxley, *Letters of Aldous Huxley*, 228; 231.

81. Aldous Huxley, *Those Barren Leaves*, 56.

82. *Ibid.*, 218.

83. *Ibid.*, 334.

84. *Ibid.*, 344–347.

85. *Ibid.*, 366.

86. *Ibid.*, 98.

87. Bedford, 155.

88. Huxley, *Letters of Aldous Huxley*, 324.

89. Aldous Huxley, *Those Barren Leaves*, 57.

90. *Ibid.*, 284.

91. Watts, 62.

92. Aldous Huxley, *Point Counter Point* (New York: Doubleday Doran, 1928), 349–350.

93. *Ibid.*, 228.

94. Bedford, 202.

95. Aldous Huxley, *Point Counter Point*, 231.

96. D. H. Lawrence, *Reminiscences and Correspondence*, as quoted in Sybille Bedford, *Aldous Huxley: A Biography* (New York: Alfred A. Knopf/Harper and Row, 1974), 207.

97. Fulke Greville, 1st Baron Brooke, "Chorus Sacerdotum from 'Mustapha,'" https://tspace.library.utoronto.ca/html/1807/4350/poem896.html (accessed July 21, 2009).

98. Huxley, *Point Counter Point*, 339.

99. *Ibid.*, 34.

100. *Ibid.*, 100.

101. *Ibid.*, 340.

102. *Ibid.*, 166.

103. *Ibid.*, 176.

104. Bedford, 207.

105. Aldous Huxley, *Point Counter Point*, 504.

106. *Ibid.*, 514.

107. *Ibid.*, 351.

108. Bedford, 199.

109. Watts, 69.

110. Aldous Huxley, *Point Counter Point*, 357.

111. *Ibid.*, 378.

112. *Ibid.*, 242.

113. *Ibid.*, 350.

114. Aldous Huxley, *Letters of Aldous Huxley*, 291.

115. *Ibid.*, 294.

116. Bedford, 199.

117. Aldous Huxley, *Letters of Aldous Huxley*, 304.

Chapter Three

1. *Ibid.*, 390; 391; 392.

2. *Ibid.*, 389; 394; 400; 401; 405.

3. *Ibid.*, 402.

4. *Ibid.*, 407.

5. *Ibid.*

6. Huxley, *Letters*, 398.

7. *Ibid.*

8. *Ibid.*, 401.

9. *Ibid.*, 406.

10. Bedford, 307.

11. Huxley, *Letters of Aldous Huxley*, ed. Grover Smith (New York: Harper and Row, 1969), 400.

12. *Ibid.*, 409.

13. Aldous Huxley, *Eyeless in Gaza* (New York: Carroll & Graf, 1995). 397; 398.

14. "Samson Agonistes," http://www.dartmouth.edu/~milton/reading_room/samson/drama/index.shtml (accessed July 27, 2009).

15. Bedford, 306.

16. Aldous Huxley, *Eyeless in Gaza* (New York: Carroll & Graf, 1995), 473.

17. Aldous Huxley, *Letters*, 404.

18. Huxley, *Eyeless in Gaza*, 21.

19. *Ibid.*, 5.

20. *Ibid.*, 380.

21. *Ibid.*, 473; 467.

22. Harold H. Watts, *Aldous Huxley* (Boston: Twayne, 1969), 89.

23. David King Dunaway, Introduction to Aldous Huxley's *Eyeless in Gaza* (New York: Carroll & Graf, 1995), ix.

24. Aldous Huxley, *Eyeless in Gaza*, 469.

25. Sybille Bedford, *Aldous Huxley: A*

Biography (New York: Alfred A. Knopf/Harper and Row, 1974), 757–758.

26. David King Dunaway, *Huxley in Hollywood* (New York: Harper and Row, 1989), 87.

27. Bedford, 758–759.

28. Aldous Huxley, *Jesting Pilate* (New York: Paragon House, 1991), 301.

29. Aldous Huxley, "Chawdron," in *Brief Candles: Four Stories* (Middlesex, England: Penguin, 1973), 30.

30. Frank Baldanza, "Huxley and Hearst," *Journal of Modern Literature* 7 (1979), 443.

31. *Ibid.*

32. Aldous Huxley, *Letters*, 440.

33. John Pfordresher, Gladys V. Veidemanis, and Helen McDonnell, eds., *England in Literature* (New York: Scott, Foresman, 1989), 968; 975.

34. Huxley, *The Letters of Aldous* Huxley, 593.

35. Charles A. Holmes, *Aldous Huxley and the Way to Reality* (Bloomington: Indiana University Press, 1970), 127.

36. Alfred Lord Tennyson, "Tithonus," in *The Norton Anthology of English Literature*, eds. M.H. Abrams, et al. (New York: W.W. Norton, 1962), 737.

37. *Ibid.*, 734.

38. Baldanza, 450.

39. Aldous Huxley, *After Many a Summer Dies the Swan* (Chicago: Ivan R. Dee, 1993), 356.

40. Dunaway, 107.

41. Baldanza, 446.

42. Huxley, *After Many a Summer Dies the Swan*, 256–258.

43. *Ibid.*, 101.

44. *Ibid.*, 118.

45. C. S. Ferns, *Aldous Huxley: Novelist* (London: Athlone, 1980), 55–56.

46. Baldanza, 449.

47. *Ibid.*, 453.

48. Huxley, *Ends and Means: An Enquiry into the Nature of Ideals and into the Methods Employed for Their Realization* (London: Chatto and Windus, 1946), 123.

49. *Ibid.*, 123–124.

50. *Ibid.*, 269–270.

51. Aldous Huxley, *After Many a Summer Dies the Swan*, 125.

52. *Ibid.*, 126.

53. Huxley, *Ends and Means*, 89.

54. *Ibid.*

55. *Ibid.*, 94.

56. *Ibid.*, 128.

57. *Ibid.*

58. Aldous Huxley, *After Many a Summer Dies the Swan*, 171–172.

59. Aldous Huxley, *Ends and Means*, 123–125.

60. Aldous Huxley, *After Many a Summer Dies the Swan*, 107.

61. Huxley, *Ends and Means*, 255.

62. *Ibid.*, 6; 7.

63. *Ibid.*, 5.

64. *Ibid.*, 9.

65. Laura Archera Huxley, "Interview with Laura Huxley," interview by Bruce Eisner, *Island Views* (November 1993), http://www.island.org/ISLAND/VIEWS3/huxley3.html (accessed October 17, 1997).

66. Aldous Huxley, *Ends and Means*, 255.

67. Aldous Huxley, *Ends and Means*, 255.

68. *Ibid.*, 5.

69. *Ibid.*, 9.

70. Aldous Huxley, *Ends and Means*, 247.

71. Jonathan Swift, *Gulliver's Travels* (New York: Bantam, 1981), 207–208.

72. Dunaway, 106–107.

73. His Holiness the Dalai Lama and Howard C. Cutler, M.D. *The Art of Happiness: A Handbook for Living* (New York: Riverhead, 1998), 294.

74. *Ibid.*, 186.

75. Huxley, *Letters of Aldous Huxley*, 445.

76. *Ibid.*, 473.

77. Aldous Huxley, *The Art of Seeing* (Seattle: Montana Books, 1975), 7.

78. *Ibid.*, 14–15.

79. Huxley, *Letters of Aldous Huxley*, 468.

80. *Ibid.*, 473.

81. *Ibid.*, 474.

82. Keith May, *Aldous Huxley* (London: Paul Elek Books, 1972), 158.

83. Huxley, *Letters of Aldous Huxley*, 499.

84. *Ibid.*, 501.

85. William Shakespeare, *King Henry the Fourth, Part One*, 5.4, lines 81–83.

86. Aldous Huxley, *Time Must Have a Stop* (New York: Berkley, 963), 228–229.

87. Guinevera A. Nance, *Aldous Huxley* (New York: Continuum, 1988), 127.

88. Aldous Huxley, *Time Must Have a Stop*, 216.

89. Nance, 128.

90. Huxley, *Time Must Have a Stop*, 117.

91. Sally A. Paulsell, "Color and Light: Huxley's Pathway to Spiritual Reality," *Twentieth Century Literature* 41, no. 1 (Spring 1995), 81–107.

92. Huxley, *Time Must Have a Stop*, 108; 110.

93. Bedford, 434.

94. Huxley, *Letters of Aldous Huxley*, 474.

95. Dunaway, 164–170.

96. Aldous Huxley, *Tomorrow and Tomorrow and Tomorrow and Other Essays* (New York: Harper Brothers, 1956), 71.

97. Aldous Huxley, *The Perennial Philosophy* (New York: Harper and Row Perennial Library, 1970), 36.

98. *Ibid.*, 92.

99. *Ibid.*, 92–95.

100. *Ibid.*, 95–119.

101. *Ibid.*, 105–106.

102. *Ibid.*, 179.

103. *Ibid.*, vii.

104. *Ibid.*

105. Huxley, *Letters of Aldous Huxley*, 474.

106. Huxley, *The Perennial Philosophy*, vii.

107. *Ibid.*, vii–viii.

108. Aldous Huxley, *Time Must Have a Stop*, 214.

109. *Ibid.*

110. *Ibid.*, 226.

111. Huxley, *The Perennial Philosophy*, 219.

112. *Ibid.*, 218.

113. *Ibid.*, 294.

114. *Ibid.*, 194.

115. *Ibid.*, 294.

116. Aldous Huxley, "How to Improve the World," in *Aldous Huxley: Between the Wars*, ed. David Bradshaw (Chicago: Ivan R. Dee, 1994), 215–229.

117. Huxley, *The Perennial Philosophy*, 79.

118. *Ibid.*, 80.

119. *Ibid.*, 91.

120. *Ibid.*, 91.

Chapter Four

1. Harold H. Watts, *Aldous Huxley* (Boston: Twayne, 1969), 73.

2. Robert S. Baker, *Brave New World: History, Science and Dystopia* (New York: Twayne, 1990), 25.

3. Richard Hauer Costa, *H.G. Wells* (Boston: Twayne Publishers, 1985), 3.

4. *Ibid.*, 7.

5. *Ibid.*, 108–116.

6. Christopher Collins, *Evgenij Zamjatin: An Interpretive Study* (The Hague: Mouton, 1973), 41.

7. Aldous Huxley, *Brave New World* (New York: Harper and Row Perennial, 1989), 54.

8. *Ibid.*, 75.

9. *Ibid.*, 246.

10. Aldous Huxley, "An Unpublished Letter," in Suzanne R. Begnoche, "Aldous Huxley's Soviet Source Material: An Unpublished Letter," *English Language Notes* 34, no. 3 (March 1997), 51.

11. Suzanne R. Begnoche, "Aldous Huxley's Soviet Source Material: An Unpublished Letter," *English Language Notes* 34, no. 3 (March 1997), 53.

12. Baker, 63.

13. *Ibid.*, 65.

14. *Ibid.*, 67.

15. William Shakespeare, *The Tempest*, 5.1, lines 185–186.

16. Aldous Huxley, *Brave New World Revisited* (New York: Harper and Row Perennial, 1989), 3.

17. *Ibid.*, 21.

18. Aldous Huxley, "Brave New World," *Life* XXV (September 20, 1948), 63–70.

19. Huxley, *Brave New World Revisited*, 20–21.

20. *Ibid.*, 55–67.

21. *Ibid.*, 138.

22. *Ibid.*, 19–20.

23. *Ibid.*, 20.

24. Huxley, *Brave New World*, 235.

25. *Ibid.*, 77.

26. *Ibid.*, 49.

27. *Ibid.*, 50.

28. Baker, 126.

29. Ian Barbour, *Ethics in an Age of Technology* (San Francisco: Harper, 1993), 3–25.

30. Huxley, *Brave New World*, 230.

31. Peter E. Firchow, *The End of Utopia: A Study of Aldous Huxley's Brave New World* (Lewisburg, PA: Bucknell University Press, 1984), 311–312.

32. Huxley, Foreword to *Brave New World*, ix–x.

33. *Ibid.*, x.

34. *Ibid.*, xvii.

35. Aldous Huxley, *Brave New World*, 35.

36. *Ibid.*, 204.
37. *Ibid.*, 208.
38. *Ibid.*, 73.
39. *Ibid.*, 74.
40. George Orwell, *1984* (New York: Signet Classic First Printing, 1950), 7.
41. Fritjof Capra, *The Turning Point, Science, Society, and the Rising Culture* (New York: Bantam, 1988), 15.
42. Brian Appleyard, *Understanding the Present: Science and the Soul of Modern Man* (New York: Doubleday, 1993), viv.
43. Huxley, *Brave New World*, 6.
44. Ayn Rand, *Anthem* (New York: Signet, 1995), 19.
45. Huxley, *Brave New World*, 15.
46. J. Bronowski, *The Ascent of Man* (Boston: Little, Brown, 1973), 19, 20.
47. Sybille Bedford, *Aldous Huxley: A Biography* (New York: Alfred A. Knopf/Harper and Row, 1974), 244.
48. Huxley, *Brave New World*, 235.
49. *Ibid.*, xi.
50. *Ibid.*, xvii.
51. *Ibid.*, 235.
52. *Ibid.*, 141.
53. *Ibid.*, 246.
54. *Ibid.*
55. *Ibid.*, 266.
56. *Ibid.*, 141.
57. *Ibid.*, 98.
58. *Ibid.*, 77.
59. *Ibid.*, 191.
60. *Ibid.*, 232.
61. *Ibid.*, 248.
62. Aldous Huxley, *Letters of Aldous Huxley*, ed. Grover Smith (New York: Harper and Row, 1969), 471.
63. *Ibid.*, 532.
64. *Ibid.*
65. David King Dunaway, *Huxley in Hollywood* (New York: Harper and Row, 1989), 199.
66. *Ibid.*, 200.
67. Aldous Huxley, *Ape and Essence* (Chicago: Ivan R. Dee, 1992), 124.
68. *Ibid.*, 126.
69. *Ibid.*, 133.
70. Shakespeare, *Measure for Measure*, 2.2, lines 121–126.
71. Aldous Huxley, *Ape and Essence* (Chicago: Ivan R. Dee, 1992), 75.
72. Aldous Huxley, *Science, Liberty and Peace* (New York: Harper and Brothers, 1946), 1–4.

73. *Ibid.*, 26–31.
74. *Ibid.*, 37.
75. *Ibid.*, 38–39.
76. *Ibid.*, 86.
77. Dunaway, 222.
78. Huxley, *Letters*, 531.
79. *Ibid.*
80. Huxley, *Letters of Aldous Huxley*, 600.
81. Philip Thody, *Huxley: A Biographical Introduction* (New York: Charles Scribner's Sons, 1973), 112.
82. Aldous Huxley, *Ape and Essence*, 62.
83. *Ibid.*, 184.
84. *Ibid.*, 148.
85. *Ibid.*, 184.
86. *Ibid.*, 190.
87. Sanford E. Marovitz, "Ape and Essence: *Fright or Fantasy?*" in *Now More Than Ever: Proceedings of the Aldous Huxley Centenary Symposium, Munster, 1994*, ed. Bernfried Nugel (Frankfurt am Main: Peter Lang, 1995), 159.
88. Aldous Huxley, *The Perennial Philosophy* (New York: Harper and Row Perennial Library, 1970), 93.
89. *Ibid.*
90. Huxley, *Letters*, 600.
91. *Ibid.*
92. *Ibid.*
93. Huxley, *Letters of Aldous Huxley*, 736.
94. Bedford, *Aldous Huxley: A Biography*, 715.
95. *Ibid.*, 645.
96. Orville Prescott, "Two Aldous Huxleys," *New York Times* (November 24, 1963), 4.
97. Aldous Huxley, *Island* (New York: Harper and Row Perennial Classic, 1989), 35.
98. Huxley, *Letters of Aldous Huxley*, 944.
99. *Ibid.*
100. *Ibid.*, 948.
101. Gerd Rohman, "*Island:* Huxley's Ecological Utopia," in *Now More Than Ever: Proceedings of the Aldous Huxley Centenary Symposium, Munster, 1994*, ed. Bernfried Nugel (Frankfurt am Main: Peter Lang, 1995), 182.
102. Dunaway, 364.
103. Aldous Huxley, *Island* (New York: Perennial Classic, 1989), 36.
104. *Ibid.*, 35.
105. *Ibid.*, 149.
106. Thody, 124.
107. Huxley, *Island*, 295.

Chapter Five

1. Sir Isaac Burton quoted in Sybille Bedford, *Aldous Huxley: A Biography* (New York: Alfred A. Knopf/Harper and Row), 573.

2. Aldous Huxley, *Letters of Aldous Huxley*, ed. Grover Smith (New York: Harper and Row, 1969), 715.

3. *Ibid.*, 706.

4. Sybille Bedford, *Aldous Huxley: A Biography* (New York: Alfred A. Knopf/Harper and Row, 1974), 548.

5. *Ibid.*, 547.

6. Huxley, *Letters*, 715 and footnote.

7. *Ibid.*, 720.

8 . Bedford, 560; 561.

9. *Ibid.*, 561.

10. Huxley, *Letters*, 706. 11. Aldous Huxley, *The Art of Seeing* (New York: Harper and Row, 1947), 180.

12. Aldous Huxley, *The Genius and the Goddess* (London: Chatto and Windus, 1955), 9.

13. *Ibid.*, 16.

14. Harold H. Watts, *Aldous Huxley* (Boston: Twayne, 1969), 121.

15. Huxley, *The Genius and the Goddess*, 44.

16. *Ibid.*, 83.

17. *Ibid.*, 84.

18. *Ibid.*, 88.

19. *Ibid.*, 97.

20. *Ibid.*, 99.

21. *Ibid.*, 102.

22. *Ibid.*, 106.

23. *Ibid.*, 107.

24. *Ibid.*, 108.

25. *Ibid.*, 109.

26. *Ibid.*, 113.

27. *Ibid.*, 126.

28. *Ibid.*, 127.

29. *Ibid.*, 49.

30. *Ibid.*, 113.

31. *Ibid.*, 45.

32. *Ibid.*, 46.

33. *Ibid.*, 94.

34. *Ibid.*, 9.

35. *Ibid.*, 87.

36. F. Scott Fitzgerald, *The Great Gatsby* (New York: Charles Scribner's Sons, 1999), 182.

Chapter Six

1. William Blake, *The Marriage of Heaven and Hell*, in *The Literature of England*, eds. George K. Anderson, William E. Buckler, and Mary Harris Veeder (New York: Harper Collins, 1979), 638, lines 10–12. Quoted by Laura Archera Huxley in "To Heal or Not to Heal," an introduction to *Jacob's Hands* by Aldous Huxley and Christopher Isherwood (New York: St. Martin's, 1998), xii.

2. Aldous Huxley, *Letters of Aldous Huxley*, ed. Grover Smith (New York: Harper and Row, 1969), 502.

3. *Ibid.*, 510.

4. *Ibid.*, 737 (Footnote to letter #690).

5. *Ibid.*, 242.

6. Bernfried Nugel, "Aldous Huxley's Revisions in the Final Typescript of *Island*," in *Now More Than Ever: Proceedings of the Aldous Huxley Centenary Symposium, Munster 1994*, ed. Bernfried Nugel (Frankfurt am Main: Peter Lang, 1995), 225.

7. Aldous Huxley quoted in David Bradshaw and James Sexton, *Introduction* to Aldous Huxley, *Now More Than Ever* (Austin: University of Texas Press, 2000), xii. Taken from "Interviews with Great Scientists (VII): Aldous Huxley" *Observer* (February 1, 1931), 15–16. Reprinted as "Mr. Aldous Huxley," in J.W.N. Sullivan, *Contemporary Mind: Some Modern Answers* (London: Humphrey Toulmin, 1942), 141–147.

8. Aldous Huxley, *Literature and Science* (Woodbridge, CT: Ox Bow Press, 1991), 40.

9. *Ibid.*, 70–71.

10. *Ibid.*, 71.

11. *Ibid.*, 72.

12. *Ibid.*, 92–93.

13. *Ibid.*, 72.

14. *Ibid.*, 109.

15. Aldous Huxley, "Foreword" to *Brave New World* (New York: Harper Perennial, 1989), xii.

16. Aristotle quoted in Epigraph to Aldous Huxley, *Island* (New York: Harper and Row Perennial, 1989).

17. Aldous Huxley, *Island* (New York: Harper and Row Perennial Classic, 1989), 35.

18. Laura Archera Huxley, *This Timeless Moment: A Personal View of Aldous Huxley* (New York: Farrar, Straus and Giroux, 1968), 308.

19. Aldous Huxley, *Island*, 35–36.

20. His Holiness the Dalai Lama and Howard C. Cutler, M.D., *The Art of Hap-*

piness: A Handbook for Living (New York: Riverhead, 1998), 15.

21. *Ibid.*, 29.

22. *Ibid.*, 33.

23. Laura Archera Huxley, "A Discussion with Laura Huxley," interview by Rick Doblin, *MAPS*, vol. 4, no. 4 (Spring 1994), http://www.maps.org/news-letters/v04n4/04438hux.html (accessed January 24, 2010).

24. Laura Archera Huxley, *This Timeless Moment*, 307–308.

25. *New York Times* (November 24, 1963), 1.

26. *Time* (November 29, 1963), 100; *Newsweek* (December 2, 1963), 67.

27. Orville Prescott, *New York Times* (November 24, 1963), 4.

28. *Ibid.*

Works Cited

Appleyard, Brian. *Understanding the Present: Science and the Soul of Modern Man*. New York: Doubleday, 1993.

Aristotle. Quoted in the epigraph to Aldous Huxley, *Island*. New York: Harper and Row Perennial, 1989.

Arnold, Matthew. *Culture and Anarchy*. Edited by Samuel Lipman. New Haven: Yale University Press, 1994.

_____. *Essays in Criticism*. London: Macmillan, 1898.

_____. *Selected Poems*. Edited by Keith Silver. Manchester: Carcanet, 1994.

Atkins, John. *Aldous Huxley: A Literary Study*. London: John Calder, 1956.

Baker, Robert S. *Brave New World: History, Science, and Dystopia*. New York: Twayne, 1990.

Baldanza, Frank. "Huxley and Hearst." *Journal of Modern Literature* VII (1979), 441–455.

Barbour, Ian. *Ethics in an Age of Technology*. San Francisco: Harper, 1993.

Bedford, Sybille. *Aldous Huxley: A Biography*. New York: Alfred A. Knopf/Harper and Row, 1974.

Begnoche, Suzanne R. "Aldous Huxley's Soviet Source Material: An Unpublished Letter." *English Language Notes 34*, no. 3 (March 1997), 51–56.

Birnbaum, Milton. *Aldous Huxley's Quest for Values*. Knoxville: University of Tennessee Press, 1971.

Blake, William. *The Marriage of Heaven and Hell*. *The Literature of England*. Edited by George K. Anderson, William E. Buckler, and Mary Harris Veeder. New York: Harper Collins, 1979, 638. Quoted by Laura Archera Huxley in "To Heal or Not to Heal," an introduction to *Jacob's Hands* by Aldous Huxley and Christopher Isherwood, xii. New York: St. Martin's, 1998.

Boethius. Quoted in Aldous Huxley, *The Perennial Philosophy*. New York: Harper and Row Perennial, 1970.

Bradshaw, David, ed. *Aldous Huxley: Between the Wars: Essays and Letters*. Chicago: Ivan R. Dee, 1994.

Bradshaw, David, and James Sexton. *Introduction* to Aldous Huxley, *Now More Than Ever*. Austin: University of Texas Press, 2000.

Bronowski, J. *The Ascent of Man*. Boston: Little, Brown, 1973.

Burton, Isaac (Sir). Quoted in Sybille Bedford, *Aldous Huxley: A Biography*. New York: Alfred A. Knopf/Harper and Row, 1974.

Capra, Fritjof. *The Turning Point: Science, Society, and the Rising Culture*. New York: Bantam, 1988.

Carson, Rachel. *Silent Spring*. Boston: Houghton Mifflin, 1962.

Collins, Christopher. *Evgenij Zamjatin: An Interpretive Study*. The Hague: Mouton, 1973.

Costa, Richard Hauer. *H.G. Wells*. Boston: Twayne, 1985.

(The) Dalai Lama and Howard C. Cutler, M.D. *The Art of Happiness: A Handbook for Living*. New York: Riverhead, 1998.

Desmond, Adrian. *From Devil's Advocate to Evolution's High Priest*. Reading, MA: Addison-Wesley, 1997.

Dunaway, David King. *Huxley in Hollywood*. New York: Harper and Row, 1989.

Eliot, T.S. "A Memorial Essay." *Aldous Huxley: A Memorial Volume*. Edited by Julian Huxley, 30–32. New York: Harper and Row, 1965.

_____. *Collected Poems 1909–1962*. New York: Harcourt, Brace, 1963.

Eulogy: "Aldous Huxley." *Newsweek* (December 2, 1963), 67.

Eulogy: "Aldous Huxley." *Time* (November 29, 1963), 100.

Fadiman, Clifton. *The Lifetime Reading Plan*. Cleveland: World Publishing, 1960.

Ferns, C.S. *Aldous Huxley: Novelist*. London: Athlone Press, 1980.

Firchow, Peter E. *Aldous Huxley: Satirist and Novelist*. Minneapolis: University of Minnesota Press, 1972.

_____. *The End of Utopia: A Study of Aldous Huxley's Brave New World*. Lewisburg, PA: Bucknell University Press, 1984.

Fitzgerald, F. Scott. *The Great Gatsby*. New York: Charles Scribner's Sons, 1999.

Greville, Fulke. Baron Brooke. "Chorus Sacerdotum from 'Mustapha.'" https://tspace.library.utoronto.ca/html/1807/4350/poem896.html (accessed July 21, 2009).

Heard, Gerald. *Pain, Sex and Time: A New Outlook on Evolution and the Future of Man*. Rhinebeck, NY: Monkfish, 2004.

Hemingway, Ernest. *The Sun Also Rises*. New York: Scribner, 2006.

Henderson, Alexander. *Aldous Huxley*. New York: Russell & Russell, 1964.

Hockenhull, Oliver, producer and director. *Aldous Huxley: The Gravity of Light*. Videocassette, VCR format. Produced by The Canada Council for the Arts, The National Film Board of Canada, BC Cultural Services, and Telefilm Canada, 1998. 70 minutes.

Holmes, Charles A. *Aldous Huxley and the Way to Reality*. Bloomington: Indiana University Press, 1970.

Horowitz, Michael, and Cynthia Palmer, eds. *Moksha: Aldous Huxley's Classic Writings on Psychedelics and the Visionary Experience*. Rochester, VT: Park Street, 1999.

Huxley, Aldous. *After Many a Summer Dies the Swan*. New York: Harper and Row, 1939; Elephant Paperbacks, 1993.

_____. *Antic Hay*. New York: Dalkey Archive Press, 1997.

_____. *Ape and Essence*. Chicago: Ivan R. Dee, 1992.

_____. *The Art of Seeing*. Seattle: Montana Books, 1975.

_____. *Between the Wars. Essays and Letters*. Edited by David Bradshaw. Chicago: Ivan R. Dee, 1994.

_____. *Brave New World*. New York: Harper Perennial, 1989.

_____. "Brave New World." *Life* XXV (September 20, 1948), 63–70

_____. *Brave New World Revisited*. New York: Harper and Row Perennial, 1989.

_____. *Brief Candles: Four Stories*. New York: Penguin Books, 1973.

_____. "Chawdron." *Brief Candles: Four Stories*. Middlesex, England: Penguin Books, Ltd., 1973.

_____. *Collected Essays*. New York: Harper Colophon, 1971.

_____. *Crome Yellow*. London: Chatto and Windus, 1921; New York: Bantam, 1955.

_____. *The Devils of Loudun*. New York: Carroll and Graff, 1989.

_____. *Ends and Means: An Enquiry into the Nature of Ideals and into the Methods Employed for Their Realization*. London: Chatto and Windus, 1946.

_____. *Essays New and Old*. New York: George H. Doran, 1925.

_____. *Eyeless in Gaza*. New York: Carroll and Graf, 1995.

_____. "Foreword" to *Brave New World*. New York: Harper Perennial, 1989.

_____. *The Genius and the Goddess*. London: Chatto & Lindus, 1955.

_____. *Grey Eminence: A Study in Religion and Politics*. New York: Harper and Brothers, 1941.

_____. "How to Improve the World." *Aldous Huxley: Between the Wars*. Edited by David Bradshaw, 215–229. Chicago: Ivan R. Dee, 1994.

_____. *Island*. New York: Harper and Row Perennial Classic, 1989.

_____. *Jesting Pilate*. New York: Paragon House, 1991.

_____. *Letters of Aldous Huxley*. Edited by Grover Smith. New York: Harper and Row, 1969.

_____. *Literature and Science*. Woodbridge, CT: Ox Bow Press, 1991.

_____. *Moksha: Aldous Huxley's Classic Writings on Psychedelics and the Visionary Experience*. Rochester, VT: Park Street, 1999.

_____. *Now More Than Ever*. Austin: University of Texas Press, 2000.

_____. "On Deviating into Sense." *On the Margin: Notes and Essays*, 81–86. London: Chatto and Windus, 1928.

_____. *On the Margin: Notes and Essays*. London: Chatto and Windus, 1928.

_____. *The Perennial Philosophy*. New York: Harper and Row Perennial Library, 1970.

_____. *Point Counter Point*. New York: Doubleday Doran & Company, 1928.

_____. "Reflections on Progress." *Vedanta for Modern Man* (1947). Reprinted in *Huxley and God*. Edited by Jacqueline Hazard Bridgeman. San Francisco: Harper, 1992.

_____. *Science, Liberty and Peace*. New York: Harper and Brothers, 1946.

_____. "Sincerity in Art." *Essays: New and Old*. New York: George H. Doran, 1927.

_____. *Themes and Variations*. New York: Harper, 1950.

_____. *Those Barren Leaves*. London: Chatto and Windus, 1928.

_____. *Time Must Have a Stop*. New York: Berkley, 1963.

_____. *Tomorrow and Tomorrow and Tomorrow and Other Essays*. New York: Harper Brothers, 1956.

_____. *Two or Three Graces and Other Stories*. New York: George H. Doran, 1926.

_____. "An Unpublished Letter." In Suzanne R. Begnoche, "Aldous Huxley's Soviet Source Material: An Unpublished Letter." *English Language Notes* 34, no. 3 (March 1997), 51.

_____. *Voices*. The Atlantic. Vol. 196, no. 1 (July 1955), 33–45.

Huxley, Aldous, and Christopher Isherwood. *Jacob's Hands*. New York: St. Martin's, 1998.

Huxley, Julian, ed. *Aldous Huxley: A Memorial Volume*. New York: Harper and Row, 1965.

Huxley, Juliette. *Leaves of the Tulip Tree*. London: John Murray, 1986.

Huxley, Laura Archera. "A Discussion with Laura Huxley." Interview by Rick Doblin. *MAPS*, vol. 4, no. 4 (Spring 1994). http://www.maps.org/news-letters/v04n4/04438 hux.html (accessed January 24, 2010).

_____. "Interview with Laura Huxley." Interview by Bruce Eisner. *Island Views* (November 1993). http://www.island.org/ISLAND/VIEWS3/huxley3.html (accessed October 17, 1997).

_____. *This Timeless Moment: A Personal View of Aldous Huxley*. New York: Farrar, Straus and Giroux, 1968.

Huxley, Leonard. *Life and Letters of Thomas Henry Huxley*. New York: D. Appleton, 1900.

Krutch, Joseph Wood. "Antic Horror." *Literary Review* IV (December 29, 1923), 403. Reprinted in *Aldous Huxley: The Critical Heritage*. Edited by Donald Watt., 93–95. Boston: Routledge and Kegan Paul, 1975.

Lawrence, D.H. *Reminiscences and Correspondence*. Quoted in Sybille Bedford, *Aldous Huxley: A Biography*. New York: Alfred A. Knopf/Harper and Row, 1974.

Marlowe, Christopher. *Edward the Second. The Complete Plays of Christopher Marlowe*. Edited by Irving Ribner. New York: Odyssey, 1963.

Marovitz, Sanford E. "*Ape and Essence*: Fright or Fantasy?" In *Now More Than Ever: Proceedings of the Aldous Huxley Centenary Symposium, Munster 1994*. Edited by Bernfried Nugel, 159–173. Frankfurt am Main: Peter Lang, 1995.

May, Keith. *Aldous Huxley*. London: Paul Elek, 1972.

Meckier, Jerome. *Aldous Huxley: Satire and Structure*. London: Chatto and Windus, 1969.

Nance, Guinevera A. *Aldous Huxley*. New York: Continuum, 1988.

Nugel, Bernfried. "Aldous Huxley's Revisions in the Final Typescript of *Island*." In *Now More Than Ever: Proceedings of the Aldous Huxley Centenary Symposium, Munster 1994*. Edited by Nugel Bernfried, 225–239. Frankfurt am Main: Peter Lang, 1995.

Obituary: "*Aldous Huxley*." *New York Times* (November 24, 1963), 4.

Orwell, George. *1984*. New York: Signet Classic First Printing, 1950.

Paulsell, Sally A. "Color and Light: Huxley's Pathway to Spiritual Reality." *Twentieth Century Literature* 41, no. 1 (Spring 1995), 81–107.

Pfordresher, John, Gladys V. Veidemanis and Helen McDonnell, eds. *England in Literature*. New York: Scott, Foresman, 1989.

Prescott, Orville. "Two Aldous Huxleys." *New York Times* (November 24, 1963), 4.

"Progress Is Overrated." *Parade* (June 14, 2009), 17.

Rand, Ayn. *Anthem*. New York: Signet, 1995.

Rohmann, Gerd. "*Island:* Huxley's Ecological Utopia." In *Now More Than Ever: Proceedings of the Aldous Huxley Centenary Symposium, Munster 1994*. Edited by Bernfried Nugel, 175–184. Frankfurt am Main: Peter Lang, 1995.

"Samson Agonistes." http://www.dartmouth.edu/~milton/reading_room/samson/drama/index.shtml (accessed July 27, 2009).

Shelley, Mary. *Frankenstein, or the Modern Prometheus*. New York: Penguin Classics, 2003.

Smith, Grover, ed. *Letters of Aldous Huxley*. New York: Harper and Row, 1969.

Swift, Jonathan. *Gulliver's Travels*. New York: Bantam, 1981.

_____. *The Writings of Jonathan Swift*. Edited by Robert A. Greenberg and William Bowman Piper. New York: W.W. Norton, 1973.

Tennyson, Alfred Lord. "Tithonus." *The Norton Anthology of English Literature*. Edited by M.H. Abrams, Stephen Greenblatt, Alfred David, et al. New York: W.W. Norton, 1931; 2001.

Thody, Philip. *Huxley: A Biographical Introduction*. New York: Charles Scribner's Sons, 1973.

Vonnegut, Kurt. *Cat's Cradle*. New York: Dell, 1988.

Ward, Mrs. Humphry. *Marcella*. London: Smith, Elder, 1894. New York: Penguin, 1985.

_____. *Robert Elsmere*. London: Smith, Elder, 1888; Lincoln, NE: University of Nebraska Press, 1967.

Watts, Harold H. *Aldous Huxley*. Boston: Twayne, 1969.

Waugh, Evelyn. *A Handful of Dust*. New York: Little, Brown, 1988.

_____. *The Loved One*. New York: Back Bay Books, 1999.

_____. "Youth at the Helm and Pleasure at the Prow." *A Critical Symposium on Huxley*. *London Magazine* (August 1955): 51–64. Review reprinted in *Aldous Huxley: The Critical Heritage*. Edited by Donald Watt., 396–399. Boston: Routledge and Kegan Paul, 1975.

Wells, H.G. *Men Like Gods*. New York: Macmillan, 1923.

_____. *The Shape of Things to Come*. New York: Penguin Classics, 2006.

Williams, Kathleen. *Jonathan Swift*. London: Routledge and Kegan Paul, 1968.

Woodcock, George. *Dawn and the Darkest Hour: A Study of Aldous Huxley*. New York: Viking, 1972.

Index